A Practical Guide to
Beauty Therapy
for NVQ Level 1

**Janet
Simms**

**Francesca
Gould**

Nelson Thornes
a Wolters Kluwer business

Published in 2006 by:
Nelson Thornes Ltd
Delta Place
27 Bath Road
CHELTENHAM
GL53 7TH
United Kingdom

06 07 08 09 10 / 10 9 8 7 6 5 4 3 2 1

A catalogue record for this book is available from the British Library

ISBN 0 7487 9605 3

Cover photograph by Royalty-Free/Corbis
Illustrations by Oxford Designers and Illustrators, IFA Design, Peter Cox, Linda Herd, Lorraine White, John Taylor and Angela Lumley
Photography by Martin Sookias
Page make-up by IFA Design Ltd, Plymouth, Devon

Printed in Great Britain by Scotprint

Contents

Foreword   iv
Acknowledgements   v
Introduction   vi

1 Working in the beauty industry   1

Overview of the beauty industry and
market trends   1
Providing beauty therapy services   5
Legal and professional framework   7
Health and safety legislation   8
Consumer protection   9
Employment legislation   10
Professional framework   12
Professional image   13
Professional relationships   15
Career opportunities in the beauty industry 16

2 Unit G1: Ensure your own actions reduce risks to health and safety 27

Health and safety legislation and
workplace policies   28
Risks to health and safety   40
Health and safety when assisting with
treatments   43
Health and safety: risks present in the
whole workplace   48
Health and safety: reporting and dealing
with risks   54
Your personal presentation   56
Treatment hygiene   61
Accidents   70
Fire safety   73
Electrical safety   76
First aid   78
Product safety   81
Salon security   83

3 Unit G2: Assist with salon reception duties 91

Reception   93
The receptionist   100
Client care   106
Making appointments   109
Handling enquiries   112
Dealing with complaints   115

4 Unit B1: Prepare and maintain the beauty therapy work area 119

Creating the right environment for client
comfort   120
Preparing the treatment area for waxing   121
Preparing the treatment area for eye
treatments   126
Preparing the treatment area for manicure
and pedicure treatment   132
Preparing the treatment area for facial
treatments   136
Preparing the treatment area for make-up
treatments   139

5 Unit B2: Assist with facial treatments 145

What is a facial?   146
Anatomy and physiology: the skin   146
Functions of the skin   149
Skin diseases and disorders   151
Contra-indications to facial treatment   155
Skin types   155
Equipment and products required to carry
out a facial treatment   158
Preparing the client for facial treatment 159
Conducting the facial treatment   159

6 Unit BT3: Assist with nail treatment on the hands 171

Benefits of receiving a nail treatment   172
Anatomy and physiology: nails   172
Nail diseases and disorders   175
Diseases and disorders of the hands and feet 180
Equipment and materials: general   186
Equipment and materials: manicure
products   188
Preparing the treatment area   191
Manicure procedure   192
Hand massage   197

Glossary   203

Index   210

Foreword

The world of beauty therapy is an exciting one. There have never been so many wonderful opportunities available to the therapist including working on cruise ships, aeroplanes and in exotic faraway places.

This book will help you begin the first step of your journey towards an interesting, challenging and rewarding career in beauty therapy. It will give you all the information needed to gain the beauty therapy Level 1 qualification. There are lots of photographs that show the facial and manicure routines so you can practise these treatments at home. There are also activities and tasks to help you learn about the different beauty treatments.

Best of luck for the future

Francesca Gould

Everyone has to start somewhere and this new Level 1 book will be the perfect friend to you as you start your career in beauty therapy. Not only will you gain valuable insight into the sorts of job opportunities available, you will learn invaluable background information about what it means to be a beauty professional and the skills and knowledge required to be successful in this exciting and rapidly growing industry.

Every job has both its serious and enjoyable sides. In tackling the 'serious' side, we have aimed to ensure you have a thorough understanding of important subjects like the law and health and safety, while, at the same time, providing you with interesting and enjoyable learning activities to lighten things up! Enjoy your first steps towards becoming a beauty professional and best of luck with your NVQ. Wishing you lots of success for the future.

Janet Simms

Acknowledgements

The publishers would like to offer special thanks to Clare Johnson and Heather Williams at Bliss (www.blisswellbeing.co.uk).

Photo credits

- **Allessandro:** p.4 (middle left), p.134 (bottom middle), p.140 (middle), p.188, p.189.
- **Aston & Fincher:** p.122 (bottom), p.133 (top left, top right, bottom left), p.141 (bottom right).
- **Bliss:** p.4 (bottom right), p.18, p.20 (bottom), p.38, p.51, p.53, p.57, p.67, p.77, p.93 (both), p.103, p.108, p.127, p.158, p.159.
- **The Carlton Group:** p.66 (bottom).
- **Clynol:** p.6 (top).
- **Corbis V94 (NT):** p.60 (bottom).
- **Corel 442 (NT):** p.19 (top).
- **Corel 664 (NT):** p.4 (middle right).
- **Ellisons:** p.33, p.135, p.186.
- **Elvele Images/Alamy:** p.74 (bottom).
- **Julie Fisher/zefa/Corbis:** p.87
- **GiGi:** p.121 (top).
- **Grafton International:** p.132 (bottom left), p.134 (top right).
- **HSBC:** p.95 (bottom left and centre).
- **Image Source 2 (NT):** p.54.
- **Instant Art/Signs (NT):** p.70, p.75, p.81.
- **JICA:** p.3 (bottom right), p.4 (top middle), p.137 (both).
- **La Remedi:** p.133 (bottom right), p.197 (bottom).
- **Natural Nail Company:** p.132 (bottom right), p.134 (top left).
- **OPI:** p.96, p.187.
- **Photodisc 67 (NT):** p.60 (top).
- **Photodisc 68 (NT):** p.22 (bottom).
- **Photodisc 75 (NT):** p.3 (bottom middle), p.58, p.126 (top), p.157, p.166 (both).
- **Photofusion/Alamy:** p.56.
- **Picturebank/Alamy:** p.59.
- **Prestige Medical:** p.66 (top).
- **Science Photo Library:** p.65, p.151, p.152, p.153, p.176, p.178, p.179 (top and middle), p.181, p.182, p.183.
- **Jane Shauck/Alamy:** p.19 (bottom)
- **Martin Sookias:** p.2, p.3 (top and bottom left), p.4 (top left), p.4 (middle centre), p.4 (bottom left), p.6 (bottom), p.15, p.16, p.21, p.22 (top), p.30, p.31, p.40, p.43, p.44, p.48, p.94, p.100, p.123, p.126 (bottom), p.128, p.130, p.132 (top), p.133 (top middle), p.134 (bottom right), p.136, p.140 (top), p.141 (top left and right), p.142, p.146, p.155, p.160, p.161, p.162, p.163, p.165, p.195, p.196, p.197 (top), p.199, p.200.
- **Sorisa:** p.4 (bottom middle), p.20 (top), p.41, p.66 (middle), p.121 (middle), p.122 (top).
- **Jack Sullivan/Alamy:** p.179 (bottom).
- **Melle Stripp:** p.4 (top right).
- **Sukar:** p.121 (bottom).
- **Virgin Vie:** p.141 (bottom left).
- **Zen:** p.84.

Introduction

Welcome to *A Practical Guide to Beauty Therapy for NVQ Level 1*, which has been specially designed to guide you through your course with ease. It will introduce you to the skills and knowledge you need to begin your career in the Beauty Therapy industry. It is packed full of diagrams and colour photos so you can see exactly what you need to do to carry out the different beauty treatments. You can also complete the activities, self-checks and multiple choice quizzes directly in the textbook and refer back to your answers when it's time to revise.

Here are the features you will notice as you work through the book:

| Learning Objectives | A list of points you will be able to understand after reading each chapter. |

Hints and tips from the authors to help you improve your skills.

A variety of different activities for you to complete. Some will require you to do some independent research and others are practical activities to help you put the knowledge you've learnt into practice.

Health and safety prompts to ensure that you are aware of the relevant laws.

GOOD PRACTICE
Reminders of what the best practice is when working in a salon environment.

Sets of questions throughout each chapter to recap and make sure you've fully understood the information that you've just learnt.

Multiple choice questions which appear at the end of each chapter for you to recap on what you've learnt in that particular section.

The important vocabulary that you will need to learn and understand.

You can check your answers for FREE by visiting www.saloneducation.co.uk

1 Working in the beauty industry

After working through this chapter you will be able to:

- describe the range and scope of beauty treatments and services
- appreciate the benefits of professional beauty services
- explain the importance of employment standards in the beauty industry
- show awareness of the laws relating to beauty therapy
- understand the importance of good customer service
- identify career opportunities in the beauty industry
- understand the personal skills, qualities and qualifications required to be successful working in the beauty industry.

If you are someone who cannot resist the beauty pages of glossy magazines and the lure of skin care and cosmetics counters in department stores, then you are already 'hooked' into the professional world of beauty. Join the club… there are millions of us!

The beauty business is *big* business and provides exciting opportunities, not only for the people who work in it, but also for the many clients and customers who benefit from it. This chapter will help you to gain insight into a professional world that might turn out to be a little different from what you expected. The beauty industry is often misrepresented and, sometimes, misunderstood. Take time to learn more about it and what it has to offer *you*.

Overview of the beauty industry and market trends

The beauty industry is huge and is growing at a dynamic rate. In the UK, there are currently over 12,000 outlets offering beauty treatments and this number is expected to reach in excess of 14,000 over the next two years.

Looking good and feeling good

Made up basically of companies that promote and sell beauty products and those which provide beauty services, the beauty business is *big* business, with salon-based outlets alone generating in excess of £1 billion each year.

It is not really surprising that the beauty industry continues to grow and thrive. In recent times, people have become much more aware of the links between health and beauty, the importance of looking after themselves and their bodies and the huge boost that looking good and feeling good gives to their confidence and self-esteem.

For most of us, feeling and looking 'the part' is very important, both at work and while enjoying our leisure time.

Product sales

The choice and types of beauty products available is vast, ranging from basic skin care and cosmetics to 'do-it-yourself' treatment kits for home use. These days, beauty products can be bought in all sorts of retail outlets, even supermarkets! No wonder that the estimated consumer spend on beauty purchases in the UK is in excess of £9 billion, with pharmacies and department stores being the most popular places for buying beauty product brands.

Of course, not all beauty purchases made 'over the counter' are successful. Most clients who attend beauty salons admit quite freely to having wasted money in the past on purchases made elsewhere, without receiving the proper advice.

Here are some interesting facts about the 'behaviour' of people when buying beauty products:

● Customers buy for their own reasons. Often these are emotional reasons, regarding how the product will make them feel.

● Customers do not buy products. They buy what they believe a product will do for them, or the feelings they associate with owning the product.

● Customers do not like high-pressure sales techniques. They prefer a professional, low-pressure approach.

● Beauty therapists, friends and family are the main people who influence what customers buy.

● Most customers change beauty product brands 'often' or 'sometimes' because they like to try new products or they think their current products are becoming less effective.

Customers do not like high-pressure sales techniques

A PRACTICAL GUIDE TO BEAUTY THERAPY LEVEL 1

- Although 58% of salon customers change brands 'often' or 'sometimes' to try new products and gain more effective results, 42% of them remain highly loyal to their brands.

(Adapted from Research – 2004 Allegra Strategies Ltd)

The most enjoyable buying decisions are made in relaxed, comfortable surroundings

Clients having professional beauty therapy treatments generally prefer to buy their products from the salon. They expect, quite rightly, that the products will be of good quality and that their therapist will give them the best advice. Selling products is an extension of the other professional services offered by a salon.

Professional beauty treatments

With such an extensive range of beauty products and beauty advice available in the media, why is there a need for professional beauty treatments? The answer is simple – apart from being able to enjoy the benefits of a pleasant and relaxing environment, the client will be treated by a trained therapist who has:

- specialist knowledge to correctly diagnose problems and give treatment advice
- technical knowledge of the treatments and products available
- professional skills which ensure that each client gets maximum benefits from the treatments
- the use of professional tools and equipment, which make treatments more effective and, sometimes, more comfortable for a client
- the knowledge and skills to provide treatments safely and hygienically
- the ability to monitor a client's progress and adapt the treatments when necessary
- the confidence that comes with having a professional qualification
- up-to-date information about new treatments and products.

This last point is important. The extensive media coverage of beauty issues, together with the ever-increasing range of products and services means that there is always popular demand for something new. As a professional, it is not enough to keep up with this demand, you have to be at least one step ahead!

The following list shows the basic categories of professional beauty therapy treatments. A large business with plenty of space, staff and resources might offer all of these treatments. A smaller business will usually specialise in treatments for which there is a good demand locally and which their staff are qualified to provide:

- Facial massage and skin care, for improving and maintaining facial skin conditions
- Eyebrow and eyelash treatments for enhancing facial appearance, particularly the eyes, by defining the eyebrows and eyelashes
- Make-up for enhancing facial appearance and for creating special effects

Skin glowing after facial

Effects of eyebrow shaping, eyelash perming and eyebrow and eyelash tinting

Natural effect evening make-up

- Hair depilatory and epilation treatments for removing unwanted facial and body hair
- Treatments for the nails, hands and feet to enhance their appearance and improve and maintain their condition
- Nail art for creating 'customised' special effects on natural or false nails

Wax depilation to underarm

Perfectly manicured nails

Dramatic nail art effects

- Nail extensions, for providing the effect of longer and stronger finger nails
- Spa treatments involving hydrotherapy (water) and heat treatments for their relaxing and therapeutic effects
- Body tanning treatments for producing an attractive, healthy looking suntan

Natural looking nail extensions

Relaxing in the spa pool (jacuzzi)

Healthy looking suntan

- Massage for relaxing the body and improving the suppleness of the muscles
- Electrical and mechanical treatments for improving a range of facial and body conditions.

All beauty therapy treatments are backed up with thorough home care advice so that their beneficial effects continue after the client has left the salon. Giving advice to clients and monitoring their home care is all part of the professional service.

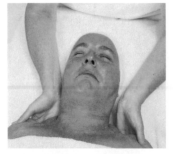
Relaxing massage to neck and shoulder

Using a facial steamer to deep cleanse the skin

Listening carefully to a client asking advice

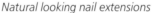

There is no doubt that the most important of all the beneficial effects of beauty treatments is the improvement they make to our self-esteem and personal well–being. Being satisfied with how we look and feel about ourselves is essential for giving us the confidence we need to be successful in all aspects of our lives. Although it is great when other people comment on how nice we look, how a certain colour suits us, how slim we look in a particular outfit, we tend to pick and choose the compliments we accept and ignore the ones we do not agree with. Most of us have at least one feature we would give anything to change and, more often than not, it is something that no one else even notices!

Providing beauty therapy services

The service side of the industry can be broken down into different types of business according to their size, location and the treatments and facilities they provide.

Some examples of different types of beauty therapy business are:

Beauty salons

These usually offer a full range of facial and body treatments, many of which are also available to male clients. Most beauty salons are privately owned, independent businesses but salons located in hotels, health clubs, on cruise liners, in-flight and in department stores usually belong to a large 'chain', often a beauty product company or leisure group.

Health farms

These are much larger businesses, usually situated in beautiful locations, which offer luxury accommodation and a very wide range of health and beauty services including a swimming pool, gym, outdoor activities and specialist hydrotherapy and heat treatments. Health farms are also known as health hydros and health resorts.

Beauty spas

Beauty salons providing some hydrotherapy facilities and heat treatments may have the word 'spa' in their title to help promote the health side of the business.

Nail bars

These are specialist beauty units providing hand and nail treatments. Their most popular treatments are usually nail extensions and nail art.

All beauty businesses, whatever their size and whatever they do, become successful by looking after their clients well and by keeping up-to-date with all the latest treatments. This also applies to freelance beauty therapists who work independently, providing treatments and services for clients in their own homes or at other venues.

Activity 1.1: Names of businesses

The name of a business usually gives clues to the scale and scope of the treatments it provides. The name also helps to project an image that attracts clients to the business.

Using the spaces provided, write a short description of what you imagine these businesses to be like. For example, what would you expect the environment to look and feel like, who would the clients be, what sort of treatments would you expect to be available, what would attract you or what would 'put you off' going to each of these businesses?

Suzie's Nail Cabin

_____
_____
_____

Hawthorpe Grange Health Farm

_____
_____
_____

Harmony Unisex Hair and Beauty Salon

_____
_____
_____

The Village Health Spa

_____
_____
_____

'Regular' beauty clients

Many men are regular clients at beauty salons

For many people, regular visits to a beauty salon or spa are as routine, and often more frequent, than visits to their hairdresser. For regular clients, beauty treatments are an important part of their lifestyle. This applies not only to women of all ages but also to men. Men have become much more confident and comfortable with the idea of using skin care products and benefiting from treatments which, up until fairly recently, were considered to be for women only. This has been good for the male clients and good for the beauty industry too!

Here are some facts we know about 'regular' beauty clients:

● over 60% of salon clients visit beauty salons and spas for beauty and relaxation treatments at least once a month
● the main reasons for choosing a salon are convenience of location and the therapist
● 80% of clients claim 'loyalty' to their salon
● salon clients claim that their 'key' health and beauty goals are 'to feel better', 'pamper myself' and 'healthier skin'
● more than two-thirds of salon and spa clients believe that they are well-informed about the types of beauty products and services on the market.

(Adapted from Research – 2004 Allegra Strategies Ltd)

Customer loyalty is built on good customer service and trust

The key to building up a good, regular clientele is excellent customer service. Customer service equals *personal* service. A service can only be truly personal when the needs of the individual clients are understood, and treatments and advice are matched to those needs. This is what being a successful beauty therapy business is all about.

A successful business looks after its regular clients well and never takes them for granted. After all, there is always competition waiting, usually just around the corner!

A PRACTICAL GUIDE TO BEAUTY THERAPY LEVEL 1

Activity 1.2: Your own experience

What is *your* experience of the beauty industry? Do you have favourite brands of make-up or skin care that you use all the time or do you like to experiment? Where do you like to buy your beauty products and why? Have you ever had treatments at a beauty salon or spa? If not, why not ? If you have, how satisfied were you with the treatments you received? Write a short account (no longer than one side of A4 paper) of your thoughts and experiences of the beauty industry and discuss them with your tutor.

The beauty industry

1   Name four different types of outlet that sell beauty products.

   _____
   _____
   _____
   _____

2   Give four benefits of having *professional* beauty treatments.

   _____
   _____
   _____
   _____

3   State three factors which contribute to the success of a business.

   _____
   _____
   _____

4   Explain, briefly, why beauty treatments have become so popular.

   _____
   _____
   _____

Legal and professional framework

Having decided on a career in beauty therapy, you will need to work within the legal and professional frameworks that set the standards for employment. High standards are essential for earning the trust and confidence of the public. They also earn you the respect of colleagues and other professionals who contribute to the success of the business.

Legal framework

'Suing' has recently become a 'fashionable' way of making money. People are much more aware of their legal rights and there are plenty of companies who have built their success on commissions earned from claims for compensation. Businesses and organisations that provide services directly to their customers are particularly at risk of being sued.

It makes sense for individuals and businesses providing beauty therapy treatments to take all possible steps to protect themselves from expensive litigation. This means working within a legal framework that protects the interests of everyone associated with the business:

- customers who buy beauty products
- clients who attend salons or other professional outlets for beauty treatments
- clients who have beauty treatments provided in their own homes
- businesses employing people to sell beauty products and provide beauty treatments
- companies providing products and equipment to the businesses providing beauty treatments.

Wherever you are in this chain, the law is there to protect you.

Types of legislation

The law is made up of different types of legislation: Acts, which are written in broad terms; and regulations, which are more specific and expand on details of the Acts. The law in the United Kingdom (UK) is influenced, increasingly, by the European Union (EU). The EU is working towards harmonising the laws in its member states. When new EU directives are issued, regulations are produced to 'tighten up' the laws in the UK.

Health and safety legislation

The law demands that every place of work is a healthy and safe place to be, not only for the people who work there but also for clients and other visitors. This even includes trespassers!

REMEMBER

As an employee, you have rights and responsibilities not only to your employer, but also to your clients, customers and colleagues. Failure to comply with the law can have very serious consequences.

The main responsibilities for health and safety lie with the employer, who must ensure that:

- appropriate health and safety policies are in place
- the premises are clean and safe
- all staff are trained in health and safety procedures.

When giving beauty treatments, you will work in very close personal contact with your clients. Some treatments will involve the use of potentially dangerous equipment and chemicals. There are considerable risks of spreading infection or causing personal injury if you do not follow the correct procedures.

GOOD PRACTICE

You must always work safely and hygienically. This is to protect yourself, your clients and your colleagues. Everyone must have confidence in your professional standards.

Health and safety legislation is part of criminal law. Failure to comply with the law has serious consequences and can be very expensive for the business, resulting in:

- claims made by injured staff
- claims made by injured clients
- prosecution and fines
- closure of the business
- loss of trade through bad publicity
- loss of staff through damaged reputation.

Would *you* want to be a client or employee of a business that neglected its health and safety responsibilities?

Health and Safety Executive

The Health and Safety Executive (HSE) is the 'lead' authority on health and safety. The HSE provides information and gives advice through its area offices. It also enforces health and safety legislation by sending inspectors from the local authority to check up on standards of health and safety. The inspectors are usually Environmental Health Officers. They have considerable powers including the right to carry out, at almost any time, an inspection of the premises or an investigation into a complaint.

If the inspectors are not satisfied with the standards of health and safety, they will issue either an **improvement notice** or a **prohibition notice**.

Improvement notice
This will allow the employer 21 days or more to make specified improvements; an employer who fails to comply with the notice by the given date, can end up in court.

Prohibition notice
This is very serious; the risks to health and safety are so severe that the business has to close down until the improvements have been made. The business will not be allowed to start operating again until the inspectors are satisfied that all problems have been dealt with to the required standards. An inspector will come back to check compliance with the notice. Failure to comply with the notice can result in prosecution.

For more details on all aspects on health and safety please see Chapter 2.

Consumer protection

As a consumer, you have legal rights that protect you from defective products and services. When they visit you as a beauty therapist, your clients have legal rights that protect them. A business that denies its clients and customers their rights will, inevitably, risk legal action.

REMEMBER
You must ensure that your clients always have realistic expectations from their treatments and that they understand how to get the best results from products they purchase for home care. This avoids disappointment later and also helps to develop their confidence in your advice.

REMEMBER
When you buy something from a supplier or a manufacturer, you are a consumer or 'customer' and have legal rights.

Activity 1.3: The law and you

Find out how the law protects *you* as a consumer. Visit your library or search the internet to find out about the following legislation. Write down key points in the spaces provided.

The Sale and Supply of Goods Act 1994

_____
_____
_____

The Trades Descriptions Act 1968 and 1972

_____
_____
_____

The Consumer Protection Act 1987

_____
_____
_____

The Cosmetic Products (Safety) Regulations 1996

_____
_____
_____

Data Protection Act 1998

This requires businesses that store details about clients on computer to register with the Data Protection Registrar and to comply with a code of practice. The Act does not apply to records that are stored manually.

Employment legislation

Once you have become employed, you will have certain statutory rights. These are legally binding and include the following:

- a detailed pay statement showing what you have earned and what deductions have been made from your earnings
- equal pay for equal work
- no discrimination on the basis of gender, race, disability or marital status
- at least one week's notice of dismissal if you have been employed for at least two months
- statutory sick pay and maternity pay
- a healthy and safe working environment
- the right to redundancy payment if you have been employed by the company for at least two years
- the right to complain to an industrial tribunal if you feel you have been unfairly dismissed
- the right to retain employment under the same conditions if the business is taken over by another company.

The Employment Rights Act 1996

Under this Act, you are entitled to ask for a written statement of the terms and conditions of your employment after you have been employed for a month. You also have the right to receive the written statement after two months of commencing employment. The statement should include:

- details of your salary or wages, including commission arrangements
- hours of work
- notice entitlements and obligations
- holiday entitlement
- date of commencement of employment
- job description
- workplace location.

If your employer does not provide you with a written statement, then you have the right to apply to an industrial tribunal who can order the employer to produce one.

Contract of employment

The written statement of employment is often referred to as the 'contract'. However, under employment law, the contract is actually made when the employer offers you the job and you accept it. This can be done verbally. It does not have to be written down. A written **contract of employment** provides legal protection for both the employer and the employee.

> **REMEMBER**
> You may have to work an initial **probationary** period in your new job. This will give you the opportunity to prove to your employer that you are able to do the job to the standards required.

The Sex Discrimination Acts 1975, 1986 and the Race Relations Act 1976

The aim of these Acts is to prevent the employer from discriminating against employees, either directly or indirectly, on the basis of their race, gender or marital status. The Equal Opportunities Commission investigates complaints of discrimination and monitors the wording of job advertisements.

The Disability Discrimination Act 1995

This Act makes it unlawful for an employer of 20 or more staff to discriminate against a current or prospective employee for any reason relating to their disability. If an employee or applicant is competent to do the job required, then the employer is responsible for making reasonable changes to the working environment and general employment arrangements so that the employee with a disability is not disadvantaged.

> **GOOD PRACTICE**
> Be proud of your profession! Project an image that instils trust and confidence in both clients and colleagues. Always treat other people as you would wish to be treated yourself.

Legal matters

1   State the main difference between the responsibilities of the employer and those of the employees for ensuring a healthy and safe working environment.

_____

_____

_____

2   What legal protection does the business have if a delivery of stock contains damaged goods?

_____

_____

_____

3   How soon after starting a new job should your employer provide you with a written statement of the terms and conditions of your employment?

_____

_____

_____

Professional framework

When you decide on a career in beauty therapy, you commit yourself to always working to the high standards set by the profession. This is the way to build your reputation as one of 'the best', gaining you the loyalty of your clients and earning you the respect of your colleagues and other professionals.

Professional associations

It will be worth your while joining one of the professional associations which represents you and your industry. A range of services and support will be available to you including:

- technical and product updating
- business advice
- news bulletins
- special rates for insurance cover
- membership badge and display materials.

Also, you will benefit by being able to meet up regularly and speak with other professionals in the beauty industry at meetings, exhibitions and social events.

Professional associations are committed to advancing beauty therapy and maintaining high standards in the profession. They provide maximum protection for the public and will work hard on your behalf. In return, you must always conduct yourself according to their **code of ethics** and maintain high standards of professional practice in all aspects of your work.

Professional code of ethics

Each professional organisation produces its own code of practice based on expected standards of behaviour. These standards are referred to as a professional code of ethics.

A professional code of ethics is not a legal requirement but the code may be used in criminal proceedings as evidence of improper practice or negligence. Professional associations will not pay out insurance on behalf of members who breach their code of ethics.

Whichever organisation you decide to join, you will have to sign a written declaration that you will:

- always work within the law
- never treat or claim to be able to treat a medical condition
- respect client confidentiality at all times
- show respect for other professions by referring clients appropriately, for example to general practitioners, chiropodists, physiotherapists
- maintain high standards of hygiene and safety in all aspects of your work
- apply certain treatments only with the written permission of the client's general practitioner
- support, help and show loyalty to other professional beauty therapists
- never 'poach' another member's clients or criticise their work
- uphold the honour of the profession at all times, for example when working with clients of the opposite sex.

Professional image

The effort you put into getting ready for work reflects your pride in the job. Clients will initially judge your professionalism on how you present yourself. You are in an industry where image and appearance are important. It is fine for you to have your own individual look provided that you appreciate that there are professional standards of dress and appearance that must be followed.

Appearance and personal hygiene

Your appearance should reflect your professional skills and knowledge. Clients will have confidence in your abilities if you always look smart, clean and well groomed. Good personal hygiene is essential, as your work will bring you into very close contact with clients and colleagues. Good personal hygiene also helps to keep the body healthy. Here are some general rules.

Body freshness

Have at least one bath or shower each day and use an antiperspirant.

Overall

Wear a clean, well-pressed overall each day. Your overall will probably be made of cotton or poly-cotton because these fabrics are easier to launder. They are also lightweight and comfortable to wear for working. Make sure your overall is not too tight. It should be loose enough for air and moisture to circulate. This helps to keep the body cool and fresh.

REMEMBER

It can be hard sometimes, but you must learn to leave your personal problems at home and always be cheerful with your clients and colleagues. Friends will want to share your problems but not during working hours.

REMEMBER

A brisk rub with the towel after a bath or shower helps to stimulate the circulation and perk up the body – particularly useful if you have difficulty getting going in the mornings!

GOOD PRACTICE

Wear a nurse's 'fob' watch pinned to your overall. This will help you to keep an eye on the time while keeping your wrist free from jewellery.

REMEMBER

Any jewellery you wear must look appropriate for work and not interfere with your professional image.

REMEMBER

If your hands are well groomed, this sets a good example for your clients and helps to promote the salon's products and treatments.

REMEMBER

The smells of cigarettes, garlic and other strongly flavoured foods stay on the breath for some time. Others can smell them long after you have tasted them!

GOOD PRACTICE

Ideally, you should wear make-up products that are available for purchase in the salon. This helps to advertise the products and promote retail sales.

Your overall should also not be too short. Knee length is usually the most appropriate. Your overall should be long enough to look respectable when you sit down or if you need to stretch or lean across a client. If you wear an underskirt make sure that it does not show below your overall.

Jewellery

Keep jewellery to the minimum. Ideally a pair of small earrings and, if you are married, a flat wedding ring. Avoid wearing bracelets, necklaces and watch straps that may get in the way during treatments or that could 'catch' the client's skin. Do not wear loose fitting chains and necklaces that could make contact with the client's skin during treatment. This is both unhygienic and uncomfortable for the client.

Hands and feet

Keep your hands clean and smooth. Wash your hands regularly throughout the day. Breaks in the skin provide a route for bacteria. Use hand cream regularly to prevent the skin from cracking. Wear protective gloves when cleaning and when mixing chemicals.

Wear correctly fitting shoes. You will spend a lot of time on your feet. Wear low-heeled shoes that are clean, smart and comfortable and appropriate for wearing with your overall. A clean pair of tights or stockings should be worn each day. They should be a natural colour, plain and not pulled or laddered. Keep a spare pair at the salon for 'emergencies'.

Oral hygiene

Brush your teeth thoroughly after every meal as well as in the morning and last thing at night. Rinse the toothbrush well afterwards. Use dental floss regularly to remove plaque from between your teeth and under your gums. Keep a spare toothbrush at work and have a breath freshener or mouthwash on hand just in case.

HEALTH MATTERS

Bad breath results from the decay of food particles left on the teeth. This is one reason why frequent brushing is so important. A build-up of food, particularly sugars, will eventually cause tooth decay and other dental problems. Stomach disorders can also cause bad breath.

Hair care

Have clean, shiny hair dressed in a smart, manageable style. Make regular visits to the hairdresser to keep your style in shape. Long hair should be worn up or secured back off the face.

Make-up

A light application of make-up is all that is required to project a professional image and set a good example to clients. Refresh your make-up during the day if necessary. This can help to give you a boost when you are getting tired. A fresh application of lipstick always brightens up the face.

For more information on the health and safety aspects of your personal presentation see Chapter 2, page 56.

Activity 1.4: Professional image

How professional do you think Tina looks? Her employer is not very impressed! She has found eight things she is not happy about.

See if you can spot them. Write your answers in the spaces provided.

1 _____
2 _____
3 _____
4 _____
5 _____
6 _____
7 _____
8 _____

Every salon has its own rules on dress because how staff dress will reflect the professional image of the business. Always stick to the rules! Do not try changing them without consulting your supervisor first.

Professional relationships

All sorts of relationships are developed and looked after in a professional beauty therapy environment, for example relationships between:

- staff and staff
- staff and clients
- employer and staff
- employer and clients
- the business and its suppliers
- the business and other local businesses
- the business and other organisations in the local community, for example the police, health services and the media.

Good professional relationships help to expand the business and build its reputation. They are built on trust, mutual respect and a sense of 'common purpose'.

Activity 1.5: Working relationships

With a friend or group of colleagues, discuss the different sets of relationships in the list above and state why you think each of them is important. Think of examples of the sorts of things that might cause each of the relationships to break down and how this could affect the business. Feed back your answers to your tutor and see what she or he has to say.

Meet the team

Discussing targets at a staff meeting

Team work

A good employer spends a lot of time and thought recruiting new people, making sure that all new employees 'fit in' with the business and the rest of the team.

A good team 'pulls together' and knows what it has to do to make the business a success. This involves agreeing targets, creating action plans and working to agreed deadlines. These occur as a result of good management, effective communication and conscientious and committed staff.

Everyone wants to work for a successful business so it is important that all staff work well together and know what they have to do to make their own contribution.

A business's staff will make the greatest contribution to the atmosphere of the salon. If clients enjoy their salon visits and are satisfied with the treatment they receive, they stay loyal and become very important to the success of the business.

Career opportunities in the beauty industry

The professional world of beauty offers a wide range of exciting career opportunities both in the UK and abroad.

Regular job searches in the beauty press and on the internet will help keep you in touch with what is out there and what employers are looking for. Popular trade publications include *Professional Beauty, Health and Beauty Salon, Guild News* and *Professional Spa*. You may be able to find some of these in your local public library or in the reference library of a further education college offering beauty therapy courses. If you are interested in subscribing to a professional journal, useful contact details can be found on www.new-concept.co.uk. You may also like to have a look at the following websites that specialise in recruitment for the beauty industry: www.beautyserve.com, www.beautyjobsonline.com and www.beautyrecruitment.com

Roles and responsibilities

Once you progress in your beauty therapy training you will probably find that you start to particularly enjoy and develop talents in specialist areas of the work. It is not unusual for beauty therapy graduates to describe themselves as a 'body' person, a 'make-up' person, a 'facials' or a 'nails' person. This is often an indication of their artistic flair and creativity or their interest in the therapeutic and health aspects of particular beauty treatments. Whether you are a generalist or a specialist, there is a job out there for you if you are qualified and committed.

Career Guide within the Spa and Beauty Industry

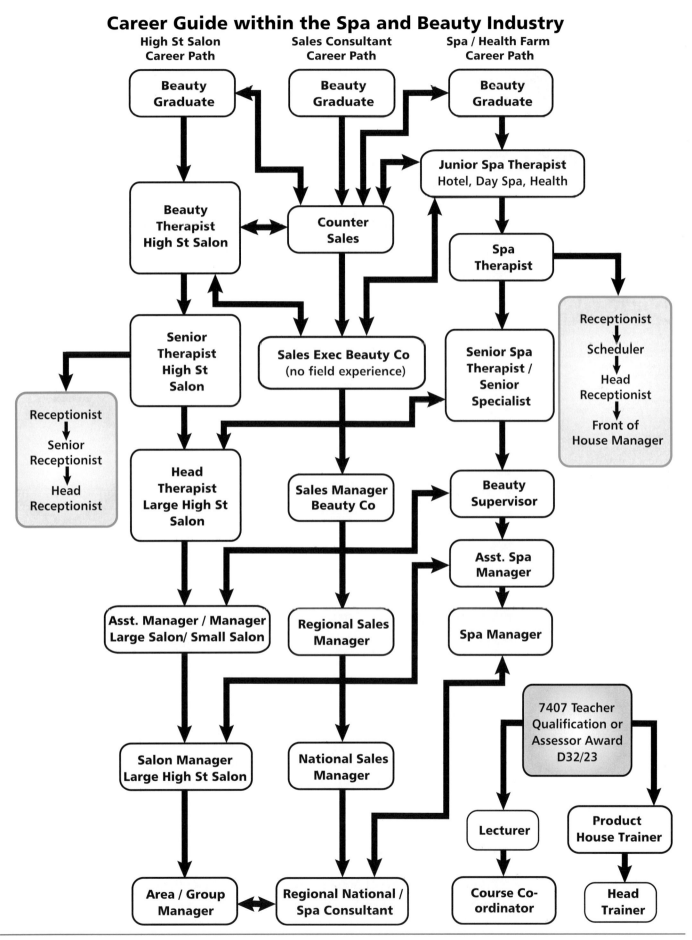

Salon-based beauty therapist

Beauty salons are located almost anywhere: on the high street, in department stores, on board cruise liners and passenger planes, within sports clubs and leisure centres and at health farms and day spas. You may be drawn towards the pace and excitement of working in a city centre salon or prefer the relative calm of a secluded health farm in the countryside.

Salon owners usually expect their staff to have attained an N/SVQ level 3 before entering employment; however, there are job opportunities at N/SVQ level 2 for beauty assistants who may provide some basic treatments and have reception duties.

Most beauty salons operate a six-day week, seven if they are situated in a health or leisure resort. The therapists work five days and either have a fixed day off or work to a rota system. If you are suitably qualified with the ability to carry out the full range of treatments, there are many different options available. Wages may be relatively low to start with but for someone competent and committed, there is the potential to earn a substantial living.

To be a successful beauty therapist you will need to be:
- technically competent
- enthusiastic and genuinely interested in other people
- friendly and welcoming with all your clients
- tactful and a good listener
- patient and good at explaining things
- well groomed
- commercially aware in order to effectively sell products and promote treatments
- confident with an artistic flair.

Beauty therapists work on a one-to-one basis with their clients, usually in private rooms or cubicles. They spend a lot of their time standing and need quite a lot of stamina for performing treatments such as body massage.

Freelance beauty therapist

If you go freelance you will be self-employed and will need good business skills as well as the technical skills and knowledge required for the job. This is because you will be responsible for your own bookkeeping, accounts, marketing, stock control, purchasing and laundry and supplies, all of which you will attend to outside normal working hours. You will need a thorough knowledge of all the treatments but will be able to choose the ones you want to offer and to whom.

Potentially, the range of clients is varied because of the different types of venues where you may provide treatments, for example in a client's own home, in a hospital or in a nursing home.

Working freelance provides a certain amount of flexibility, which may suit you. However, it is definitely *not* the 'soft' option! To run your own, successful 'portable' beauty salon, you will need to invest in a suitable vehicle and a good range of quality products and 'transportable' equipment. You will also need to be self-motivated and have good organisational skills to plan your appointments and journeys in the most cost-effective way.

A PRACTICAL GUIDE TO BEAUTY THERAPY LEVEL 1

Cruise therapist

For the passengers, life on board a cruise liner consists of relaxation and more relaxation! Therapists employed in the ship's beauty salon have a lot to contribute to this, providing a full range of relaxing beauty treatments and the all-important makeovers for the many formal evenings on board. The companies managing salons on cruise liners aim to recruit the best. They expect outstanding professionalism, excellent technical skills, immaculate appearance, flexibility and the ability to communicate effectively with a very diverse range of people. Team work is essential on a cruise liner where staff work together to ensure top quality service to a demanding, international clientele.

Cruise therapists learn all aspects of business management and ship life. Training includes promotion, presentation, retail skills and customer service, which indicate the importance of 'selling' to the job. It goes without saying that a willingness to travel is essential for working on a cruise liner! Although an N/SVQ level 3 qualification is preferred, there are opportunities for N/SVQ level 2 candidates with the right personal qualities and commitment.

Beauty technician

Some large beauty businesses, colleges and training schools employ technicians who are usually fully qualified beauty therapists, sometimes with an additional assessor qualification. Beauty technicians organise the day-to-day running of the salons from ordering stock and setting up the salons to managing resources, carrying out risk assessments, implementing the Control of Substances Hazardous to Health (COSHH) regulations and helping to supervise trainees. Beauty technicians need to be well organised, computer literate and efficient with paper work. They also need to be patient, energetic, outgoing and be able to handle situations diplomatically, especially when things go wrong!

Make-up artist

There is a glamorous and exciting side to being a make-up artist and a serious, very rewarding side. Every fashion model and catwalk show needs a make-up artist and that is where the glamour and excitement is. On the other side, opportunities as a make-up artist are also available in the health and caring professions, helping patients with disfigurements or following injury or surgery. This type of make-up is called cosmetic camouflage and requires special corrective techniques and make-up products.

Whichever type of make-up artist you aim to be, you will need to have a strong visual sense, to be creative and to have excellent technical skills developed to N/SVQ level 3 standard. If you want to work in the fashion world, you will also need a certain amount of luck and be in the right place at the right time. It will help if you build up a portfolio of your make-up work to show prospective employers. If you want to work in the health or care service, you will need to be very patient and sensitive and have excellent interpersonal skills for dealing with patients who are often very low in confidence and self-esteem.

Media make-up artist

Although there are not nearly as many openings for media make-up artists as there are for beauty therapists generally, the opportunities in the television and film industry are out there if you are creative, determined, talented, resilient, hardworking, outgoing and have stamina. Some television and film companies have an entry requirement of two A levels, including Art and English or History and/or N/SVQ level 3 qualifications in hairdressing and beauty therapy.

Entrants are usually required to be at least 21 years old in order to be considered for 'on the job' training in the world of television and film. This is an indication of the importance placed by employers on the personal skills and experiences they consider important for working in the media industry.

The first six months of training is usually spent learning the basic skills of media make-up. This is followed by six months on secondment to a make-up department before becoming a full member of the team, working under supervision.

Media make-up artists are responsible for the research, design and execution of all make-up and hair creations for the productions. Their work involves a lot of preparation and planning. Make-up artists work closely with lighting directors and set designers as well as liaising closely with producers, directors, costume staff and performers. The working hours are long and a willingness to travel and live away from home are important considerations when applying for this type of work. Although the work of a film and television make-up artist sounds quite glamorous, it does not always feel like that when you are working on an outside broadcast in the freezing cold and rain! Despite this, competition is intense for the limited number of jobs available.

Electrologist

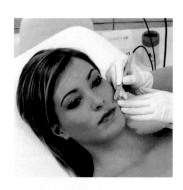

Electrologists specialise in the permanent removal of hair using a fine needle and an electrical current. The treatment is called electrical epilation and is provided to both male and female clients for destroying unwanted facial or body hair. There are often underlying medical causes for superfluous hair and some clients are referred to an electrologist by their GP. To practise electrical epilation you must be qualified to N/SVQ level 3, be sensitive and sympathetic and be able to put clients at their ease. Electrologists may provide their services in a beauty salon, a private clinic or a clinic within the dermatology department of a hospital.

Nail technician

'Nails' are very big business and if you are interested in becoming a nail expert, you will need to be qualified at N/SVQ level 3, have a strong visual sense, be creative and keep up-to-date with all the latest fashions and techniques. Nail technicians work in specialist nail studios, beauty salons and hairdressing salons. Freelance nail technicians work on a mobile basis, visiting clients in their homes or providing their services on a part-time basis in someone else's business. Nail treatments do not need a lot of workspace, so they can be set up quite quickly and easily. However, many treatments involve the use of products which have a very pungent smell so good ventilation is required. Clients will need to know this when preparing for treatments in their homes.

Massage

Manual massage is probably one of the most relaxing and therapeutic treatments provided by a beauty therapist, particularly when it involves the wonderfully fragranced essential oils used in aromatherapy. Any beauty business specialising in the health aspects of beauty therapy will offer body massage and facial massage treatments, for example beauty salons, spas, health farms and health clubs. There are also opportunities for freelance massage therapists.

If you are interested in becoming a massage therapist you will need to be qualified to N/SVQ level 3 and have in-depth knowledge of anatomy and physiology. You will also need to be able to identify and advise on certain medical and non-medical conditions and understand the science relating to the use of massage equipment.

Sales (beauty consultant)

People who sell cosmetics and skin care in a retail environment are called beauty consultants. Beauty consultants help customers to choose and buy the right products and make the most of their personal appearance. They work in places such as department stores, large hotels, airports, on cruise ships, or in an overseas branch of a cosmetic company.

If you do become a beauty consultant, you will be given targets to reach and routine paperwork to complete. You will also be responsible for cleaning and maintaining displays, carrying out promotions and ensuring adequate stock levels.

Although beauty consultants do not always need formal qualifications, many of the 'serious' skin care companies prefer to recruit beauty therapists qualified at N/SVQ level 2 or 3 to their sales teams because of their specialist knowledge and expertise.

To be a successful beauty consultant, you must have a smart appearance, be well groomed, have excellent interpersonal skills and be good at selling. You will also need good literacy and numeracy skills. Previous experience in retail, sales, or customer service will be an advantage. Customer service and people skills are important in this job, so maturity can be an asset.

Beauty consultants work between 37 and 40 hours a week, and do some weekend and evening work.

If you enjoy the busy and competitive environment of an in-store cosmetics department and have the stamina to be on your feet for most of the day, advising potential customers and promoting your products, sales offers very good career opportunities.

Sales (field sales representative)

A company with products to sell is constantly seeking to increase its sales. Field sales representatives work for companies who supply products to other companies such as beauty salons and spas. They are responsible for ensuring that existing key customers continue to expand their business with the company while, at the same time, seeking out and developing new business opportunities.

As a field sales representative, you will manage your own portfolio of customers and provide a technical, professional and customer-focused service. This is a challenging and varied role involving responsibility for running promotional initiatives, preparing sales forecasts, delivering sales presentations and planning strategies for gaining new business.

On the 'professional' side of the beauty business, there are many opportunities available for N/SVQ level 3 qualified beauty therapists, with sales ability, to become field sales representatives. This usually involves having responsibility for an area or region, promoting products and services to practitioners in the beauty business and providing after-sales customer service. Some field sales representatives also provide training to salon staff and staff and students in colleges that use their products.

There is a lot of travelling involved but the work is interesting and varied. Field sales representatives are usually very committed to their products and enjoy promoting them. They also enjoy the relationships they develop with the businesses they sell to and feel part of their success.

Spa assistant

If you are qualified at N/SVQ level 2 and considering working in a health farm or beauty spa environment, there are opportunities for you to become a spa assistant, supporting the work of therapists qualified at N/SVQ level 3 who carry out the treatments. This includes preparing the areas for water, heat and spa treatments, cleaning, maintaining and monitoring the spa environment, assisting with treatments and shutting down the treatment areas afterwards.

You need to be very vigilant in a spa environment and monitor clients closely. This is particularly important in relation to the communal use of spa pools, saunas and steam rooms where individual clients are not under the direct supervision of a qualified therapist.

Working as a spa assistant gives you the opportunity to decide if you are interested in pursuing your career along a N/SVQ level 3 Beauty Therapy, Body Massage or Spa Therapy route.

Salon owner

Running your own business is probably one of the hardest and most rewarding things you can do! The hours are often long because, in addition to the work undertaken in the salon during opening hours, there is a lot of paperwork and administration and this has to be done outside normal working hours, after the salon has closed. This includes financial accounts and bookkeeping, PAYE, banking, stock control and dealing with health and safety and other business management issues.

Marketing and recruiting the right staff are essential for the success of the business as are ongoing close relationships with your bank manager and accountant. It is important to prepare a thorough business plan before committing finance and other resources to your new venture. You will need to show evidence of good market research and detailed plans for your business, based on well-researched information.

Competition is fierce but a well-run salon offering a valuable service in a caring environment will succeed. To be a successful salon owner, you will need technical skills developed to N/SVQ level 3 with, ideally, additional Continuing Professional Development (CPD) qualifications. If you do not already have an N/SVQ level 4 qualification, you should register for this so that your management and business skills can be developed and assessed 'on the job'. Additionally, you will need the strength of character, resilience and self-motivation to succeed in the knowledge that things very rarely go smoothly in business.

Lecturer/trainer

Opportunities exist for beauty therapists to go into teaching. It is preferable for trainers to be qualified to N/SVQ Level 3, either full-time or part-time, in colleges of further education or private training schools. Colleges require their teachers to 'top up' with a further education Teachers' Certificate or a Postgraduate Certificate of Education. These qualifications can be gained in one or two years, depending on the requirements of the teacher training awarding body. Many qualified beauty therapists combine part-time teaching with running their own business.

Full-time college lecturers spend approximately 21 hours per week teaching and 9 hours on administration, preparation, marking and assessments. Lecturers and trainers are required to keep themselves updated with Continuing Professional Development courses. As a lecturer, you could make your career in teaching or progress through a college management route. As a qualified trainer and assessor, you could also be employed by a private training organisation, delivering N/SVQs in the workplace. The N/SVQ awarding bodies must comply with the requirements of the Hairdressing and Beauty Industry Authority (HABIA) when registering a centre's assessors. Assessors must have five years' experience and the relevant level N/SVQ.

Her Majesty's Prison Service

The main focus of work for the Prison Service is preparing prisoners for employment when they return to the outside world. There are opportunities for beauty therapists, who are also qualified trainers and assessors, to help inmates create a new life for themselves once they have been released. Training usually takes place in a small, equipped training salon on prison premises.

If you become a trainer in one of Her Majesty's prisons, you will have to go through a series of security checks and follow stringent policies, procedures and security arrangements. These will be covered in a one-week induction when you join the service.

Prisons are increasingly under pressure from the Home Office to provide vocational training courses so, although there are relatively few training posts available currently, the number is expected to rise in the future.

ACTIVITY

Activity 1.6: What job will you do?

Now that you know a bit more about employment opportunities in the beauty industry, what sort of job do you think you would like in the future? Write a short summary of what appeals to you about the job and why you think you might be good at it.

_____

_____

_____

_____

_____

_____

_____

Qualifications

Qualifications are proof of your knowledge, skills and experience so the more you have, the more choices and opportunities you will have for progressing your career. The main qualifications providing the career pathways in beauty therapy are N/SVQs (National/Scottish Vocational Qualifications).

N/SVQs are designed by the industry for the industry and employers contribute to keeping them up to date, in line with changing needs of the industry. N/SVQs are 'doing' qualifications that acknowledge technical skills and knowledge developed 'on the job'. The national occupational standards create the framework for N/SVQ qualifications, which are structured in 'units' and are available at different levels for different job roles:

Level 1
An introductory level, developing awareness of the industry and the skills and knowledge required for carrying out some basic beauty treatments and assisting with others. You will also be able to work on reception.

Level 2
The minimum standard required to be a competent beauty therapist. Having achieved N/SVQ level 2 you will be qualified to provide a range of treatments for the face, hands and feet and, depending on the optional units you complete, to assist with spa treatments. Important aspects of client care – selling, health and safety and working relationships – are also covered at level 2.

Level 3
At level 3 you will need far less supervision in your own work and, with some experience, could be supervising the work of others. N/SVQ level 3 develops further the technical skills acquired at level 2 and covers specialist body treatments and electrical treatments with their related sciences. Aspects of finance and basic business practice are also covered at N/SVQ level 3.

Level 4
Level 4 is aimed at salon management and covers all aspects of financial management, operational planning and control, human resources, training and development, business strategies and management information systems. An N/SVQ level 4 or equivalent qualification is essential if you aim to run your own business.

REMEMBER

All N/SVQs with the same name, and at the same level, contain identical core units but offer additional 'optional' units for providing specialist employment opportunities. These specialisms are identified in brackets after the main title of the qualification.

The full suite of beauty therapy N/SVQs currently available are:
- N/SVQ Level 1 Beauty Therapy
- N/SVQ Level 2 Beauty Therapy (General)
- N/SVQ Level 2 Beauty Therapy (Make-up)
- N/SVQ Level 3 Beauty Therapy (General)
- N/SVQ Level 3 Beauty Therapy (Make-up)
- N/SVQ Level 3 Beauty Therapy (Massage)
- N/SVQ Level 2 Nail Services
- N/SVQ Level 3 Nail Services
- N/SVQ Level 3 Spa Therapy

One big advantage of N/SVQs are that there are no external exams to sit. Progression is measured through continuous assessment at a pace to suit the student. There is no time limit and courses are open to students of any age and experience.

Skills and knowledge are developed and assessed 'on the job' in the professional working environment of either a commercial beauty salon, a private training school or a college of further education.

In addition to N/SVQs there are non-N/SVQs available, some of which provide a grounding in the skills and knowledge required to achieve the N/SVQ itself. Others allow for career development into specialist beauty therapy skills or related areas.

For more information on qualifications and training providers in the beauty industry, contact:

HABIA (the Hairdressing and Beauty Industry Authority)
Oxford House
Sixth Avenue
Sky Business Park
Robin Hood Airport
Doncaster
South Yorkshire DN9 3GG
Tel: 08452 306080 Fax: 01302 623171
http://www.habia.org.uk

Career paths

There are three main pathways for progressing a career in beauty therapy. These are shown on page 17. The High Street Salon Career Path can also be applied to other, specialist 'high street' beauty outlets such as those providing nail services.

ACTIVITY

Activity 1.7: Know your N/SVQ

Show you have understood how the N/SVQ system works by identifying the N/SVQ level which applies to each of the jobs on page 17, 'Career paths in the beauty industry'. Decide on a colour code for each of the N/SVQ levels 1 – 4 (For example level 1 = yellow, level 2 = red) then colour in each of the boxes containing a job title with the appropriate colour. Some of the jobs will be easier to decide than others. If you get stuck, have a word with your tutor.

Continuing Professional Development (CPD)

Once qualified, beauty therapists continue their professional development by completing a designated amount of professional training each year. This enables them to learn advanced techniques or other specialist skills and help keep them up to date with developments in the industry. CPD also helps beauty therapists to develop their career plans.

For example, as an electrologist you could learn to remove thread veins and skin tags. Some therapists take the 'business' route and move into areas such as marketing, sales and retailing. For people whose main ambition is to own their own salon, it is important that their continuing professional development equips them with the skills and knowledge required to succeed in business.

CPD provides you with opportunities to gain more qualifications, which are your 'currency' when moving up the career ladder. Keep your CPD under review and be clear about where you want to go and what you need to get there.

Careers in the beauty industry

1 List five personal qualities which are essential for a beauty therapist.

(1) _____

(2) _____

(3) _____

(4) _____

(5) _____

2 State three of the main differences between working in sales as (i) a beauty consultant and (ii) a field sales representative.

(1) _____

(2) _____

(3) _____

3 Name the qualification that sets the minimum standard required for practising as a beauty therapist _____

4 Identify with a ✓ which of the following treatments you would be qualified to provide at N/SVQ level 2. When you have finished, write the number of treatments you have ticked in this box ☐

☐ Cleanse and make-up   ☐ Leg waxing   ☐ Nail wraps

☐ Pedicure   ☐ Body massage   ☐ Body wraps

☐ Electrical epilation   ☐ Eyelash tinting   ☐ French manicure

☐ Bikini waxing   ☐ Facial massage   ☐ Face mask

☐ Acrylic nail extensions   ☐ Ear piercing   ☐ Cosmetic camouflage

5 Explain (i) the meaning of CPD and (ii) why CPD is important.

(i) _____

(ii) _____

_____

KEY TERMS

You should now understand the following words or phrases. If you do not, go back through the chapter and find out what they mean:

Beauty industry	**Consumer protection**	**Beauty therapist**
Product sales	**Employment rights**	**Career path**
Professional beauty	**Health and Safety Executive**	**Continuing Professional**
treatments	**Professional standards**	**Development (CPD)**
Customer service	**Code of ethics**	**National /Scottish**
Regular clients	**Professional image**	**Vocational Qualifications**
Legislation	**Team work**	

2 Unit G1

Ensure your own actions reduce risks to health and safety

After working through this chapter you will be able to:

- understand your legal duties and responsibilities for health and safety
- know the impact of specific health and safety legislation on your job role
- understand the importance of **workplace policies** for controlling risks to health and safety
- know the responsible persons to whom you report health and safety matters
- understand **hazards** and **risks** in the workplace and how to deal with them
- know the importance of personal presentation and conduct for maintaining health and safety in the workplace.

Before you work through this chapter: Be wise and revise!
Revision topics to help you achieve this unit:

Ensure your own actions reduce risks to health and safety

TOPIC	CHAPTER	PAGE

Although the employer is legally accountable for the health and safety of people working in or visiting the salon, it is the staff who, on a day-to-day basis, are at the forefront of business operations. All employees have a professional responsibility for ensuring high standards of health and safety. These standards should be set out in the salon's policies and procedures.

Health and safety legislation and workplace policies

It is important to know where you stand legally in terms of health and safety. You must apply your knowledge of health and safety to everything you do:

- dealing with clients
- assisting with treatments
- working in the stock room
- helping on reception
- taking 'time out' in the staff room.

Never take short cuts or try 'getting away' with things that you know are 'skimping' on health and safety. One act of negligence can be very 'expensive' for a business.

ACTIVITY

Activity 2.1: Revision

Think back to Chapter 1 and try to remember four ways in which negligence with health and safety can be 'expensive' for a business. Write your answers in the spaces below.

_____

_____

_____

_____

_____

_____

_____

_____

_____

Your legal duties

The law says that your main duty is to always work without endangering yourself or others. You must not misuse or interfere with anything provided for your health, safety and welfare and you must always work safely and hygienically. This is to protect yourself, your clients and the people you work with.

Your job role

Your duties for health and safety are affected by legislation which covers all businesses. The legislation is made up of Acts and Regulations relating to the different types of work you do and your working environment.

A PRACTICAL GUIDE TO BEAUTY THERAPY LEVEL 1

Specific legislation covering your job role includes:

The Health and Safety at Work Act 1974 (HASAWA)

This Act covers all aspects of health, safety and welfare at work. It identifies the responsibilities of employers and employees to provide a safe working environment, not just for themselves but for anyone present on the business premises.

Your duties are to:

- take reasonable care to avoid injury to yourself and others
- co-operate with others in matters of safety
- avoid interfering with or misusing anything provided to protect your health and safety
- take part in all health and safety training provided by your employer
- read and make sure you understand all safety information provided for you
- know the salon's health and safety procedures.

The Management of Health and Safety at Work Regulations 1999

Employers have responsibility for safeguarding, as far as possible, the health, safety and welfare of themselves, their employees and members of the public. This means that health and safety must run through all aspects of the business.

Your duties are to:

- make sure you know all the safety procedures in your workplace
- read all safety information and take part in all safety training
- always work safely; take all protective and preventative measures relevant to what you are doing
- take part in all employer/staff consultations on health and safety matters
- store, handle and dispose of all substances safely
- report any equipment which you feel is not up to standard
- take precautions to avoid a build-up of toxic fumes
- ensure safe systems of work; do not 'skip' or 'cut corners' on safety matters
- report all accidents and incidents relating to health and safety so that they can be recorded and dealt with appropriately.

REMEMBER

Under the **Health and Safety at Work Act**, everyone working in the salon must always work safely and have consideration for their fellow workers.

ACTIVITY

Activity 2.2: Learning about health and safety

1 Take a look around you, not just in the beauty treatment rooms but also in other areas such as reception, sauna, stock room, dispensary and corridors. What health and safety information can you see? Make notes as you go round and compare your answers with colleagues.

2 What health and safety information were you given at the start of your training? What was the information about, how was it provided and what did you learn? Discuss this with your supervisor and check that you have not missed any important information.

GOOD PRACTICE

If there are more than five employees, your employer must provide you with a health and safety policy statement, which must be kept updated.

The Workplace (Health, Safety and Welfare) Regulations 1992

These Regulations relate to the maintenance of business premises and safety facilities.

Your duties are to:

● keep your workplace clean and tidy

● ensure adequate heating, lighting and ventilation in the areas you are working

● ensure waste does not accumulate; store and dispose of waste material appropriately

● keep floors, staircases and passageways free from obstruction

● report any fixtures, fittings and floorings which appear insecure

● know the location of fire exits and how to use firefighting equipment

● use the secure storage space provided by your employer for storing personal items

● use the protective clothing and equipment provided by your employer for ensuring your safety.

HEALTH MATTERS

Adequate and suitable lighting is needed in order to:

● enable people to see what they are doing and where they are going

● show up potential hazards such as a step

● encourage and highlight cleanliness

● prevent eye strain.

The Provisions and Use of Work Equipment Regulations 1998

All equipment at work must be properly constructed, suitable for its purpose and kept in a good state of repair. All employees must be trained to use and maintain the equipment properly and written records must be kept of maintenance work carried out.

Your duties are to:

● always ensure equipment is clean and in good working order before use

● take all necessary electrical and other safety precautions when setting up and using equipment

● clean and store all equipment and accessories appropriately after use

● follow workplace procedures for reporting faulty equipment

● do not use equipment that you are not qualified to use.

Personal Protective Equipment (PPE) at Work Regulations 1992 (amended 2002 paragraph 5)

Your employer is responsible for ensuring that all employees who may be at risk of being exposed to health risks or injury are provided with appropriate protective equipment.

Your duties are to:

● always use the protective equipment provided for your safety

● take care of your personal protective equipment and maintain and dispose of it appropriately.

Wearing disposable apron and gloves for depilatory waxing

A PRACTICAL GUIDE TO BEAUTY THERAPY LEVEL 1

The Health and Safety (Display Screen Equipment) Regulations 1992 (amended 2002)

Employers must ensure that people who use a visual display unit (VDU) more or less continuously in their job, are protected from possible adverse health effects. These include eye strain, headaches, back pain, stress and fatigue.

As a beauty assistant or beauty therapist, you will not spend much time continuously working at a computer so these regulations do not really apply to you. However, during your training, be aware of the possible effects of spending too much time working at a computer when completing assignments. You need to look after your health!

Make sure you:

- give yourself regular breaks from keyboard work, preferably involving some exercise
- don't sit in the same position for too long; change position as often as possible
- make sure the screen surface is clean
- adjust brightness and contrast controls on the screen to suit lighting conditions in the room
- adjust your chair and VDU to find the most comfortable position for you
- make sure the computer screen is positioned away from sunlight to prevent reflective 'glare'.

Manual Handling Operations Regulations 1992 (amended 2002)

Employers are required to make an assessment of the risks to their employees, of injuries at work from incorrect lifting, carrying and handling techniques and to take steps to prevent injury.

Your duties:

- ensure you lift only 'safe' weights
- adapt your posture appropriately to avoid injury when lifting, putting down, pushing, pulling, carrying or moving stock and other 'heavy' items
- take part in all manual handling training provided by your employer
- use equipment provided for your own safety when lifting or moving heavy loads.

Incorrect lifting and carrying can cause serious injuries

Activity 2.3: Manual handling

Correct lifting and handling techniques are just as important wherever you are and whatever you are doing, not just at work. Once someone has damaged their back, they can have continuing back problems throughout their life. Think of everything you have done over the last 48 hours that has involved lifting, putting down, pushing, pulling, carrying or moving something heavy. Examples might be carrying heavy shopping or moving furniture. Make a list and think about what you did, if anything, to protect your back.

_____

_____

_____

_____

_____

_____

The Local Government (Miscellaneous Provisions) Act 1982

This Act is concerned primarily with standards of cleanliness and the registration of businesses and people carrying out treatments, in particular those involving the use of needles and skin piercing. These include:

- acupuncture
- ear and body piercing
- tattooing
- epilation.

Your duties are to:

- always follow the correct workplace procedures for cleaning and maintaining your work area
- maintain high standards of personal hygiene and clean your hands thoroughly before each procedure
- ensure all instruments, equipment and materials required for treatment are clean and hygienically prepared for use
- ensure all instruments, equipment and materials used during a treatment are cleaned and stored hygienically
- keep vigilant. If you see something that looks dirty and unhygienic, do something about it!

Activity 2.4: Salon cleanliness

Does your salon stand up to close inspection? Imagine you are someone from the Health and Safety Executive, carrying out a routine inspection. With a partner, make a very detailed examination of all the salon areas, looking hard at standards of hygiene and cleanliness. Include things like floors, decorations, equipment, couch covers…everything! Write down your observations as you go along and discuss them with your supervisor afterwards.

Health and Safety (First Aid) Regulations 1981

Businesses must be able to provide emergency treatments for minor accidental injuries and unexpected situations that can happen from time to time in the salon. This means having someone available who is qualified to give first aid treatment, having a well-stocked first aid kit available and making sure that everyone knows where to find it and how to use it. A first aid certificate is valid for three years and a two-day refresher course must be completed before the expiry date of the certificate.

Your duties are to:

- know where the first aid kit is kept; be familiar with its contents and how to use them
- know who has overall responsibility for first aid in your salon and how to contact them in an emergency
- assist with basic first aid procedures as required
- take part in any first aid training offered by your employer.

REMEMBER

It is usual for somebody to have overall responsibility for first aid in the salon. Find out who is responsible in your salon and the procedures for contacting them in an emergency.

REMEMBER

If you are interested in becoming a qualified 'first aider', details of courses and examinations can be obtained from your local college or by contacting the British Red Cross, St John's Ambulance or St Andrew's Ambulance Association.

First Aid box

The Fire Precautions Act 1971, The Fire Precautions (Workplace) Regulations 1999

Staff must be trained in fire and emergency evacuation procedures and the premises must have adequate means of escape in cases of fire. All workplaces must carry out a fire **risk assessment** and have regular fire drills.

Your duties are to:

- not do anything which obstructs access to fire escape routes
- keep fire exit doors closed
- know the location of and how to use the firefighting equipment
- know what to do and what not to do in the event of a fire
- know and follow the fire drill procedures of your workplace
- report anything you think looks like a fire hazard.

REMEMBER

A fire can close the business temporarily or permanently, destroying important papers and records at the same time. It can cause extensive damage to property and result in serious injuries or even death. Everybody in the business must know how to prevent a fire from happening and how to deal with one if it happens.

The Reporting of Injuries, Diseases and Dangerous Occurrences Regulations 1995 (RIDDOR)

Personal injuries occurring at work to staff or members of the public must be reported in the salon's **Accident Book** and serious ones must be reported to the local council.

Your duties are to:

- know and use your workplace's procedures for reporting work-related injuries
- know the location of and how to fill in the salon's Accident Book
- enter details of injuries to a client, during a treatment, on their treatment record card.

Control of Substances Hazardous to Health Regulations 2002 (COSHH) (amended)

Employers are required to control people's exposure to hazardous substances in the workplace and to ensure that staff are appropriately trained in the handling of hazardous substances.

Your duties are to:

- understand the risks associated with substances you come into contact with at work
- take appropriate safety precautions when handling hazardous substances.

Know how to protect yourself from potentially hazardous substances

HEALTH MATTERS

The four main ways by which a substance may harm the body are by:

- entering the eyes
- inhalation
- swallowing
- skin contact (either by absorption or entry through a break in the skin).

The employer needs to consider these when assessing risks in the salon. Effective controls can then be introduced, backed up with staff training.

HAZARDOUS SUBSTANCES ASSESSMENT FORM

SUBSTANCE NAME: **Thick Bleach (Johnson's)**
DATA SHEET: No (**X**) Yes ( ) (attach to this form)

STORAGE DETAILS
Stored in original container in cleaning/store cupboard

CLASSIFICATION
Toxic ( ) Very toxic ( ) Harmful ( )
Irritant (**X**) Corrosive ( ) Other ( )

RISKS
Irritating to eyes and skin

PRECAUTIONS – Including PPE (Personal Protective Equipment)
1 Avoid contact with eyes and skin (wear rubber gloves and if there is a greater risk of splashing in the eyes, wear goggles).
2 Not to be used in conjunction with any other cleaning agent.
3 Not to be used on enamel or other plated surfaces.
4 Always keep upright in the original container with cap secured.
5 Use with windows open.
6 Wash hands after use

Measurement/Monitoring Necessary Yes ( ) No (**X**)
Health Surveillance Yes ( ) No (**X**)
Instruction/Training Yes (**X**) No ( )

PROCESS/HOW USED
Squirted in toilets and generally used on hard surfaces.
Used directly and also diluted in hot water and mopped.

FIRST AID
If in contact with eyes, rinse immediately with plenty of water and seek medical advice. After contact with skin, wash immediately with plenty of water.
If swallowed, seek medical advice immediately and take/show the label on the side of the bottle.

OTHER INFORMATION/ACTION
Users to read the instructions and warnings on the label.

DISPOSAL
Dispose of empty container in normal waste bins at rear of building.

DATE: 10. 05. 04

NAME: Neeta Laing

DATE OF REVIEW: 10.05.05

SIGNATURE: **Neeta Laing**

The Environmental Protection Act 1990

Some of the substances available in the salon can cause harm. The way that these substances are used and disposed of is important for protecting the environment.

Your duties are to:

- understand the risks associated with different substances and materials you come into contact with at work
- follow workplace procedures and take appropriate safety precautions when disposing of hazardous substances and waste.

Electricity at Work Regulations 1989

Electrical equipment must be inspected regularly and its maintenance and repair monitored and controlled.

Your duties are to:

- always carry out safety checks before using electrical equipment and appliances (this includes the kettle in the staff room!)
- take all necessary safety precautions when preparing, setting up and using electrical equipment
- ensure electrical equipment used during a treatment is cleaned and stored properly afterwards
- be careful when moving electrical equipment around the salon
- know and use your workplace's procedures for reporting electrical faults.

HEALTH MATTERS

If you spot an electrical fault or potential electrical hazard in the salon, report it to your supervisor. Never use equipment or an appliance that you know is unsafe.

Employer's Liability (Compulsory Insurance) Act 1969

Employers must have everyone on their payroll covered by this insurance for claims that might arise when an employee suffers injuries or illness as a result of negligence by either the employer or another employee. Employees who are injured as a result of their own negligence are not covered by this Act.

GOOD PRACTICE

Public liability insurance should be taken out by an employer to cover them for claims made by members of the public as a result of injury or damage to personal property caused by the employer or employee at work. Special **professional indemnity** insurance extends this liability to cover named employees against claims, by clients, of personal injury resulting from a treatment. All employees who give treatments should be covered by professional indemnity insurance. See www.hse.gov.uk/pubns/hse40.pdf for guidance document.

It is a good idea to display the public liability insurance certificate in reception

SELF-CHECKS

Health and safety legislation

1 Give two main responsibilities of an employer for ensuring health and safety in the workplace.

_____

_____

2 What is the main reason for the Manual Handling Operations Regulations 1992?

_____

_____

3 Why must a salon be registered with the local authority for carrying out ear piercing treatments?

_____

_____

4 State three requirements of the Fire Precautions Act 1971.

_____

_____

_____

5 What does **RIDDOR** stand for?

_____

6 Under the **COSHH** regulations, what sort of training is required for employees?

_____

_____

7 Name the special insurance that covers employees against claims, by clients, of personal injury resulting from a treatment.

_____

8 What is the proof that an employer has their employees covered by the Employers' Liability (Compulsory Insurance) Act?

_____

_____

9 What is the name of the authority that enforces health and safety legislation?

_____

Health and safety workplace policies

Health and safety policies apply to everybody working in the business. They set out the 'ground rules' and make it clear who is responsible for what and when and how things are done in order to minimise risks to health and safety.

Employers are able to control the risks to health and safety by ensuring that:

- all risks are assessed and covered by their policies
- their policies are carried out by everyone in the business
- their policies are carried out across all work activities.

There should be a range of policies in place to ensure that the salon is a safe and healthy place to be for staff, clients and visitors alike.

Some of these policies will relate directly to standards of conduct and behaviour. The way you conduct yourself and your general behaviour is very important for maintaining the health and safety of yourself and others. For example:

- Smoking should never be allowed in the salon; besides being unhealthy and smelling unpleasant, many of the substances contained in beauty products are inflammable and there is increased risk of fire where there are cigarettes and lighters present.
- Eating should not be allowed in the salon. Separate facilities should be made available for staff to take refreshments although supplies of fresh drinking water are usually readily available for clients relaxing after hydrotherapy and heat treatments.
- The consumption of alcohol is not normally allowed on salon premises although this might be permitted, in a limited way, at a social evening event planned to promote the business.

REMEMBER

Employees turning up for work under the influence of alcohol or drugs risk immediate dismissal for gross misconduct. They present an unprofessional image and cannot be trusted to work safely or competently.

You need to know where you stand with regard to your workplace's policies, especially when starting a new job. Written policies make it clear what is acceptable and what is not acceptable behaviour at work.

GOOD PRACTICE

The Health and Safety (Information for Employees) Regulations 1989 require employers to display a poster and provide leaflets telling employees what they need to know about health and safety.

Details of your salon's policies will usually be contained in a company handbook, issued to you when you start your job. Failure to comply with workplace policies can have serious consequences.

Activity 2.5: Workplace policies

In the following table, complete the boxes by writing down what policies are in place where you are training, to cover the health and safety issues listed in the first column. Ask your supervisor if you are not sure where to find the answers.

What the policy covers	What the policy says	Consequences
1 Your dress and appearance for practical work		
2 Smoking at work		
3 Drinking alcohol during your lunch break		
4 Looking after your personal tools and equipment		

Your job description

As a beauty assistant, your job description will contain at least one statement that covers your responsibilities for health and safety. Some examples are:

- 'Be committed to the health and safety of the business'
- 'Ensure health and safety policies are adhered to at all times'
- 'Ensure the salons and stock rooms meet the necessary health and safety requirements, including storage, handling and use of chemicals'
- 'Comply with all relevant Health and Safety regulations and assist the business in the implementation of its own Health and Safety Policy'
- 'Ensure that treatment areas are adequately and safely supplied with equipment and materials and that security is maintained'

Although these statements are written in general terms, they cover all the legal responsibilities you have as an employee, to avoid harming yourself or others through the work that you do.

Reporting health and safety matters

It is important for you to know the responsible person to whom you should report health and safety matters. Although the employer has overall responsibility for managing the health and safety side of the business, it is usual for them to delegate some of that responsibility to their managers and supervisors. Make sure you know the manager or supervisor to whom you should report health and safety matters. This may change depending on your job role at the time and the area of the salon in which you are working.

Ian – Leisure Manager

Sam – Spa Manager

Jenny – Nail Technician   *Lisa – Beauty Therapist*   *Vicky – Beauty Therapist*

Risks to health and safety

An injured client could sue on the grounds of professional negligence if they felt that adequate safety precautions had not been taken during their treatment. You need to know the possible risks to health and safety in your salon and how to prevent anything that could result in personal injury or damage to property. Should an emergency occur, you need to be able to do whatever you can to protect yourself and others.

Hazards and risks in your workplace

A **hazard** is something that can cause harm. A **risk** is the chance, high or low, that a **hazard** will actually cause somebody harm.

Employers have a legal duty to carry out risk assessments across all work activities to identify what hazards exist in the workplace and how likely these hazards are to cause harm. They must then decide what must be done to eliminate the hazard altogether or, if that is not possible, how to control risks so that harm is unlikely.

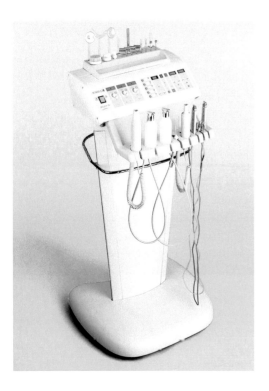

- Using a piece of electrical equipment is a typical salon activity requiring a risk assessment.
- A hazard associated with using electrical equipment is the potential for an electric shock.
- Control measures are the actions taken to prevent an electric shock as a result of using electrical equipment, for example regular visual inspections to ensure there is no damage to the cable or the plug, making sure the cable is gripped correctly, making sure the right fuse is fitted, making sure sockets are not overloaded, arranging for an annual check by a competent person (that is, a qualified electrician) and so on.
- The risk is the likelihood of an electric shock occurring after the control measures have been carried out.

REMEMBER

A risk assessment is a careful examination of what, in your work, could cause harm to people.

HAZARD OR AREA	WHO MIGHT BE HARMED	WHAT ARE THE EXISTING CONTROL MEASURES	FURTHER ACTION TO CONTROL THE RISK	PRIORITY H (HIGH)/ M (MEDIUM)/ L (LOW)	ACTION: WHO/WHEN
Electricity	Employees Clients	User's visual checks of electrical equipment before use.	Employees to report any damage or electric shocks.	H	All employees/ ongoing
		Electrical equipment purchased to British/ European standards.			
		Annual inspection of all electrical equipment (logged).	Taped cable to kettle to be removed and replaced	H	Heather Small/ Immediately
		Testing of all electrical equipment every 3 years Salon equipment tested annually.			

A sample risk assessment form

Activity 2.6: Hazards and risks

Working with a partner, see if you can think of all the risks relating to these hazards and write your answers in the spaces provided.

Hazard	Risks
Electrical flex trailing across trolley	
Therapist wearing high-heeled open-toed shoes	
Cup of tea on reception desk	
Light bulb flickering in stock room	
Loose floor tile in treatment room	
Strong fumes from the nail extension products	
Puddle of water outside shower	

Risks present in your job role

You should be aware of the particular risks to health and safety in your job role and know the precautions you must take.

As a beauty assistant, your work is varied, bringing you into contact with a wide range of clients and different areas of the salon, for example treatment areas, stock rooms and reception. You need to be conscious of the varying risks in different areas of your work.

Health and safety when assisting with treatments

When providing assistance with treatments, your main responsibilities are to:

- prepare the work areas for treatments
- clean, maintain and monitor the environment
- assist with facial treatments and nail treatments on the hands.

In order to do these effectively, you need to:

Before treatment

Ensure that everything required for treatment is available in the right condition, in the right place, at the right time, according to legal and workplace requirements.

What you should know:

- your workplace's standards and procedures in terms of cleaning, preparing and maintaining the treatment area
- the consumables required, where they are located and any special instructions for mixing or preparing them
- the equipment required and how it should be cleaned and maintained to keep it in good working order
- how the equipment and any accessories should be prepared for treatment and how much time to allow for preparing them.

The treatment area must look and be scrupulously clean and tidy for each client

What you must do:

- always follow the workplace's standards and procedures when selecting and using cleaning products
- until you are sufficiently experienced, read and follow the written instructions regarding the correct cleaning, preparation and use of equipment and accessories
- inspect equipment and accessories before treatment and report faults or breakages promptly to the relevant person
- always wear the recommended protective clothing when cleaning and preparing the treatment area.

During treatment

Assist the therapist as required and ensure the health, safety and well-being of clients during treatment, according to legal and workplace requirements.

What you should know:

- the specific tasks you are required to do in order to assist the therapist with treatment

- the limits of your responsibilities when assisting with treatment
- the workplace's standards and procedures in terms of maintaining and monitoring the treatment area and equipment
- the possible contra-actions which may occur during treatment and necessary follow up actions
- the relevant person to whom problems during the treatment should be reported.

What you must do:
- monitor the treatment area and equipment at regular intervals
- monitor the clients at regular intervals
- take immediate action if you suspect that there is a problem.

After treatment

Ensure that the treatment area is left clean and tidy according to legal and workplace requirements.

What you should know:
- the correct procedures for tidying and sanitising the area after treatment
- the person with whom you should liaise regarding the completion of duties.

What you must do:
- assist the client away from the treatment area
- remove soiled towels and linen
- return stock and equipment to store
- dispose of waste safely and correctly
- make sure that the treatment area is left in perfect condition for the next treatment.

Providing treatments: client care

You are responsible for ensuring the health and safety of your clients by taking all possible precautions to avoid injuries and adverse reactions to treatments. At level 1 you will be qualified to carry out basic facial and manicure treatments.

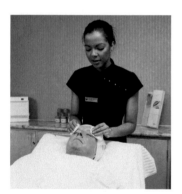

Providing a basic facial

What you must do:
- check that the client is suitable for treatment, with no contra-indications
- check that equipment, machines and tools are in good working order
- explain treatments clearly to the client beforehand so that they know what to expect
- use correct techniques; never 'skimp' on treatments
- adapt treatments appropriately to suit the needs of individual clients
- keep a check on the client's facial expressions and skin reactions during treatment to ensure that they are comfortable and reacting normally
- always apply skin tests before treatments when required and write details of the tests and their results on the client's record card
- keep accurate records of treatments given and note any abnormal reactions or problems
- know the possible contra-actions to treatment and how to treat them.

Providing a basic manicure

Contra-indication

This is a condition that makes a client unsuitable for treatment. The condition may be visible or may be revealed during your discussion with a client. Never treat a client with a contagious skin disease or any other contra-indication. If you do, you risk spreading the disease, worsening the condition or harming the client.

REMEMBER

Never allow a client to talk you into giving them a treatment that you know is contra-indicated. Their health and your reputation could be at stake.

Contra-action

A contra-action is an adverse reaction of a client to treatment. This can sometimes happen even when all the necessary safety precautions have been taken. You should be able to respond quickly to a contra-action that occurs in the salon. You should also be able to advise a client how to recognise and deal with a contra-action that occurs after they have left the salon.

Record keeping

Regrettably, we live in a society where people are inclined to sue for all sorts of things. It is very important that people who provide beauty treatments keep written records, with dates, of all the steps they have taken to ensure the suitability of the client for treatment. A client's record card should contain:

- relevant personal and contact details
- main findings from the initial consultation, including health checks
- the client's agreement to the treatment plan
- details of any 'tests' given before treatment
- the client's reactions to the treatment
- any special advice given to the client for home care, including possible contra-actions
- any retail purchases.

Written records, dated and signed by the client and yourself, will provide evidence that proper procedures have been followed.

A sample record card – front and back

This side of the record card has the client's personal details. Some of these influence the treatments given and others provide useful practical information.

(i) The initial of the client's surname is printed in the top right-hand corner of the card so that the card can be retrieved quickly from the index storage system.

(ii) The information given here is important for effective communication with the client. It is more polite to ask a client their date of birth rather than their age. Knowing this will help you to assess the condition of the skin and advise the most suitable treatments and home care.

(iii) Details of the client's doctor may be needed in an emergency. It is important to know health and medication details when assessing the skin.

(iv) These details are necessary to make an accurate diagnosis and plan appropriate beauty care.

BEAUTY BOX SALON		
Mr/Mrs/Ms	Address	Tel. no.
Surname		Home
Forenames	Date of birth	Work
Doctor's name	General state of health	Recent illness/operation
Doctor's address	Current medication	Allergies
Basic skin type	Skin history/treatment	Recommended home care
Skin tone		
Skin colour	General comments	
Muscle tone		Date of consultation
Problems		Given by
Contraindications		Signed
Recommended salon treatments		I have understood and agreed the treatment plan. Client signature Date

This side of the record card records details of the client's visits to the salon.

(i) This shows the frequency and regularity of the visits/treatments.
(ii) This shows which treatments the client has received, including skin tests.
(iii) Details of the client's reaction to treatments may be recorded; the information may be important to recall for the next visit.
(iv) It is necessary to know which therapist has treated the client. This information may be needed when making a follow-up appointment or when referring to details of the purchases made. This information is used for recommending further purchases.
(v) Client home care may be monitored by referring to details of the purchases made. This information is used for recommending further purchases.

Date	Treatment record	Comments	Initials	Retail purchases
(i)	(ii)	(iii)	(iv)	(v)

Health and safety when assisting with stock

When providing assistance in the stock room, your main responsibilities are to store and handle stock correctly and safely. A lot of money is tied up in stock. The salon loses money on old stock that has to be sold off cheaply or thrown away due to damaged packaging or 'out-of-date' products.

What you should know:

- the layout of the stock room and where everything is kept
- the COSHH regulations for storing, handling and disposing of stock
- the location of tools and equipment for dealing with new consignments of stock.

What you should do:

- lift only 'safe' weights and carry containers of stock correctly to avoid damaging your back
- keep the stock room tidy and handle stock carefully to avoid damaging containers and packaging
- use any special equipment provided for opening cases of stock, do not use your nails and fingertips as tools!

Be careful when using the special equipment for unpacking stock

Health and safety when assisting with salon reception duties

The reception is usually the busiest part of the salon because it is the control centre for salon operations. Everyone in the salon should know who is allowed at reception and how to behave there. Health and safety is just as important at reception as it is in other areas of the salon.

When providing assistance on reception, your main responsibilities are to look after clients and other visitors, maintain retail stock and displays and contribute to the efficiency and professional image of the reception.

What you should know:

- the layout of the reception and where everything is kept
- the correct, safe way of using electrical and other equipment at reception
- the workplace procedures for cleaning and maintaining the reception desk and client waiting areas.

Reception is the hub of the salon operations

What you should do:

- work cleanly and tidily at reception
- monitor the reception and waiting areas and deal promptly with any risks to health and safety
- inspect equipment at reception and report faults or breakages promptly to the relevant person
- always follow the workplace's standards and procedures when selecting and using cleaning products.

Health and safety: risks present in the whole workplace

Everyone needs to keep alert to the presence of risks in the whole workplace and to take the necessary precautions. The 'whole' workplace refers to all the areas of the business, not just the areas in which you spend most time. The whole workplace is your working environment, including the staff room.

Controlling the salon environment

Your salon should offer the same high standards of hygiene, safety and comfort throughout the working day. This is to ensure that all clients receive the same quality of service, whatever the time of their appointment. At all times, the salon must be:

- clean and tidy
- maintained at a reasonable temperature
- well ventilated
- well lit.

Maintaining a clean and tidy salon

If careful thought has gone into designing the salon, all work surfaces, wall and floor coverings, furniture and fittings will have been chosen to not only look attractive, but also to be fit for purpose and easy to clean. This is particularly important for items that will be coming into direct contact with clients or for materials and equipment that will be used during treatments.

Couches, stools and worktops should be wiped over regularly with a mild liquid detergent that cleans, deodorises and disinfects. Most products of this type are safe for use on plastics and metal and can also be used effectively for cleaning other surfaces such as countertops, sinks, workstations, footbaths, tanning beds and telephones.

REMEMBER

Cleaning products contain chemicals, therefore the **COSHH** regulations apply. Always read and follow the manufacturer's instructions carefully when preparing, using and disposing of cleaning products.

What you must do:

- make sure you know the salon's cleaning policy and follow the procedures
- practise quick but effective tidying and cleaning routines in between your work with clients
- know which cleaning methods are used in your salon and for what purpose
- understand the special care that must be taken when using different types of cleaning products.

GOOD PRACTICE

If a spillage occurs, wipe it up immediately and make sure the floor is dry to prevent slipping.

Accidents can happen at any time

Dealing with waste

Waste should be dealt with promptly. It should not be allowed to build up on trolleys and work surfaces.

What you must do:

- dispose of waste in a covered bin
- remove salon waste daily
- place contaminated needles in a yellow 'Sharps' container: when full, this should be taken to a local hospital or Drug Line for disposal
- clear away and dispose of broken glass carefully after an accident.

GOOD PRACTICE

Make sure that the waste resulting from your treatments is placed directly into a lined container and disposed of in a large, sealed refuse sack with other salon waste.

GOOD PRACTICE

When dealing with broken glass:

- clear it away immediately
- try to avoid handling broken glass; use a dustpan and brush
- if you have to touch broken glass, wear strong gloves to protect your hands
- ensure broken glass does not cause injury to anyone else once you have disposed of it; wrap it up securely in several layers of newspaper before placing in a waste bin.

Water supply

The salon needs a constant supply of clean hot and cold water. Problems with plumbing and drains are a risk to health and safety and may mean that treatments have to be delayed or even cancelled. This can cause financial loss to the business.

GOOD PRACTICE

Do not waste water. It is becoming increasingly expensive and, in some areas of the country, less plentiful in supplies. Water is heated by gas, oil or electricity, all of which have to be paid for. Heating costs are a major expense for the salon. Wasting hot water is literally pouring money down the drain!

The S bend waste trap beneath a wash basin

What you must do:

- report a blocked sink immediately to your supervisor
- do not leave the hot water tap running longer than necessary; this is both wasteful and expensive
- do not flush solid or semi-solid materials down the sink; they may cause a blockage in the pipes that carry water away from the salon to the drains outside
- in the event of a pipe bursting, turn off the water at the stopcock; this will stop the supply of water to the salon from outside
- if water comes out of the tap discoloured or with a strange smell, report it to your supervisor who should contact the local Water Authority for advice.

HEALTH MATTERS

Do not delay in attending to a blocked sink. Wastewater left standing smells unpleasant. Also, bacterial growth increases which may spread disease.

HEALTH MATTERS

In the event of a water pipe bursting, it is advisable to turn off the electricity as well as the water. Until you have done this, you should not touch any light switches or electrical appliances because if you do, you could get electrocuted.

The plumbing beneath the basin has a waste trap that holds water and stops gases and smells from the drains travelling back up the pipes. If a small object accidentally falls through the plughole, the waste trap can be investigated to see if it has settled there.

Heating and ventilation

The working temperature of the salon should be 16°C (60 – 80°F) after the first hour. Thermostatically controlled heating systems keep the salon at a comfortable temperature. They include a device that switches off the heat when the required temperature has been reached and then turns it on again as the temperature begins to fall. The heating method should not give out dangerous or offensive fumes.

There should be enough ventilation to keep the air fresh and to prevent the build-up of fumes. Extractor fans and open windows help to remove pungent smells, for example those produced by solvent-based manicure preparations and some nail technology products.

Too much exposure to pungent smells can cause nausea and headaches. Where possible, the layout of the salon should ensure that treatments creating fumes take place near an open window.

A full air-conditioning system is ideal for keeping the salon comfortable and fresh. This method recirculates air and replaces it with clean, fresh air heated to the correct temperature. It also helps to control humidity levels where water vapour is being produced, for example by a steam bath or shower.

GOOD PRACTICE

Mechanical ventilation and air conditioning systems should be cleaned and tested regularly to keep them in good working order.

What you must do:

● know how to control the heating and ventilation systems in your salon

● if possible, open a nearby window when using products that smell strongly.

HEALTH MATTERS

The air must be kept fresh. Stale air makes us feel tired and listless. This is because of the build-up of carbon dioxide in the air. If the salon is warm and air is not circulating, sweat does not evaporate as readily from the skin's surface. The body does not cool and, therefore, feels very uncomfortable.

Lighting

The lighting in the salon should be bright enough for everyone to move around safely but not so bright as to create glare. Adequate and suitable lighting is needed in order to:

● enable people to see what they are doing and where they are going

● show up potential hazards such as a step

● encourage and highlight cleanliness

● prevent eye strain.

Natural daylight is the best type of light and has the advantage of showing up 'true' colours. Artificial lighting often distorts colours. Warm white fluorescent tubes are nearly as good as daylight for colour matching. The special lighting needed for close work is usually provided by a magnifying angle-poise lamp containing a circular fluorescent tube.

The special lighting needed for close work is usually provided by a magnifying angle-poise lamp containing a circular fluorescent tube

REMEMBER

A client would be very disappointed to find that the colour of a nail enamel or lipstick looked quite different once they had left the salon, particularly if it had been bought to match with a special outfit.

Bad lighting can cause eye-strain and headaches.

What you must do:

● always make sure that you have enough light to work safely and accurately

● ensure that neither you or your client are dazzled by a bright light

● report glaring light bulbs and flickering tubes to your supervisor so that they can be checked or replaced.

To get the best out of a lighting system, light fittings should be kept clean and the ceiling should be a pale colour to reflect the light. Windows should be cleaned regularly to let in as much natural daylight as possible.

SELF-CHECKS

Your working environment

1 Who is responsible for the health, safety and comfort of the client during a treatment?

_____
_____
_____

2 Give two reasons why special care is needed when cleaning the salon.

_____
_____

3 How should salon waste be disposed of?

_____
_____
_____

4 List three precautions that should be taken when clearing away broken glass.

_____
_____
_____

5 Give two reasons why a blocked sink should be dealt with promptly.

_____
_____

6 State one reason for a sink becoming blocked.

_____

7 Why is good ventilation important in the salon?

_____
_____
_____

8 Describe two methods of ventilation.

_____
_____

9 State two ways in which bad lighting can affect health.

_____
_____

10 Which is the best type of light for colour matching?

_____
_____
_____

Health and safety in the treatment areas

- All equipment should be serviced regularly according to the contract with the supplier and follow up servicing agreements. This is the responsibility of the salon manager.
- The manufacturer's instructions should always be followed. These should be made available to all staff concerned with maintaining health and safety in the treatment areas.
- Hygiene is of utmost importance. All furniture and equipment should be cleaned and maintained according to the manufacturer's instructions.
- Spillages should be cleared up immediately.
- There should always be sufficient supplies of clean towels and gowns, which are replaced regularly.
- Laundry baskets containing soiled gowns and towels should be emptied regularly and not allowed to accumulate.
- Clients must always be checked for contra-indications before treatment.
- Clients should be monitored for contra-actions throughout treatment and appropriate action taken.
- Records of treatments and equipment usage should be maintained.
- Waste should not be allowed to build up in the treatment area.

There should always be sufficient supplies of clean towels and gowns

Health and safety in the stock room

- Stock should be stored in a cool, dark place.
- Products should be stored correctly so that they do not deteriorate or become damaged.
- Boxes should not be stacked too high; stretching up to reach stock is dangerous.
- Care should be taken with flimsy packaging; heavier goods should be stocked on low shelves and not on top of fragile items.
- Large, glass bottles and jars should be stored at low level.
- Aisles or passage ways must not be blocked with containers of stock.

A computerised till

Health and safety at reception

- The reception desk and waiting areas should be kept clean and tidy at all times.
- Waste should not be allowed to build up at reception.
- Furniture, decorations and fittings should be kept clean and maintained in good order.
- Smoking should not be allowed at reception.
- Electronic equipment such as computers, telephones, tills and fax machines should be used properly and kept clean; flexes, wires and plugs should be checked regularly for electrical safety.
- Retail samples and testers should be checked regularly to ensure they are clean and undamaged; damaged testers should be removed due to the risk of contamination.
- Correct procedures should be followed to ensure the safety of clients, visitors and colleagues in an emergency.

Health and safety: reporting and dealing with risks

Everyone at work must take responsibility for dealing with risks associated with their own job role and for reporting those that are not.

If you spot a hazard, you should report or deal with it promptly so that the risks associated with it can be removed before causing harm. The person to whom you should report any health and safety issues or hazards is referred to as the responsible person. This could be your supervisor, your line manager or your employer.

You are responsible for ensuring that:

- your own actions do not create any health and safety risks
- you do not ignore significant risks in your workplace
- you take sensible action to put things right
- you report situations which pose a danger to people in the workplace
- you seek advice when you need it.

GOOD PRACTICE

Always read the supplier's and manufacturer's instructions for the safe use of equipment, materials and products. These may be written on the packaging or containers or be issued as a separate leaflet. Always read labels and make sure the guidance or instructions on them does not get worn off or covered. Read any leaflets provided by manufacturers and keep them for reference.

Activity 2.7: How your workplace handles risks you are unable to deal with

Working in pairs, fill in the following table to show what you think are the risks, who you think is responsible for dealing with each of the risks and what they should do.

Hazard	Risk	Responsible person	Action
Dirty water running through taps			
Faulty thermostat on depilatory wax heater			
Broken top on bottle of acetone			
Frayed flex on kettle in staff room			

Activity 2.8: Safe working practices

You must know the safe working practices for your own job role. Choose one aspect of your work, for example assisting on reception, assisting with treatments or helping in the stock room and then find one example of each of the following that relates to that aspect of your work. In the spaces provided, give details of what you have found.

1　A risk assessment carried out in the area.

_____

_____

_____

2　A hazard safety sheet relating to a piece of equipment in the area.

_____

_____

_____

3　A **hazard data sheet** relating to a chemical product used in the area.

_____

_____

_____

4　A **product data sheet** listing all the general characteristics or components of a product used in the area.

_____

_____

_____

Your personal presentation

The way you present yourself is important, not just so that you look 'professional' (see Chapter 1, pages 13-15) but also for health and safety reasons.

Your overall

Your overall must always look spotlessly clean and well pressed. Wear a clean overall every day. An overall that looks dirty is dirty and harbours germs. A tight overall will be uncomfortable to wear and, particularly if tight under the arms, will increase sweating. The sweat will remain 'trapped' in the fibres of your overall, discolouring and damaging the fabric. If you wear a tight overall, you will become too warm and feel tired and listless. You will also risk BO (body odour).

The longer you wear your overall the more likely it is to pick up smells. For example, your clients and colleagues will be able to tell if you have been wearing your overall while smoking. Don't do it! Stale smells are very unpleasant and give the impression that you are not clean.

REMEMBER

Sweat evaporates freely from skin that is exposed to air, but not from areas where two surfaces of skin meet or where clothes and shoes fit tightly. The evaporation of sweat helps to cool the body and keep it at a comfortable temperature.

GOOD PRACTICE

Always wear an apron or tabard when preparing or giving treatments to protect from spills which could stain or damage your overall.

REMEMBER

Wear clean fresh underwear every day. If you wear an underskirt make sure that it does not show below your overall.

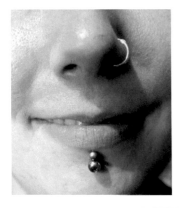

Jewellery

Rings harbour germs that could be transferred to your client during a treatment if brought into contact with their skin. Rings with stones in are particularly unsuitable as they can scratch the client, causing discomfort and possibly damaging the surface of their skin.

Piercings, especially facial ones, also harbour germs. Do not touch these and then a client or you risk the possibility of spreading these germs.

HEALTH MATTERS

If you wear a ring there could be as many germs under it as there are people in Europe... this is a fact! Millions of germs can also hide under watches and bracelets.

REMEMBER

Broken skin provides a route for germs to enter into the deeper layers of the flesh.

Hands

Your hands need to be kept clean and in very good condition. Germs collect on your hands all the time and these are easily transferred to your client during a treatment, particularly if the skin of your hands is broken or rough. Wash your hands before, during and following treatments and regularly throughout the day. Dry them well after washing and keep them moisturised with hand lotion to soften the skin and prevent it from cracking. Wear gloves to protect your hands when doing jobs that could damage them, for example when using cleaning products or mixing chemicals.

Feet

It is important to look after your feet. You will be on them for most of the day! The most important part of looking after your feet is wearing the correct shoes. Shoes that are too small or too narrow cause your toes to 'bunch up', putting stress on the joints and damaging the skin. Shoes that are too high get very uncomfortable over the course of the day and affect your posture. The shoes you wear for work should have low heels and fully cover your toes.

REMEMBER

The majority of foot problems are caused by ill-fitting shoes. Shoes that fit properly provide space for your feet and toes to spread and prevent them from getting too hot and uncomfortable. Foot sprays and medicated foot powders help to keep the feet cool and dry. The skin of the feet, particularly between the toes, needs to be kept dry to avoid diseases such as athlete's foot.

HEALTH MATTERS

Tight shoes are very unhealthy. They cause the feet to sweat more and become hot. Warmth and moisture provide an ideal environment for germs to grow and spread. Also, because tight shoes are uncomfortable, they 'throw' your posture out when walking. This affects your balance and puts a strain on other parts of your body.

'You'll have to break them in!'

Nails

The shorter the nails are, the easier they are to keep clean. Germs collect under long nails and are easily transferred to the client's skin. Your fingernails should be no longer than the end of the fingertips when looking at your hands with your palms facing you. Regular scrubbing with a nailbrush helps to loosen dirt trapped underneath your nails.

GOOD PRACTICE

As well as keeping your nails short, you should make sure that their edges are smooth and rounded. Broken nails or nails that are pointed can scratch the client's skin.

REMEMBER

Do not wear nail polish when preparing or providing facial treatments. Your nails may come into direct contact with the client's skin and they could be allergic to your nail polish. This could cause an unpleasant skin reaction.

Nails that are free from enamel can be seen to be clean and this is reassuring for a client. Only wear nail enamel if you are employed as a manicurist or nail technician.

Teeth

Your teeth, gums and breath are often a reflection of your general health. A dentist can pick up all sorts of clues from examining your teeth. You should have regular appointments to see your dentist and look after your teeth well in between visits. Regular brushing, flossing and use of mouthwash helps prevent the build-up of food, particularly sugars, which eventually causes tooth decay and other dental problems.

REMEMBER

Cigarettes, garlic and other strongly flavoured foods can linger and cause 'bad breath'. This can be very offensive to other people.

Hair

Your hair and scalp collect grease, dust, scurf and parasites that need to be removed with regular washing and brushing and not brought into contact with your client. A smart, manageable style is best for work. If your hair is long enough to fall forward over a client when you are working on them, tie it back, away from your face, in a neat style.

GOOD PRACTICE

Wash and disinfect your combs and brushes regularly. Infection can occur if the scalp is scratched with dirty hair equipment.

HEALTH MATTERS

Did you know that a 1mm hair follicle can harbour 50,000 germs?

Body freshness

Have at least one daily bath or shower. This removes the build-up of sweat and loose, dead skin cells. Bacteria thrive in warm, moist areas of the body such as the armpits and feet. If you do not wash them away regularly, the bacteria produce unpleasant body odour (BO) that everybody notices but no one likes to mention!

Use an antiperspirant. This has a cooling, astringent (tightening) effect, preventing the build-up of sweat that causes body odour. Most antiperspirants are also bactericidal. Under normal circumstances, antiperspirants stay effective all day but it is a good idea to keep one at work just in case. By all means wear perfume but just a light fragrance to help you feel and smell fresh. Strong perfumes can be too heavy and are a bit overbearing for day wear.

HEALTH MATTERS

Deodorants are not generally as effective as antiperspirants. Although most have some bactericidal properties, they only mask smells. They do not deal with the real cause of the problem, which is a build-up of sweat. Some people, however, prefer to use a deodorant as their skin can be sensitive to the extra ingredients contained in an antiperspirant.

Your posture

Good posture is important for your health. With good posture, the muscles and joints of your body are lined up correctly and this means that they can function efficiently. Poor posture increases the stress on joints, bones, ligaments and muscles. This can lead to changes which affect the way muscles work. The muscles suffer through lack of circulation, causing aches and pains. Nerves can become 'trapped' producing numbness or tingling.

Always stand or sit 'tall' with your back straight and your head held up. Apart from being good for your posture this shows that you are confident.

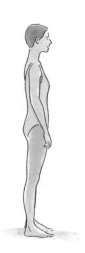

REMEMBER

Your workplace will have policies regarding appearance and dress code. These are the rules and you *must* stick to them.

ACTIVITY

Activity 2.9: Risks and behaviours

Working with a partner or in a small group, discuss the possible risks to health and safety of each of these behaviours. Check out your answers with your supervisor.

- Taking a call on your mobile when working on your own in the stock room.
- Wearing your long hair 'down' for work because your supervisor is on holiday and you think you won't get caught.
- Having a couple of glasses of wine with a friend, during your lunch break, to celebrate their birthday.
- Rushing in late for work because you have overslept.
- Wearing your *huge* solitaire diamond engagement ring at work because you cannot bear to take it off!

Your lifestyle

Although the atmosphere in a beauty salon is usually calm and very relaxing, the work can be quite demanding. Apart from always having to look your best and appear on top form for your clients and colleagues (even when, sometimes, you don't feel like it!) you may have to spend quite a lot of time on your feet or sitting in certain positions providing treatments. You may need to do quite a lot of lifting and carrying, for example if a consignment of new stock arrives or when assisting clients on and off the treatment couch.

Whatever the work is on any particular day, you will need to be strong and healthy with lots of energy. This means looking after yourself and ensuring you get enough:

- sleep
- exercise
- fresh air
- nourishment
- enjoyable leisure time.

Not looking after yourself means doing any of the following:

- smoking
- taking 'recreational' drugs
- drinking excess alcohol
- eating 'junk' food
- eating hardly anything or nothing at all
- eating too much
- neglecting your personal hygiene
- staying up very late and waking up tired and bad-tempered
- spending most of your 'spare' time indoors, doing nothing in particular.

You must put as much effort into looking after yourself as you do looking after your clients!

ACTIVITY

Activity 2.10: Assess your lifestyle – are you healthy enough to be a beauty assistant?

Using all the information in the previous section, write an account of your own lifestyle behaviours, highlighting the good aspects of how you live your life but also where there is room for improvement. Your account should be contained on one side of A4 paper. When you have finished, award yourself a mark out of 10 to show how healthy you think your lifestyle is and set yourself three action points for improving it! Ask your supervisor and colleagues for their opinions. Your library or study centre will be able to help you. Professional associations, the internet, beauty recruitment agencies and trade journals are also sources of information.

1 _____
_____
_____

2 _____
_____
_____

3 _____
_____
_____

Personal presentation

1 Explain the causes of body odour.

_____

_____

2 State the main difference between a deodorant and an antiperspirant.

_____

_____

3 Give three reasons for wearing an overall.

_____

_____

_____

4 What are the main reasons for not wearing jewellery at work?

_____

_____

5 Give two reasons why nail enamel should not be worn when giving a facial treatment.

_____

_____

6 Why should long hair be styled off the face?

_____

_____

7 Give three reasons why make-up should be worn for work.

_____

_____

_____

8 In your own words, explain what 'having a professional image' means.

_____

_____

_____

Treatment hygiene

We spend our lives surrounded by what are commonly known as 'germs'. Some germs are harmless, some are even beneficial, but others present a danger to us because they cause disease. The germs that cause disease are usually spread by:

- unclean hands
- contaminated tools
- sores and pus
- discharges from the nose and mouth
- shared use of items such as towels and cups
- close contact with infected skin cells
- contaminated blood or tissue fluid.

Germs can easily be spread and cause infections

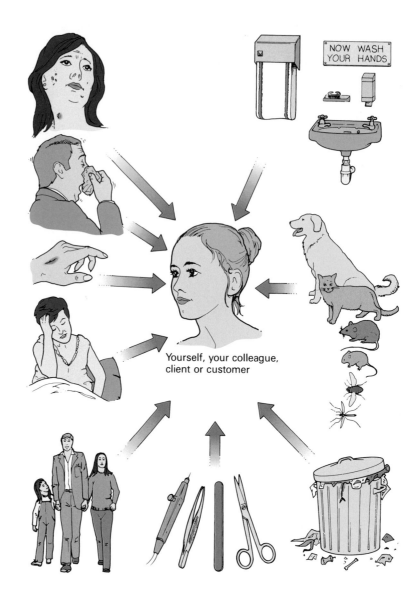

Yourself, your colleague, client or customer

Infection

Infection occurs when the body becomes contaminated, usually with bacteria, parasites or a virus. The reaction to the infection will depend on its cause and the part of the body that is infected.

The general signs of infection are:

● inflammation

● swelling

● pus.

Pus is a yellowish substance that forms when the body fights bacteria. It consists of white blood cells, dead and living bacteria and fragments of dead tissue destroyed by the bacteria. Pus is sometimes greenish in colour, depending on the type of bacteria present.

Cross-infection

Cross-infection occurs directly, through personal contact, or indirectly, through contact with an article or implement that has been contaminated. Always work hygienically and do everything you can to avoid the spread of infection.

What you must do:

- make sure you can recognise the signs of infection
- avoid any form of contact that might put your client, your colleagues or yourself at risk
- provide a clean gown and towels for each client
- wash your hands regularly, before, during and after treatments
- use only scrupulously clean tools and equipment
- wear disposable gloves when handling waste and during a treatment when appropriate
- dispose of all materials, including used gloves, in a sealed plastic bag
- put sharp items in containers for disposal
- advise clients about applying their own aftercare if a treatment has produced spots of blood or tissue fluids on the skin.

Secondary infection

Secondary infection occurs following injury when the skin is broken and open to infection.

What you must do:

- always practise safe techniques using tools and equipment that are in perfect working order
- look after your hands, keeping the skin soft and pliable; cuts and grazes should be covered with a waterproof dressing
- if the skin (yours or your client's) is accidentally broken, immediately clean the area and apply a suitable antiseptic.

Viruses

Viruses are the tiniest germs, yet they are responsible for an enormous range of human diseases. Viruses can only survive in living cells. The following are examples of viral infections:

- common cold: the virus is spread by coughing and sneezing and is carried through the air as a droplet infection
- cold sore: this virus remains dormant in the mucous membranes of the skin and is triggered by sunlight or general debility. Cold sores are most likely to spread when they are weeping tissue fluid
- warts: there are several types of wart. Verruca plantaris is a wart that occurs commonly under the feet and is spread by close contact.

AIDS (Acquired Immune Deficiency Syndrome)

AIDS is caused by a virus (HIV). The virus attacks the body's natural immune system and makes it very vulnerable to other infections, which may eventually cause death. Some people are known to be 'HIV positive', which means that they are carrying the virus yet without having the symptoms of AIDS. HIV carriers are able to pass on the virus to someone else through infected blood or tissue fluid, for example through cuts or broken skin. The virus does not live for long outside the body.

Hepatitis B

Many people feel most threatened by AIDS but, in fact, there is a much higher risk of cross-infection with hepatitis B. This disease of the liver is caused by a virus (HBV), which is transmitted by infected blood and tissue fluids. Hepatitis B is one of the most infectious diseases there is. The virus is very resistant and can survive outside the body. People can be very ill for a long time with a hepatitis B infection. It is a very weakening disease and can be fatal. Strict hygiene practices are essential to prevent hepatitis B from spreading in the salon.

Bacteria

Bacteria are tiny and highly resistant. They can enter the body by:

- entry through breaks in the skin
- being breathed in
- being taken in with food.

Bacteria are capable of breeding outside the body and can, therefore, be caught easily through personal contact or by touching a contaminated article. The following are examples of bacterial infections of the skin.

Impetigo

Bacteria enter the body through broken skin and cause blisters which weep and crust over. The condition is highly infectious and can be spread easily by dirty tools.

Boils

Boils occur when bacteria enter the hair follicle through a surface scratch or by close contact with an infected person.

Whitlow

A whitlow can be caused by the bacteria invading the pad of the finger through a break in the skin, for example from a splinter.

Impetigo

Parasites

Vegetable parasites are fungi that feed off the waste products of the skin they invade. Some vegetable parasites confine themselves to the surface of the skin. Others invade the deeper tissues. Infections caused by vegetable parasites are very easily transmitted by personal contact or by touching contaminated articles. The following are examples of infections caused by vegetable parasites.

Tinea pedis

In this condition, the fungus thrives in the warm, moist environment between the toes and, sometimes, under the feet. The condition is picked up easily by direct contact with recently shed infected skin cells.

Tinea unguium (*ringworm of the nail*)

This condition may result from contact with the fungus present on other parts of the body. For example, toenails may become infected during an outbreak of athlete's foot, which, if touched, could then spread to the hands.

Animal parasites are small insects that cause disease by invading the skin and using human blood or protein as a source of nourishment. Diseases caused by animal parasites usually occur as the result of prolonged contact with an infected person. The following are examples of disease caused by animal parasites.

Scabies

These tiny mites burrow through the outside layer of the epidermis and lay their eggs underneath the skin surface. The condition is very itchy and causes a rash and swelling. Characteristic line formations show where the burrows have been formed.

Head lice

Lice are small parasites that puncture the skin and suck blood. They lay eggs on the hair close to the scalp. The unhatched eggs are called nits and can be seen as shiny, pearl-coloured oval bodies that cling to the hair shaft.

Sanitisation

'Sanitisation' refers to any procedures undertaken in the salon to remove dirt and reduce the risk of infection. Effective sanitisation procedures ensure that hands, tools, equipment and implements are safe to use directly on the client during treatment.

Sterilisation

Sterilisation is the complete destruction of germs and bacteria. In an ideal world all tools and equipment coming into contact with the client during a treatment would be sterile. Unfortunately, this is not possible. Once a sterilised object is exposed to the air, it is no longer sterile.

Articles that have been cleaned, sterilised and stored hygienically are safe to use on the client, particularly when kept soaking in or wiped over with a sterilising solution or disinfectant before use.

There are different methods of sterilisation available but not all are reliable or suitable for a beauty salon. The one you are most likely to see is steam sterilizing, which is done in an autoclave.

Autoclave

An autoclave

Using an autoclave is the most effective method of sterilisation. It involves steaming at high pressure. Steam is produced from a reservoir of water and is contained under pressure at a minimum of 121 °C (250 °F) for 15 minutes. Special indicators change colour to show the required temperature has been reached. Articles can be 'stacked' at different levels in an autoclave so they can fit quite a lot in. Sterilisation by autoclave is suitable for stainless steel and glass items. Other items may be suitable but you should check first that they are made of a material that can withstand the process.

The very high temperature required to kill some germs destroys certain materials in much the same way that over-cooking ruins food!

Other, less effective, forms of sterilisation you may come across are:

Ultraviolet cabinet

An ultraviolet cabinet

Ultraviolet rays have a very low rate of penetration. They sterilise only the surface of objects, so are suitable only for solid tools such as cuticle nippers. Items have to be turned halfway through the sterilisation process to ensure that all surfaces have been treated with the rays. The generally recommended exposure time is 15 minutes each side. Micro-organisms such as bacteria may hide in little cracks and other shaded areas. Therefore, this method is often used in addition to another sterilisation technique to ensure items are completely sterilised. Items such as manicure tools are often stored in the cabinet as it provides a sterile environment until required for use.

Glass bead steriliser

Glass bead sterilisers reach a temperature of between 190 and 300 °C (374 – 572 °F) depending on the model. The temperature has to be maintained for 30–60 minutes. If extra items are put into the steriliser during this period, the temperature of the beads drops and the effects are lost. Glass bead sterilisers can hold only very small items and have limited use in a beauty salon.

Disinfection

Glass bead steriliser

Disinfectants are used to clean work surfaces, trolleys and equipment. They remove contamination but they do not kill all the germs. Disinfectants only reduce the number of germs but this is usually enough for maintaining hygienic conditions.

Chemical sterilisers and disinfectants

Concentrated liquid chemical agents are available, which need to be diluted for use. Some chemical agents can act as sterilisers or disinfectants, depending on the strength of the solution used and the time items need to be kept soaking in them.

Tools should always be washed in warm, soapy water and rinsed well in clean running water, then dried with a clean paper towel before being placed in the disinfectant or sterilising fluid. This ensures the removal of dust, dirt and grease, which could act as a barrier. It also prevents contamination of the soaking solution.

HEALTH MATTERS

Some liquid chemicals used for disinfecting and sterilising are very harmful to the skin and great care is needed when handling them. Remember the **COSHH** regulations. Always read and follow the manufacturer's instructions carefully.

ACTIVITY

Activity 2.11: Know your cleaning and tidying procedures

Find out about the cleaning and tidying procedures used in the reception, stock room, facial and manicure treatment areas of your salon including:

- waste removal
- cleaning procedures
- frequency
- materials/products used
- special instructions.

Complete the form on the following page.

AREA:				
	RECEPTION DESK	STOCK ROOM	FACIAL TREATMENT ROOM	MANICURE STATION
WASTE REMOVAL				
SPECIAL INSTRUCTIONS				
MATERIALS/ PRODUCTS				
FREQUENCY				
CLEANING PROCEDURES				

Activity 2.12: Sanitising your hands

We all think we know how to wash our hands but many of us don't do it properly. Wash your hands, following the instructions provided and compare this with your usual hand washing treatment.

Simply rinsing the tips of fingertips under cold water does not count. Here are some reminders:

- Always use warm water.
- It is better to wet hands before applying soap as this prevents irritation.
- Rub hands together vigorously for about 15 seconds, making sure both sides of the hands are washed thoroughly, around the thumbs, between each finger and around and under the nails.
- Then, rinse with clean water.

Germs spread more easily if hands are wet so dry them thoroughly. Use a clean dry towel, paper towel or air dryer.

HEALTH MATTERS

1,000 times as many germs spread from damp hands than dry hands.

SELF-CHECKS

Treatment hygiene

1 List four ways of spreading infection in the salon.

_____
_____
_____
_____

2 What are the general signs of infection?

_____
_____
_____
_____

3 Distinguish between cross-infection and secondary infection.

_____
_____
_____
_____

4 Why does infection with Hepatitis B present a greater risk in the salon than infection with AIDS?

_____
_____
_____
_____

5 Explain the difference between sanitisation and sterilisation.

_____
_____
_____
_____

6a State two items of beauty equipment that may be sterilised effectively in an autoclave.

_____
_____
_____
_____

6b Name two items of beauty equipment that would not be suitable for sterilising in an autoclave.

_____

_____

7 Give three disadvantages of sterilisation by ultraviolet rays.

_____

_____

_____

8 State three ways of ensuring the effectiveness of disinfectants and sterilising fluids.

_____

_____

_____

Accidents

Accidents can happen not just when you are treating clients, but also when taking breaks, returning equipment to store, dealing with stock, cleaning up or even just moving around the salon. The employer is responsible for ensuring that the layout of the salon is safe and that staff have been trained to protect themselves from physical injury. Accidents are far less likely to occur in a 'safe' working environment. The main cause of accidents is negligence.

What you must do:

● keep alert; as soon as you spot a potential danger, either do something about it or report it to someone who can

● be conscientious in all aspects of your work; protect yourself and those around you.

REMEMBER

A hazard is something with the potential to cause harm, for example a trailing cable from a piece of electrical equipment.

A risk is the likelihood of the hazard's potential being realised, for example if the cable is trailing across the floor where it is likely to trip someone up. Ensuring that the cable runs along a wall, out of the way, reduces the risk.

GOOD PRACTICE

All accidents in the salon must be recorded on a report form and entered in the **accident book**. This is a requirement of the **Health and Safety at Work Act**. The report should state the names of the people involved, details of the accident, any injuries sustained and any follow-up action taken.

Lifting and handling

Serious injuries can result from lifting, carrying and moving heavy loads. You must be able to identify 'safe' weights for lifting and know how to adapt your posture to avoid straining your back. This is particularly important when moving equipment, assisting clients on and off the beauty couch and when dealing with stock.

What you must do:

- ensure your route is clear
- grasp the load firmly with the palms of your hands (not fingertips)
- hold the load close to your body
- do not change your grip while carrying
- let your legs, not your back, take the strain
- keep your spine straight
- avoid jerking; never twist your body while picking up a load
- lift in easy stages e.g. floor to knee to start with
- avoid over-stretching.

REMEMBER

Lowering heavy objects can be just as dangerous as lifting them. Take your time. Keep your back straight with feet apart and bend at your knees and hips. This will take the strain off your back.

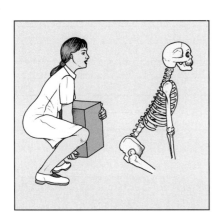
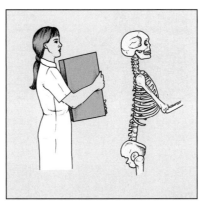

Correct lifting and carrying technique: avoid straining your back when moving heavy stock

ACTIVITY

Activity 2.13: Hazards and risks

Oh no! What's happening in each of these pictures and how could it have been prevented? Tell the story in each of the spaces provided. Identify the hazards and risks involved.

HEALTH MATTERS

When lifting, keep your knees bent and your back straight at all times. If you lift incorrectly, you could strain a ligament or a joint in your spine.

▶▶

Accidents

1 Give two responsibilities of the employer for ensuring the safety of staff.

2 State four responsibilities of the employee for ensuring the safety of themselves and others.

3 When are accidents most likely to occur in the salon?

4 List four ways of avoiding back strain when lifting and carrying a heavy load.

5 Name three pieces of legislation that cover the health and safety of clients in the salon.

6 Distinguish between a hazard and a risk. Give one example of each to explain your answer.

Fire safety

A fire can close the business temporarily or permanently, destroying important papers and records at the same time. It can cause extensive damage to property and result in serious injuries or even death. Everybody in the business must know how to prevent a fire from happening and how to deal with a fire if one happens.

GOOD PRACTICE

Smoking is now generally recognised as being anti-social as well as dangerous to health. Smoking should not be allowed in the salon and particularly anywhere near stock.

The common causes of fires are:

- electrical faults
- smouldering cigarette ends
- open flames
- matches
- heaters.

All electrical work in the salon should be undertaken by a qualified electrician. Ideally, smoking should not be allowed anywhere on the business premises. Main supplies of flammable materials should be stored well away from sources of heat in a closed, metal cupboard. Loose paper and cardboard should not be left lying around.

REMEMBER

Many beauty products are flammable. This means that they are capable of catching fire and burning. Flammable products must be kept away from heat and electricity.

What you must do:

- keep flammable products away from sources of heat
- avoid overloading electrical circuits
- never leave the flex of an electric heater trailing where it could be tripped over
- switch off and disconnect electrical appliances after use
- do not smoke
- avoid placing towels over electric or gas heaters
- use a safety lighter in preference to matches for lighting a gas heater
- before leaving at night, check that bins are emptied and that all electrical appliances are unplugged.

REMEMBER

You should not expose yourself to danger when fighting a fire. Your personal safety is a priority.

Firefighting equipment

A fire should be detected and tackled within a few minutes of it breaking out. Employees should be trained in the correct use of firefighting equipment. This may be used to put out a small fire but, more usually, it helps to keep control of the fire until the fire brigade arrives.

The local fire authority will provide advice regarding the best locations and types of equipment for the business.

REMEMBER

Water or foam extinguishers are not normally suitable for a fire in the salon because such a fire would usually involve flammable products or electrical equipment. A carbon dioxide gas or dry powder extinguisher is the type normally recommended for salon use.

Fire extinguishers

There are different types of extinguishers for different types of fires. Using the wrong type could make the fire worse.

Know your fire extinguisher colour code

RED	*BLUE*	*CREAM*	*BLACK*	*GREEN*
Water	Dry powder	Foam	CO_2 Carbon dioxide	Vapourising liquids
Unsafe all voltages	Safe all voltages	Unsafe all voltages	Safe all voltages	Safe all voltages
Wood, paper, textiles etc.	Flammable liquids	Flammable liquids	Flammable liquids	Flammable liquids

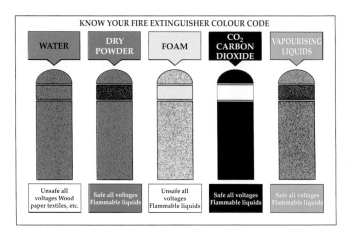

Colour coded fire extinguishers

Fire blanket

A blanket is used to smother a small, localised fire or if a person's clothing is on fire.

Sand

A bucket of sand is used to soak up liquids which are the source of a fire and, also, to smother the fire.

Water hoses

Hoses are used to extinguish large fires, for example those caused by paper. Buckets of water may be used to extinguish a small fire caused by paper.

Once it has started, a fire can rip through the premises in minutes. The most important thing is to get away from the fire to safety. This means getting everybody out of the salon, even if they are in the middle of a treatment. If it is safe to do so, a designated person should take the appointment book and visitor's book with them as they leave the building. When everybody is outside, they should gather at a muster point. Their names should be checked against the names in the books. The emergency services must be told if anyone is missing.

GOOD PRACTICE

If you have time, shut windows and doors and turn off electric and gas appliances. This will help to prevent the fire from spreading.

REMEMBER

In the event of a fire:

- do not use lifts
- do not waste time collecting personal belongings before evacuating the premises.

What you must do:

- never ignore the smell of burning: if there is a fire, the sooner you know the better
- sound the fire alarm if there is one
- know where the firefighting equipment is kept and how to use it
- know the emergency evacuation procedures for your salon
- know the location of the nearest fire exit
- know where to assemble outside the building on evacuation
- know how to call the emergency services
- find out where the nearest phone is
- check for injuries and continue to take care of your client and others while you wait for the emergency services to arrive.

REMEMBER

There are other times when you might need to call the emergency services, for example, flooding, gas leak, an intruder, bomb scare. By dialling 999 or 112, you can get connected directly to the Fire, Police and Ambulance services. Emergency 999 calls are free, even when they are made from a public telephone box.

GOOD PRACTICE

The salon should have regular fire drills to prepare staff for a real emergency. The fire alarm should be checked regularly to make sure it is working properly. New staff should be trained in fire and emergency evacuation procedures as soon as they start their job.

Calling the emergency services

It is very important to try not to panic and to speak clearly and not too quickly when calling for help from the emergency services.

What you must do:

- dial 999
- tell the operator you want the Fire Service
- give your telephone number and location. If you are in a public telephone box, these details will be displayed

- wait for the Fire Service to come on the line
- give the full address of the emergency and other relevant details of the fire
- report any injuries
- listen carefully to any questions you are asked and answer them calmly
- listen very carefully to any instructions you are given
- after the call, replace the receiver and wait with the others, in a safe place, for the Fire Service to arrive.

Electrical safety

All electrical items must be tested for safety, at least once a year, by a qualified electrician. Records should be kept of the tests. The main risks associated with unsafe electrical equipment are electric shock and fire.

REMEMBER

You must not treat clients with any piece of electrical equipment for which you have not received training. A record must be kept of when the training took place.

A PRACTICAL GUIDE TO BEAUTY THERAPY LEVEL 1

Electric shock

If a fault develops in an electrical appliance, the outer casing may become 'live'. This may cause anyone using or touching the appliance to receive an electric shock. The current will pass straight through the body from the mains to earth, contracting the muscles in its path. The muscles may stay contracted, causing both breathing and the heart to stop. A mild electric shock is unpleasant. A severe electric shock can be fatal. For the treatment of electric shock, see the table on page 80.

Fire

A fire can occur as the result of poor electrical maintenance, for example faulty or damaged flexes, plugs and switches; or if the electrical circuit becomes overloaded. This can happen when two or more machines are being operated from one socket using an adaptor. If the correct fuse is not fitted, the socket may become overloaded with current and get dangerously hot.

> **REMEMBER**
> Electrical safety is just as important in the staff room as it is in the salon. A kettle that is unsafe can present as big a risk to health as a faulty piece of salon equipment.

Electrical precautions

Basic safety checks should be carried out before using any piece of electrical equipment. Machines should be handled carefully and stored safely between treatments.

When using any electrical appliance or piece of equipment, always check that:
- cables and flexes are in good condition with no signs of fraying or worn insulation
- there are no trailing flexes which could cause someone to trip
- the plug is intact; if it is cracked or broken it must be replaced
- there are no loose connections; leads should feel firmly attached and switches secure
- the appliance is on a level and stable base
- there is no water in the immediate area
- the appliance is switched off and disconnected from the mains after use
- the appliance is left clean and stored properly
- cables and flexes are wound up and secured to avoid them becoming damaged in between uses
- sockets are not overloaded or broken.

> **REMEMBER**
> Repairs must be attended to promptly. The salon loses business for each day it is unable to use the equipment for providing treatments.

> **HEALTH MATTERS**
> Do not touch equipment, plugs, sockets or flexes with hands that are damp or wet. This could give you an electric shock.

GOOD PRACTICE

Written details of the fault should be attached to the machine, together with the date it became faulty. This will help to identify the problem and determine if the machine is still under guarantee.

Identifying and reporting faulty equipment

Once a beauty therapist has been trained on a piece of equipment, they will know the characteristic features which show that the machine is working properly. Having carried out the basic safety checks, they always test the equipment on themselves in front of the client. This is particularly important if the client has not had the treatment before and is feeling a little nervous. If anything feels, sounds, smells or appears wrong to the therapist when testing the equipment, they do not proceed with treatment.

GOOD PRACTICE

If you are asked to 'deal with' a piece of equipment that has been found to be faulty, take it out of use immediately and report it to the responsible person. This could be your supervisor, the salon manager or technician.

SELF-CHECKS

Electrical safety

1 What are the two main risks associated with electrical equipment?

_____

_____

2 Give four indications that a piece of electrical equipment is not safe to use.

_____

_____

_____

_____

3 Explain the action that should be taken if a machine develops a fault.

_____

_____

_____

_____

4 Why are electrical appliances 'earthed' for safety?

_____

_____

_____

5 Name the main piece of legislation that applies to the safety of electrical equipment in the salon. Outline the main requirements of this legislation.

_____

_____

_____

First aid

You need a basic knowledge of first aid so that you can assist with minor accidental injuries or unexpected situations that happen from time to time in the salon. For a list of situations you may help with, see the table on page 80. More serious injuries, for example those involving acute pain, loss of consciousness or serious bleeding, should be dealt with by a qualified first aider, doctor or nurse.

First aid kit

Health and Safety regulations require the salon to have a first aid kit readily available. All staff should know what the first aid box looks like and where it is kept. It is recommended that the box is green with a white cross marked on it and that it is dust proof and free from damp. The contents should be sufficient to cover most emergency situations.

Essential items are:

- a first aid guidance card
- ten assorted plasters (preferably waterproof)
- different sizes of sterile dressings: three medium, one large, one extra large
- one sterile eye pad
- two triangular bandages
- two crepe roller bandages
- six safety pins
- disposable gloves.

Useful additions to this list are:

- surgical adhesive tape and lint
- antiseptic liquid or cream
- an eye bath
- gauze
- antihistamine cream
- cotton wool
- medical wipes.

Gloves give some protection from hepatitis B and AIDS if an infection is present. Dispose of contaminated cotton wool and dressings in a plastic bag that has been tied up. (For more information on AIDS and hepatitis B, see page 64).

What you may have to assist with

PROBLEM	PRIORITY	ACTION
Minor cuts	To stop the bleeding and minimise risk of infection	Ask client to apply pressure over cotton wool/towels taking care to avoid contact with the blood (see AIDS and hepatitis, page 64).
Severe cuts	To stop the bleeding and minimise risk of infection	Keep applying pressure over a clean towel until qualified help arrives. Put on disposable gloves as soon as possible.
Electric shock	To remove from source of electricity	Do not touch the person until they are disconnected from the electricity supply. If breathing has stopped, artificial respiration will need to be given by a qualified person. Ring for an ambulance (see Calling the emergency services, page 75).
Dizziness	To restore the flow of blood to the head	Position the person with their head down between the knees and loosen their clothing.
Fainting	To restore the flow of blood to the head	Lie the person down with their feet raised on a cushion.
Nose bleed	To constrict the flow of blood	Sit the person up with the head bent forward. Loosen the clothing around the neck. Pinch, firmly, the soft part of the nose, until the bleeding has stopped. Make sure breathing continues through the mouth during this period. If bleeding has not stopped after half an hour, medical attention must be sought.
Burns	To cool the skin and prevent it from breaking	Hold the affected area under cold, running water until the pain is relieved. Serious burns should be covered loosely with a dry sterile dressing and medical attention sought.
Epilepsy	To prevent self-injury and relieve embarrassment after an attack	Do not interfere forcibly with a person during an attack. Gently prevent them from injuring themselves. Ensure the person's airways are clear and wipe away any froth which forms at the mouth. After the attack, cover with a blanket, comfort and give reassurance until recovery is complete.
Objects in the eye	To remove the object without damaging the eye	Expose the invaded area and try stroking the object towards the inside corner of the eye with a dampened twist of cotton wool. If this is not successful, help the person to use an eye bath containing clean warm water.
Falls	To determine if there is spine damage. To treat minor injuries if the fall is not serious	If the person complains of pains in the back or neck, then do not move them: cover with a warm blanket and get medical aid immediately. For less serious falls, treat the bruises, cuts, sprains or grazes as appropriate.
Bruises	To reduce pain and swelling	Apply cold compresses for 30 minutes using a towel wrapped round an ice-pack or soaked with very cold tap water. Keep the compress in place with a bandage. Replace it if it dries out.
Grazes	To clean wound and prevent infection	Soak a pad of cotton wool with antiseptic and gently clean the graze, working outwards from the centre. Replace the cotton wool regularly throughout the cleaning. Apply a sterile gauze dressing, preferably a non-adherent type, to protect the wound as it heals. If dirt or foreign matter has become embedded in the graze, the person should be referred to a doctor who may want to give a tetanus injection.
Sprains	To reduce swelling and pain	Apply cold compresses to the area (see treatment for bruises) and support the affected joint with a bandage firmly applied. Refer the person to a doctor.

Activity 2.14: First aid

1 Find out where the first aid kit is kept in your salon and who is in charge of first aid procedures. Ask if you can have a look at the first aid kit. Check the contents to see if there is anything missing. If there is, inform your supervisor.

2 Working with a partner, role play the first aid procedures for each of the following:

- a nose bleed
- dizziness
- object in the eye
- fainting.

Product safety

Many of the products used in the salon are safe under normal use but can become unsafe if not stored, handled or disposed of properly. This is because of the chemical ingredients they contain, which require particular conditions to keep them safe.

Specific hazard warning symbols and guidance phrases have been introduced for labelling such products. These show, at a glance, what the dangers are. Products may be very toxic, toxic in contact with skin, by inhalation or if swallowed.

Flammable

REMEMBER

The employer is required by law to assess the risks with chemical products used in the salon and to provide guidance and training for staff. Trainees must always be supervised when carrying out treatments using dangerous substances.

Hazardous substances

Hazardous substances may enter the body by inhalation through the nose, by ingesting through the mouth, by absorption or penetration through the skin and via the eyes.

What you must do:

- know the potential hazards in your salon and carry out the necessary safety precautions
- always read labels and make sure the guidance on them does not get worn off or covered
- read any leaflets provided by manufacturers and keep them for reference
- check with your supplier if you are unsure about a product
- mix products in a well-ventilated area
- try not to breathe in dust, vapour or spray
- wear protective clothing where necessary
- dispose of waste chemicals and unused mixtures safely: small amounts may be rinsed away down the sink to dilute and remove them
- ensure that damaged and leaking containers are handled with care when disposing of them.

REMEMBER

If you understand all the risks involved in using a product, there is less chance of anything going wrong.

HEALTH MATTERS

Seek medical advice if you feel unwell or if you develop symptoms which you think are a reaction to a product or chemical ingredient, for example a skin reaction, eye irritation, nausea, bad headache, difficulty in breathing.

As with all beauty products, substances that are hazardous should be stored in an area that is:

- secure
- inaccessible to children and other unauthorised people
- dry and well-ventilated
- away from sources of ignition
- cool (room temperature or slightly cooler)
- away from direct light.

HAZARDOUS SUBSTANCES ASSESSMENT FORM
SUBSTANCE NAME: **Thick Bleach (Johnson's)**   DATA SHEET: No (**X**) Yes ( ) (attach to this form)
STORAGE DETAILS   **Stored in original container in cleaning/store cupboard**
CLASSIFICATION   Toxic ( ) Very toxic ( ) Harmful ( )   Irritant (**X**) Corrosive ( ) Other ( )
RISKS   **Irritating to eyes and skin**
PRECAUTIONS – Including PPE (Personal Protective Equipment)   **1 Avoid contact with eyes and skin (wear rubber gloves and if there is a greater risk of splashing in the eyes, wear goggles).**   **2 Not to be used in conjunction with any other cleaning agent.**   **3 Not to be used on enamel or other plated surfaces.**   **4 Always keep upright in the original container with cap secured.**   **5 Use with windows open.**   **6 Wash hands after use.**
Measurement/Monitoring Necessary Yes ( ) No (**X**)   Health Surveillance Yes ( ) No (**X**)   Instruction/Training Yes (**X**) No ( )
PROCESS/HOW USED   **Squirted in toilets and generally used on hard surfaces.**   **Used directly and also diluted in hot water and mopped.**
FIRST AID   **If in contact with eyes, rinse immediately with plenty of water and seek medical advice.**   **After contact with skin, wash immediately with plenty of water.**   **If swallowed, seek medical advice immediately and take/show the label on the side of the bottle.**
OTHER INFORMATION/ACTION   **Users to read the instructions and warnings on the label.**
DISPOSAL   **Dispose of empty container in normal waste bins at rear of building.**   DATE: 10. 05. 04
NAME: Neeta Laing   DATE OF REVIEW: 10.05.05   SIGNATURE: **Neeta Laing**

An example of a hazardous substance assessment form which has been completed for a cleaning item in the salon

Hazardous substances

1 State the four routes by which hazardous substances can enter the body.

_____
_____
_____
_____

2 What is the effect of a caustic substance upon the skin? Give one example of a caustic manicure preparation.

_____
_____

3 Why is special care required when disposing of aerosols?

_____
_____

4 Name three different types of flammable products used in the salon. State the precautions that should be taken when handling flammable products.

_____
_____
_____

5 State the main health risks associated with handling fine powder products.

_____
_____
_____

6 List three ideal conditions for storing beauty products.

_____
_____
_____

Salon security

A salon owner is required by law to ensure adequate security of the business premises. This is particularly important for obtaining insurance cover in the case of theft from or damage to the property, also for leasing and mortgaging purposes.

It is virtually impossible to make the salon completely burglar-proof, but steps can be taken to make it more difficult to burgle and minimise the possible damage once the property has been entered:

- locks and/or bolts should be fitted on all doors and windows, including basements and attics
- a burglar alarm system should be installed
- glass window panels should be checked to make sure they are intact and that they are not loose: double glazing and window bars give extra security
- metal shutters should be fitted to external doors and windows
- video cameras should be installed.

Strict salon procedures are required to ensure the security of the building both during and outside business hours.

Security outside business hours

There is obviously a greater risk of burglary when the salon is closed.

Particular attention must be paid to locking up at the close of business:

- There should be a minimum number of key holders, with every key accounted for at all times; the police should be given details of key holders in case they need to contact them outside business hours.
- A light should be left on all night, preferably at the front of the salon; this may deter a burglar and will help patrolling policemen to keep watch on the premises.
- Money should not be left in the till overnight; large sums of money should be banked during the day or deposited in the night safe after banking hours.
- The till drawer should be left open at night; a thief would try opening it anyway and cause unnecessary damage.
- All entrances, lockable cupboards, doors and windows should be checked and the burglar alarm tested before leaving the premises.
- External doors should be locked while the internal checks are being carried out.

The person responsible for opening up the salon usually has tasks to perform in preparation for the day's business. This person is normally expected to arrive early, before the rest of the staff, which means they are on their own for a short while.

During this period:

- the main entrance should remain locked until the opening time of the salon; staff can be let in as they arrive, preferably through an alternative staff entrance
- the burglar alarm should be switched off
- the till and lighting for shop window and display areas should be switched on
- post that has arrived should be put in a safe place for collection
- all internal doors and fire exits should be unlocked to satisfy health and safety regulations.

REMEMBER

Every salon has rules regarding the security of money, equipment and stock. Make sure you know the rules and stick to them.

Security during business hours

It is important to establish the identity of anyone entering the premises and their reason for being there. In most cases, visitors will be attending the salon on legitimate business and will have an appointment card or carry professional identification. Casual callers will expect to be attended to at the reception. If you are suspicious about someone who you think is not authorised to be in an area of the premises, politely ask for their identity and offer them assistance. If you are still not happy, alert your supervisor or another member of staff.

REMEMBER

If you spot an intruder, do not put yourself in danger. If the intruder runs away, report the incident immediately to your supervisor who will contact the police.

GOOD PRACTICE

Details should be written down as soon as possible after an incident. Check the area for damage or theft. It will help the police if you can also provide them with an accurate description of the intruder.

Stealing by staff and clients

Regrettably, theft by burglary is not the only way in which stealing may take place in the salon. Pilfering by staff and clients (politely known as 'shrinkage') is something that the salon owner must protect against. Pilfering by staff can take the form of 'a hand in the till' or stealing from stock. In the retail industry, stealing by customers or clients is known as shoplifting and refers to the theft of items on display for re-sale. Shoplifting is not a big problem in beauty salons, but there are obviously risks where items are displayed at reception or in treatment rooms. This type of stealing is much less likely to occur in a salon that operates efficient stock control and reception procedures, such as:

- limited staff access to retail, payment and product storage areas
- use of replica 'dummy' stock for 'open' retail displays
- well-lit shelves and display stands which are stocked up neatly
- locked display cabinets for retail products
- an electronic cash till
- random checks of stock and money taken through the till.

Security of money

Money payments are safest when recorded and stored in an electronic cash till. The till can be kept locked in between uses. Where only one or two named people have the authority to handle cash and have keys for the till, the risk of theft becomes very small.

An electronic till keeps a running total of takings and updated information can be provided instantly for cashing up purposes throughout the day. In this way, discrepancies between the takings and till receipts can be spotted and acted upon quickly.

GOOD PRACTICE

It is a good idea to have a system of signing out for stock and equipment needed for a treatment and signing back in when the items are returned to store.

Ideally, money that is cashed up during the working day should be paid straight into the bank but this is not always possible. Most banks provide a night safe for depositing money outside business hours. The salon should have a safe for the short-term storage of money and valuables.

It is up to the employer to decide which staff should be entrusted with the special combination code that opens the safe, but clearly, confidentiality is essential for providing security.

REMEMBER

Be careful in your attitude to salon stock. It does not belong to you until you have paid for it. Your salon will have rules regarding employee's own purchases. These will probably qualify you for a discounted price. Helping yourself to goods without paying for them is stealing.

Security of stock

A good system of stock control monitors the use of consumable and retail products and keeps supplies stored safely in a locked storeroom or cupboard. Usually only one or two people will have keys to the storage areas and they will have responsibility for issuing items to staff and keeping stock records. In this way, general access to stock is limited and the rate of replacement is monitored closely.

Personal property

Staff and clients also need protecting against theft. Ideally, each member of staff should be provided with a lockable cupboard in which to store their personal belongings. If the salon does not provide secure storage facilities for staff, it is best to keep personal possessions in a small purse or wallet that can be kept safely, nearby, throughout the working day. In larger businesses particularly, leaving handbags and purses on open display in staff rooms or other shared areas is asking for trouble.

The reception should provide secure facilities for storing clients' outerwear and other belongings that cannot be taken into the treatment room. The therapist is responsible for ensuring that the client's handbag and jewellery are kept safely in the treatment area, preferably where they can be seen by the client, or in a locked cupboard. The client's property should not be visible if the treatment area is left unattended.

REMEMBER

Security in the salon relies to a large extent on the day-to-day vigilance of staff. Stay alert and notice what is going on around you! Make your contribution to protecting the business that employs you. What you must do:

- keep the amount of money and valuables you take to work to a minimum; this reduces the risk of disappointment and upset caused by loss or theft

- give your client a small bowl for their jewellery and show them where you are placing it for safe keeping

- show your client the safe place where you are putting their handbag

- do not leave the client's belongings unattended; if they have to move between different treatment areas of the salon, it may be preferable to place valuable items of jewellery in the safe

- always remember to return your client's jewellery and possessions after a treatment.

An employer would be justified in feeling very angry about losses to the business and personal losses suffered as a result of staff negligence.

Personal safety

Sometimes you may need to work quite late at night. This is not unusual for salons with extended opening hours. Let your supervisor know when you are leaving. Try and avoid walking on your own after dark. If you need to take public transport, travel with colleagues or friends at night rather than on your own. Keep to well-lit main streets where possible. Carry a personal alarm for extra reassurance.

Activity 2.15: Salon security

Effective security measures are essential in the salon. A lot of money is tied up in the till, in salon stock and in consumables. If things go 'missing' this impacts on the business, not only because it represents a breakdown in trust, but also because it affects the financial success of the business. Most successful businesses share their success with employees. Businesses are less likely to reward staff if they feel they cannot trust them.

For this activity, use the following observation sheet to record your assessment of the effectiveness of the security arrangements in your salon. Go on a 'tour of inspection'. Find out your salon's procedures with regard to monitoring and controlling the use and movement of stock, consumables and money in the areas of the stockroom, salon and reception. Talk to the people with responsibility for the security. See if the procedures are actually working in practice and comment/make recommendations where you feel they are not.

Assessment area	Salon's security arrangements/controls	Effective? Yes/No	Comment/ recommendations
Linen: blankets, sheets and towels – treatment areas			
Linen: blankets, sheets and towels – stockroom			
Linen: blankets, sheets and towels – laundry			
Treatment products/ equipment: treatment areas			
Treatment products/ equipment: stockroom			
Retail products: reception			
Retail products: stockroom			
Money: reception			

Health and safety

There may appear to be more than one correct answer. Read each question carefully before making your final decision. Discuss your answers with colleagues and supervisor and see if you all agree. If you don't, talk through the issues raised and let your supervisor have the last word!

1 During a beauty treatment, the safety of a client is the responsibility of the:
☐ employer
☐ client
☐ supervisor
☐ employee (you).

2 The main role of the **Health and Safety Executive** is to:
☐ provide information and advice on health and safety
☐ write health and safety legislation
☐ carry out health and safety inspections
☐ prosecute employers in breach of health and safety.

3 The safety of a salon's electrical equipment is the responsibility of the:
☐ electrician
☐ employer
☐ employee (you).

4 The **COSHH** regulations were introduced to:
☐ ban hazardous substances from the workplace
☐ prevent abnormal reactions to hazardous substances in the workplace
☐ control exposure to hazardous substances in the workplace
☐ control the number of hazardous substances in the workplace.

5 Details of abnormal reactions or problems with treatments should be recorded so that:
☐ the treatment is no longer offered in the salon
☐ accurate information is available for insurance purposes

☐ the salon cannot be held responsible for accidents
☐ the manufacturer can be informed.

6 The **Employers' liability** (Compulsory Insurance) Act covers claims that may arise from:
☐ injury to the employer in the workplace
☐ injury to a client in the workplace
☐ injury to an employee in the workplace
☐ any accidents that may happen in the workplace.

7 Professional indemnity insurance covers employees against claims of:
☐ professional negligence
☐ damage to property
☐ injury to a client
☐ damage to reputation.

8 Long nails are less hygienic than short ones because:
☐ they spread infection easily
☐ they are more prone to infection
☐ they collect more germs underneath
☐ they break and cause germs to enter.

9 An overall should be loose enough to:
☐ disguise figure faults
☐ allow freedom of movement
☐ prevent sweating.
☐ allow sweat to evaporate.

10 Good personal hygiene is essential for:
☐ creating a professional image
☐ avoiding the spread of infection
☐ removing surface bacteria
☐ improving personal appearance.

KEY TERMS

You should now understand the following words or phrases. If you do not, go back through the chapter and find out.

Health and Safety Executive	Professional indemnity	Hazard data sheet
Hazard	Risk	Product data sheet
Accident Book	Employers' liability	Environmental Health
RIDDOR	Product liability	Officers
COSHH Regulations	Workplace policies	Health and Safety at Work
Public liability	Risk assessment	Act

3 Unit G2

Assist with salon reception duties

After working through this chapter you will be able to:

- understand the importance of reception to the success of the business
- know how to look after clients at reception
- know how to prepare and maintain the reception area
- understand your responsibilities on reception and the limits of your authority
- understand why confidentiality is important
- know how to make appointments
- know how to communicate effectively on reception
- know how to prepare products for sale and look after stock.

Before you work through this chapter: Be wise and revise!
Revision topics to help you achieve this unit:

Assist with salon reception duties

TOPIC	CHAPTER	PAGE

The reception desk is the control centre for salon operations. Everybody's working day is planned according to the **appointment book** and then adapted as visitors come and go. Regular clients are welcomed back for treatments. Casual enquirers become new clients. The building up of a successful business starts at the reception, where good first impressions (and bad!) have lasting effects.

ACTIVITY

Activity 3.1: First impressions

Use this checklist to assess the first impressions people are likely to have of your salon reception. Discuss your findings with colleagues and report back to your supervisor.

Checklist	Y/N	Observations/recommendations
1. Does the reception look and feel welcoming?		
2. Is the receptionist busy, friendly and attentive?		
3. Do people who are waiting look comfortable and relaxed?		
4. Are telephone calls being dealt with politely and helpfully?		
5. Are the magazines appropriate, current and in good condition?		
6. Are notices, posters and pictures on the wall eye-catching, interesting and well presented?		
7. Are there attractive retail displays?		
8. Is there information about the treatments and products available?		
9. Do the décor and furnishings look clean, attractive and well maintained?		
10. Are there diplomas and certificates on display?		
11. Do people appear to be being seen to on time?		
12. Do clients paying at reception appear pleased with their treatment?		

Give three suggestions for improving or enhancing your salon's reception area:

(a)_____

(b)_____

(c)_____

A PRACTICAL GUIDE TO BEAUTY THERAPY LEVEL 1

Reception

The receptionist should arrive at least 15 minutes before the first appointment of the day. This is to ensure that everything is in its place and that furniture and equipment is clean and ready for use. Everyone in the salon should know who is allowed at reception and how to behave there. Nothing should be allowed to interfere with the efficiency and professional image of the reception.

The reception desk

The following items should be readily available at the reception desk:

- **appointment book** with spare pages
- visitors' book
- appointment cards
- price lists
- promotional leaflets
- pre-treatment/aftercare advice leaflets
- client record cards
- forms, letter paper and envelopes
- pencils, pens, a ruler and eraser
- note/message pad
- calculator
- bill heads/receipt pads
- **petty cash** slips
- gift vouchers
- business cards
- first aid kit
- credit card payment vouchers
- address and telephone book
- accident/incident report book.

It is important to keep an eye on supplies of equipment, price lists and stationery at reception. Running out of essential items during the working day is inefficient and causes unnecessary delays.

Electronic equipment

At the very least, every salon should have a telephone and an electronic or computerised cash register (till).

Telephone and answering machine

A telephone is essential for any business. For many clients, it is their first contact with the salon. The telephone is the means by which appointments can be made, changed or cancelled quickly or advice sought and received. It is a good idea for the salon to have a telephone answering machine. This can be used for recording messages outside business hours.

REMEMBER

Staff must not be allowed to eat, drink or smoke at reception.

GOOD PRACTICE

Supplies of stationery and other consumable items should be monitored and reordered before stocks run out.

Using a computerised salon system

Computer

There are many benefits to the business of having a computer. All sorts of information such as clients' details, stock records and sales figures can be stored on a disk. The information can be input and retrieved easily by a trained person. Some manufacturers produce special computer software (programs) for salon use.

Depending on the system purchased, the computer at reception could be used for:

- keeping a database of clients and suppliers
- maintaining records of clients' treatments and purchases
- managing an appointment system
- producing standard letters and price lists
- creating personalised mail shots
- producing promotional literature
- keeping stock records.

Most salons have a computerised or electronic cash till on reception that adds up bills, records payments, issues receipts and keeps money safe. A computerised till is more sophisticated than an electronic cash till and may be programmed to provide a lot of other information which is useful to the business.

Computerised 'card' payments

Electronic point of sale (EPOS) technology allows clients to make card payments which are authorised from a central computer, holding details of the client's account. 'Swipe' refers to the action of passing the card through a special terminal so that the client's details and payments can be registered. A receipt is issued which the client has to sign.

'Chip and PIN' is gradually being introduced into the UK. This involves the cardholder keying their PIN (Personal Identification Number) into a handheld device rather than signing a receipt. From 2006, everyone in the UK who wants to pay by debit or credit card will have to be able to remember their PIN number to complete the transaction.

A 'swipe' machine for processing card payments

A credit card

A debit card

A charge card

Facsimile transmission service (fax)

A fax transmits black and white documents, letters and photographs. The document is fed into a machine and a copy of it is immediately transmitted via a telephone line to a fax machine somewhere else. Although fax machines are 'older' technology, some businesses, particularly those without a computer, like to have a fax machine because they are more convenient than the normal postal service when written information is required quickly.

Activity 3.2: The reception area

There are at least eight reasons why you would not want to return to *this* salon – and they are all happening in reception!

Find eight things that are wrong and then fill in the table explaining why they are wrong.

WHAT IS WRONG?	WHY IS IT WRONG?
1	
2	
3	
4	
5	
6	
7	
8	

Retail displays

The reception is usually the main site in the salon for displaying and promoting retail products. This is not surprising as every client has to pass through reception at least twice – when they arrive and when they leave!

Time spent waiting in reception is time that clients can use to browse through promotional literature and ask advice or take a closer look at products available for purchase. People working on reception are responsible for keeping the retail area clean and tidy and displaying stock attractively.

When assisting at reception, you will help to maintain the **retail displays** and handle stock.

A floor standing retail display

What you must do:

- read all the information about the products you sell: this is so that you can advise and make recommendations to the clients
- inform clients of current promotions: draw the attention of clients to special offers and make sure that promotional material is available and displayed where it will 'catch the eye' of people waiting in reception
- check that shelves are clean, safe and undamaged and strong enough to take the weight of the products on display
- dust the counter, shelves, display cabinets and stock every day: where possible, have regular changes of display
- have samples and testers available: check that they are clean and remove any that are damaged
- display stock attractively: packaging should be displayed with the product
- use 'dummy' stock under bright lighting, this way the colour, texture and fragrance of products will not spoil
- do not display stock in direct sunlight; this is to prevent the packaging from fading and the product from spoiling
- display related products together to encourage clients to buy more than one thing from the range
- price the retail products: check that identical products are not priced differently
- if all retail stock is to be displayed, extra space is needed for the fastest selling lines.

Handling stock

Stock that is not on display is usually kept secure in a locked cupboard or storeroom. The way that stock is stored and handled is important for keeping its value.

What you must do when assisting with stock:

- store stock in a cool, dark place
- do not pile boxes too high
- when an order arrives, bring older stock to the front of the shelves and store new stock behind. This method is called FIFO (First In First Out)
- take care with flimsy packaging and stack heavier goods lower down than more fragile items
- store products correctly so that they do not deteriorate or become damaged: keep fast moving lines at the front of the shelves and slower moving ones nearer the back.
- carry out regular stock checks to monitor how well different products are selling and to make sure that popular lines are reordered before being sold out
- store stock in straight lines: this makes counting easier at stock checks
- check price tickets as part of the regular stock checks: old price tickets should be removed before putting on new ones so that a lower price is not disguised
- keep accurate stock records

GOOD PRACTICE

When preparing products for sale, be sure to check over them for any signs of damage, loose packaging, cracks, leaks or anything that might affect the quality of the product. Clients will not be prepared to pay the full price for damaged goods.

REMEMBER

Displays should be set up and dismantled with minimum disruption to the business. Take care when dismantling a display. Put back equipment where it will not become damaged and keep tools and accessories safe in a box.

REMEMBER

Do not block aisles or passageways with containers of stock. Stock should be kept in a locked cupboard or secure storeroom where it does not present a safety risk.

Remember the COSHH regulations when storing, handling and disposing of stock. For safety reasons, some products may need dealing with in a particular way.

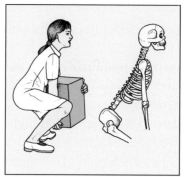
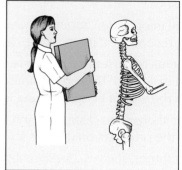

Remember to look after your back when handling stock

REMEMBER

The quality of a product cannot be guaranteed once its expiry date has passed. Stock that has been stored beyond its 'shelf life' has either to be sold off cheaply or disposed of.

ACTIVITY

Activity 3.3: Health and safety at reception

1 What are the main health and safety issues relating to the reception area? Produce a list, identifying the relevant legislation.

2 List the responsibilities of the receptionist relating to health and safety.

Accurate stock records are essential for tracking the movement of stock in and out of the business. Update dates on stock book pages.

	STOCK LIST		STOCK LIST
1	Dermalesse Cleansing Oil 75ml	21	
2	Dermalesse Cleansing Milk 150ml	22	
3	Dermalesse Cleansing Cream 150ml	23	
4	Dermalesse Exfoliant 100ml	24	
5	Dermalesse Cleansing Milk 100ml	25	
6	Dermalesse Cleansing Cream 300ml	26	
7	Dermalesse Skin Freshener 150ml	27	
8	Dermalesse Skin Tonic 150ml	28	
9	Dermalesse Skin Freshener 300ml	29	
10	Dermalesse Skin Tonic 300ml	30	
11		31	
12		32	
13		33	
14		34	
15		35	
16		36	
17		37	
18		38	
19		39	
20		40	

Different colours may be used to record the figures in each column. This is useful if you need to find figures quickly. For example:
Stock = blue

STOCK BOOK

NO	PRODUCT CODE	PRODUCT	BASE STOCK	DATE: 27/2/06 Counter stock	Stockroom stock	Total stock (i)	Order	Received	Total stock (ii)	Sold	DATE: 5/3/06 Counter stock	Stockroom stock	Total stock (i)	Order	Received	Total stock (ii)	Sold
1	00191	Dermalesse Cl. Oil 75ml	10	6	2	8	2	/	8	2	4	2	6	/	2	8	/
2	00192	Dermalesse Cl.Mlk 150ml	10	4	2	6	4	/	6	/	4	2	6	/	4	10	2
3	00193	Dermalesse Cl. Oil 75ml	10	4	2	6	4	/	6	4	2	/	2	4	4	6	1
4	00194	Dermalesse Exfol 100ml	6	4	/	4	2	/	4	1	3	/	3	1	2	5	2
5	00195	Dermalesse Cl.Milk 300ml	5	2	2	4	1	/	4	2	2	/	2	2	1	3	2
6	00196	Dermalesse Cl. Crm 300ml	5	2	/	2	3	/	2	/	2	1	2	/	3	5	1
7	00197	Dermalesse Sk Frsh 150ml	8	4	2	6	2	/	6	4	2	/	2	4	2	4	1
8	00198	Dermalesse Sk Tonic 150ml	8	5	/	5	3	/	5	1	4	/	4	1	3	7	2
9	00199	Dermalesse Sk Frsh 300ml	5	2	1	3	/	2	5	1	3	1	4	1	/	4	2
10	00200	Dermalesse Sk Tonic 300ml	5	3	1	4	1	/	4	3	1	/	1	3	1	2	/
11	00201	Dermalesse Cr Mask 75ml	4	2	1	3	1	/	4	3	1	/	1	3	1	4	2
12	00202	Dermalesse Ampoules	6	3	/	3	3	/	3	2	1	/	1	2	3	4	1
13	00203	Maqui Base Ivory	6	2	3	5	1	1	6	2	3	1	4	2	1	5	/
14	00204	Maqui Base Cream	6	4	/	4	2	/	4	2	2	/	2	2	2	4	1
15	00205	Maqui Base Beige	6	2	/	3	2	1	4	/	3	1	4	/	/	4	2

Reception

1   State four ways of creating a good first impression at reception.

_____
_____
_____
_____

2   Explain three things that the receptionist needs to do to ensure that reception is ready for business.

_____
_____
_____

3   List six items that should always be available on the reception desk.

_____
_____
_____

4   Why is a 'float' required in the till at the beginning of the day?

_____
_____

5   Name three items of electronic equipment that may be available at reception.

_____
_____
_____

6   Give three reasons why security is important at reception.

_____
_____
_____

7   List four ways of promoting retail sales at reception.

_____
_____
_____
_____

8   Give three reasons for carrying out regular stock checks.

_____
_____
_____

9   When are the best times for changing displays and attending to stock?

_____
_____
_____

10 State three ways in which the salon can use a computerised **client database**.

_____
_____
_____

The receptionist

Not all salons have a full-time receptionist. The duties may be shared by the rest of the staff. Everyone in the salon should be trained in reception skills so that they can confidently take over when needed. It is important that the salon always presents the same professional image at reception.

Lovely to see you!

The receptionist should always look smart, be efficient and communicate pleasantly and politely with everyone who enters the salon.

The main responsibilities of a receptionist are:

- maintaining the reception and retail areas
- looking after clients and visitors
- handling enquiries
- taking messages
- making appointments
- dealing with problems
- processing payments.

Most of these tasks involve dealing with people either directly or over the telephone. They also include giving, receiving and recording information that is important for the business to run efficiently. While you are assisting on reception, look and learn!

GOOD PRACTICE

It is very important for you to be able to do what you do with confidence. You are bound to be a little nervous at first but your confidence will grow with the more experience you get. Most beauty therapy clients are very pleasant and will want to help you to succeed. The important thing is that you know what you can and what you cannot do (this is called knowing the limits of your authority) and who you should go to if you are unsure. Find out who is the responsible person with the authority to help you.

Communication skills

A good receptionist manages to make every client and potential client feel 'special'. This comes from having good **communication skills**. It is important that everyone, whoever they are and whatever they want, is dealt with in the same, professional way. Remember this particularly when you are tired or very busy and working under pressure.

GOOD PRACTICE

A smile works wonders! Always smile and look happy to see all visitors to reception. News spreads about a business that offers a friendly welcome.

GOOD PRACTICE

Reading, writing, speaking and listening are essential skills for ensuring effective communication in the salon. When communication breaks down, problems occur. Good communication starts at the reception.

You must be able to:

- read information essential to carrying out your work safely and effectively; identify those details which are important

- write clearly in the appropriate format; check that what you have written can be read by others and makes sense

- speak clearly and confidently; make sure that information is accurate and explained well

- listen carefully and 'hear' what is being said; be sure of the facts.

Reading

Some of the information that you need will be written down. You will not be able to use the information unless you can first make sense of it! Effective reading involves selecting and reading for a particular purpose, getting the information you need, checking your understanding of what you have read and summarising the information obtained. The following are examples of written information you will need to read in the salon:

- appointment details
- client records
- product labels
- treatment information
- price lists
- promotional material
- instruction leaflets
- journals.

Can you think of any more?

GOOD PRACTICE

When taking messages, always read back over what you have written. Check that it contains all the relevant information and that it makes sense. This is particularly important when dealing with people over the telephone.

Writing

Any written information you provide must be clear, accurate and easily understood by other people. This way, misunderstandings are avoided. At work, you may have to adapt your writing to suit different purposes and know how to use different types of written material for obtaining, providing and keeping information. Sometimes this will mean using abbreviations or codes, for example when making an entry in the **appointment book** or filling in a client's record card. Always follow the salon's procedures. Do not introduce abbreviations or codes that only you understand!

GOOD PRACTICE

Always read back over what you have written. Check that it contains all the relevant information and that it makes sense. This is particularly important when taking messages and dealing with information over the telephone.

Here are some examples of activities that require good writing:

- entering details in the appointment book
- making out appointment cards
- filling in client record cards
- writing out a bill
- passing on a message.

Speaking

During a normal working day, you will speak to many different types of people about a wide range of things. It is important that you do this well. Good speaking skills are essential for keeping up the salon's image with clients, suppliers, members of the public and other professional colleagues. Most of your speaking will take place on a one-to-one basis, either directly or indirectly over the telephone.

GOOD PRACTICE

It will help you both as a speaker and a listener to learn how to 'paraphrase'. Paraphrasing is summarising what was said in your own words. This is not the same as repeating exactly what someone else has said. Paraphrasing gives you the opportunity to clarify things and check that there are no misunderstandings.

Whatever the situation, you will need to:

- speak clearly
- use language that is appropriate
- emphasise key points
- ask the right sorts of questions
- know how to respond to others
- say things that are relevant to the subject
- say things that keep the discussion going
- check and show understanding of what has been said.

Listening

Listening is quite a hard thing to do. This is because we can think much faster than we can speak. There is a time delay between someone's speech and our mental thought processes when we are listening. If we allow ourselves to get distracted from what someone is saying, by thinking of other things, we stop listening and information gets 'lost'.

REMEMBER

It is much easier to give the speaker your attention when dealing with them face to face. **Body language** and facial expressions help you to pick up things that are more difficult to grasp on the telephone. During a phone conversation you have to work harder at listening and checking your understanding of what is being said.

Here are some points to help you become a good listener:

- be interested in what is being said; even if it doesn't sound interesting, it might turn out to be!
- concentrate on what the speaker is saying
- resist the temptation to anticipate what is going to be said
- do not interrupt, wait until there is a pause or you are asked to speak
- ask questions to check your understanding of what has been said
- ask questions to check that others have understood you
- take notes if necessary.

Things to avoid when listening:

- being too tired to pay attention properly
- deciding in advance there's no point in listening
- external noises and distractions
- switching off because of 'information overload'
- listening only for the bits you want to hear
- switching off because you think you know where the conversation is going
- thinking of what you are going to say when it is your turn.

GOOD PRACTICE

Clients very often have limited knowledge and understanding of what is available in the salon. Sometimes, what they think they want is not always what they need. To find out what the client needs, you must ask the right sorts of questions and listen carefully to the answers.

Asking questions

All information passed on and used in the salon must be accurate and relevant. This is particularly important, for example, when advising clients about the best choice of treatments and products or needing a colleague to help you with a problem. The way you ask questions will determine the usefulness of the information you get back.

Examples of 'closed' questions:

- Are you available at 10 o'clock on Monday morning?
- Have you had treatment at the salon before?
- Do you have a regular nail care routine?
- Does your skin normally feel dry?

Examples of 'open' questions:

- When are you available on Monday?
- What treatments have you had at the salon before?
- How do you normally look after your nails?
- Why have you been using this skin treatment cream?

ACTIVITY

Activity 3.4: Asking questions

Compare the above examples of closed and open questions. Decide which version of each question is the more useful, the closed question or the open question. It could be that both types are useful, but in different circumstances. Explain your answers.

_____

_____

_____

_____

_____

_____

_____

_____

_____

_____

_____

_____

_____

_____

_____

_____

_____

_____

_____

What you must do:

- use 'closed' questions only to get short, straightforward answers (usually yes or no). Closed questions do not check understanding. They just help to confirm or eliminate ideas

- use 'open' questions to get fuller and more detailed answers. Open questions are good because they help to develop the conversation and provide more information. Open questions give the person more room to say whatever they need to say. They often begin with how, what, when, where, who or why?

- ask probing questions – 'tell me more about ...' or 'so why was that?' These questions also tend to include how, what, when, where, who and why

- ask one question at a time

- wait for a good time to ask a question

- ask questions sensitively to avoid embarrassment or reluctance by the person to give you a full or honest answer

- wait for the answer before asking another question

- keep asking questions until you are satisfied with the answer.

GOOD PRACTICE

Keep your questions short, direct and to the point. Long, rambling questions confuse people. They forget the beginning of the question or do not realise exactly what you are asking.

Body language

The way you present yourself is a form of communication. Your gestures, poses, movements and expressions are all part of your **body language** and help you to communicate. You can use your body language to project a professional image that helps other people develop trust and confidence in your work.

- Stand or sit 'tall', that is with your back straight and your head held up. Apart from being good for your posture, it shows that you are confident. Clients trust a person who appears confident. People who slouch give out the wrong 'signals'.

- Use positive hand movements and open gestures. These are friendly and welcoming. Avoid finger pointing or folding your arms across your chest. These can be considered aggressive.

- Keep your facial expressions relaxed and smile genuinely and often. People always feel better and respond well to a smile. It is very difficult not to smile back at someone who is smiling at you!

- Always face the person and maintain good eye contact when speaking or listening. People who avoid eye contact or look down give the impression of being dishonest.

- Tilt your head slightly and nod occasionally when listening. This shows that you are concentrating and are interested in what is being said.

- Try to move smoothly in a relaxed manner. People who are confident use steady, unhurried movements.

- During a conversation, keep a reasonable space between yourself and the other person. Getting too close to somebody when speaking to them can feel very intimidating.

ACTIVITY

Activity 3.5: Communication skills

Working with a partner or in small groups, discuss how you think a receptionist should use and adapt their **communication skills** in the following situations:

- dealing with a telephone enquiry from a person who has difficulty speaking your language

- attending to a deaf client arriving at the salon for treatment

- looking after a client in a wheelchair.

The receptionist

1   State three ways of developing good relationships with clients.

   _____

   _____

   _____

2   List four essential communication skills.

   _____

   _____

   _____

   _____

3   Give five examples of problems that might occur in the salon if there is a breakdown in communication.

   _____

   _____

   _____

   _____

   _____

4   Give examples of three 'closed' and three 'open' questions that a client might be asked at reception.

   _____

   _____

   _____

   _____

   _____

   _____

5   Give three 'messages' a receptionist should convey using body language.

   _____

   _____

   _____

6   Explain why personal presentation is important for a receptionist.

   _____

   _____

Client care

Every visitor to the salon should be greeted with a smile and be shown where to wait while the relevant person is informed of their arrival. Visitors such as company representatives or trades people doing work on the premises should be asked to sign the visitors' book.

Dealing with clients

Expected clients who have already made an appointment may show you their appointment card or may have made their appointment on the telephone. Either way, you need to check the client's name, date, time and treatment against details recorded in the appointment book. You must then look after them until they go for treatment.

GOOD PRACTICE

Record cards should be kept in strict alphabetical order, using the clients' surnames. Where two or more clients share the same surname, the cards should be filed according to the initial letter of their first name.

What you must do:

- welcome the client and help them with their coat and belongings
- estimate the waiting period and inform the client if this is to be longer or shorter than originally expected
- record the client's arrival at the salon by drawing a diagonal line in pencil across their details in the appointment book
- ensure the comfort and care of the client while they wait, offering magazines and hospitality as appropriate
- when the client has gone through for treatment, draw a diagonal line across the first one to record that they are being attended to
- after treatment, help the client with retail purchases and arrange a convenient time for their next appointment
- help the client with their coat and belongings
- confirm how nice it was to see them and, if possible, accompany them to the door
- keep the client's records up-to-date and well organised.

REMEMBER

Never leave a client's record card on top of the reception desk where the card could be seen by others. The information is private and confidential between the client and their therapist.

ACTIVITY

Activity 3.6: Record cards

1   Work out the order in which the following clients' record cards should appear in the filing system: Sue Mackintosh, Malini Malik, Helen Makerfield, Elaine McKinlay, Mary Killeen, Elsie MacIntyre, Margaret Killeen, Kim Kerindi, Sue McLintock, Sundus Salam. Check your answers with your supervisor.

_____

_____

_____

_____

_____

_____

_____

_____

_____

_____

2   Find out the basic information that is kept on the clients' record cards in your salon. With your supervisor, discuss the importance of keeping this information and the ways in which it may be used.

REMEMBER

Clients who arrive unexpectedly may be treated provided that there is a therapist available. The receptionist should always check first and then record the client's details in the appointment book.

GOOD PRACTICE

In some salons, the receptionist prepares a list for each therapist at the beginning of the day showing the names of their clients, their expected time of arrival and what they are booked in for. This helps to keep them on schedule. It is kept by the therapist throughout the day and provides a useful, quick reference, particularly if an unexpected client arrives.

Dealing with problems

However well you prepare for the clients, problems can still happen. For example:

- a client may be late for their appointment (the bus was late, the car park was full, an unexpected visitor arrived)

- a client may arrive without an appointment (a regular client who has suddenly been invited out)

- someone could have overbooked (two Mrs Greens may turn up for the same appointment)

- a treatment may take longer than the time allowed so that later appointments start running behind schedule (unexpected complications during a treatment or an extra service may have been provided)

- a member of staff is suddenly absent due to illness (remember to refer this immediately to your supervisor so that bookings can be rescheduled).

If there is a problem with the bookings, keep cool, calm and do not appear flustered! Politely ask the client to take a seat while you explain the situation to your supervisor. An alternative therapist may be suggested, another appointment made or a short wait may be necessary.

It is your job to look after the client until their treatment can start. Use your initiative to make best use of the time. This should include:

- explaining the delay to the client, giving an indication of how long they may have to wait

- offering the client tea, coffee or a soft drink

- offering the client a magazine to read

- informing the client as soon as the therapist is ready and apologising to them for the delay.

REMEMBER

If the client refuses to wait and cannot spare the extra time, tell your supervisor immediately. Do not wait until the client has left the salon!

ACTIVITY

Activity 3.7: Dealing with problems

Discuss the following problem in a small group and see if you can agree on a solution:

A client arrives ten minutes late for her manicure appointment and explains, very apologetically, that she has been held up by the arrival of an unexpected visitor. The appointment book shows that another client is expected with the same therapist in twenty minutes.

Should you:

1 Apologise and explain that there is not enough time left for a manicure and ask her to make
☐ another appointment?

2 Tell her not to worry: assure her that she can have the manicure and, when the next client
☐ arrives, explain that there will be a slight delay.

3 Explain to the client that she can have a manicure but that it will have to be 'cut down' so that
☐ it is completed in twenty minutes?

A PRACTICAL GUIDE TO BEAUTY THERAPY LEVEL 1

If your answer is 1, do you think that the client should be charged for the treatment she has not had? (After all, you were not able to offer the appointment to someone else.)

_____

_____

_____

_____

If your answer is 2, would it make any difference if the client expected for the later appointment is a regular or new client, visiting the salon for the first time?

_____

_____

_____

_____

If your answer is 3, should the client have the price of the manicure reduced because she has not had the full treatment?

_____

_____

_____

_____

Are there any other possible solutions to this problem?

_____

_____

_____

_____

Making appointments

Details of all appointments should be recorded in the appointment book. Pages should be prepared a few weeks in advance so that courses of treatments can be booked, follow-up appointments made and details of each therapist's availability identified well in advance.

GOOD PRACTICE

Making up pages a few weeks ahead gives the receptionist an opportunity to get staff holidays and days off put in the book before appointments are being made.

What you must do:

- as appointments are arranged, transfer details to the appointment book in pencil, stating the name of the client, their telephone number (or alternative contact details) and the treatment or service required
- keep the pages neat and tidy: do not 'doodle' or use the appointment book as a note pad!
- make sure that the correct codes and abbreviations are used and that the start and finish times are made clear
- make out an appointment card for the client, recording details in pen and stating the day, date, time and therapist's name
- check the accuracy of both sets of records and repeat the details back to the client before handing them their appointment card.

REMEMBER

Always use a pencil to record details in the appointment book. Sometimes clients have to cancel or change their appointment. Their details can be rubbed out neatly and the space used for another client.

The amount of time you allow in the book for a client's appointment depends very much on whether they are a 'first time' client or a 'regular' client. It is usual, for a 'first time' client, to allow a little extra time for a chat and consultation with the beauty therapist so that they can agree a treatment plan. The time allowed for a 'regular' client's appointment will depend on the treatments they are having.

Here are some recommended commercial timings for beauty therapy treatments. They give a general indication of how long each treatment is expected to take under normal circumstances. These may vary slightly, depending on the specific products and methods used in your salon. Make sure you know the recommended timings for all the treatments offered by your salon.

SERVICE (EXCLUDING CONSULTATION AND PREPARATION)	MAX TIME (MINUTES)
1 Eyebrow shape	15
2 Eyelash tint	20
3 Facial	60
4 Make-up	45
5 Manicure	45
6 Pedicure	60
7 Eyebrow wax	15
8 Underarm wax	15
9 Half leg wax	30
10 Bikini-line wax	15
11 Arm wax	30
12 Full leg wax	45
13 Half leg, bikini, underarm	45
14 Full leg, bikini, underarm	60
15 Facial, including eyelash tint and eyebrow shape	75
16 Eyebrow shape and eyelash tint	30
17 Eyebrow tint	10
18 Eyebrow tint, eyebrow shape and eyelash tint	30
19 Ear piercing	15
20 Nail art	5-10 per nail
21 Facial and make-up	90
22 False eyelashes	15

This table has been produced by HABIA, the Hairdressing and Beauty Industry Authority

Date	Tuesday February 9th		Beauty Box Salon	
	Emma	Mel	Nusreen	Joss
8.30	Mrs Ledgard Lash/brow tint			
8.45	953-2417		Mrs Shacklady	
9.00	Mrs Wolf Oil man	Mrs Ledgard Lash/brow tint C	Fac/DHS **DNA** 954-1000	
9.15		954-7897		
9.30	943-2136	Mrs Smith	Sue Jones	Morning Off
9.45	Mrs D House	Fac/man	Bridal M/U	
10.00				
10.15	Top/toe Special	943-9995	942-1892	
10.30		Mrs Gilbert	Mrs Poole	
10.45				
11.00		Gal/facial	steam /facial	
11.15				
11.30	951-2221	950-9930	942-1892	
11.45	Mrs Poole Ped	Mrs Ross s/p lashes		
12.00		948-3626		
12.15	942-1892	Mrs Kelly		Mrs Stewart
12.30			LUNCH	Consultation (F)
12.45	LUNCH	Fac/man		942-3344
13.00				Mrs Gibson Man
13.15		943-9191	Mrs Gordon 1/2 leg wax,	940-7632
13.30	Mrs Cronin Gel/tips	LUNCH	Eyebrow shp 942-8344	
13.45	763-4265			

☐	Available time	☒	Client has been taken for treatment	C	'Last minute' cancellation
◩	Client arrived and is awaiting treatment	DNA	Did not attend – client did not inform, make a note on the record card		

The appointment book provides a 'snapshot' of what is happening in the salon

ACTIVITY

Activity 3.8: Recording appointments

Each salon has its own system for recording appointments. It is important that you follow the system used in your salon.

1 Find out the abbreviations used in your salon for recording appointments and the amount of time to be allocated for each treatment.

2 Make out a chart, preferably on a computer, presenting the information in three columns, that is, treatment, abbreviation, time. Refer to your chart when making appointments at reception.

3 Check the next day's page in the appointment book: are there any gaps? If there are, how long are they for and which treatments could be booked in to them?

Here are some examples:

TREATMENT	ABBREVIATION	TIME
Cleanse/make-up	C1/MU	45 mins
Facial	F	1 hr
Manicure	Man	45 mins
Eyebrow shape	EBS	15 mins

ACTIVITY

Activity 3.9: Limits of your authority

Get hold of a copy of your salon's treatment list and, next to each treatment, write a symbol to show whether you have the authority (√) or do not have the authority (X) to make an appointment for that treatment. If you are not sure, write a question mark (?). Get your supervisor to check your answers.

SELF-CHECKS

Making appointments

1 Why should the pages in the appointment book be prepared a few weeks in advance?

_____

_____

2 State two reasons why it is important not to allow too much time for treatments in the appointment book.

_____

_____

3 State two reasons why it is important to allow sufficient time for treatments in the appointment book.

_____

_____

4 Give three details required when recording an appointment in the appointment book.

_____

_____

5 Why should details in the appointment book be recorded in pencil?

_____

_____

Handling enquiries

Although people may call into the salon to make enquiries, most requests for information will be made over the telephone. Remember that the salon telephone is for business and should not be used for chatty personal calls. Clients who cannot get through may give up and make an appointment somewhere else.

Many enquiries will be about the services offered, their effects, how much they cost, how long they take and the availability of appointments.

What you must do:

- keep details of treatments, services, products and price lists available at reception close to the telephone
- know which types of enquiries can be dealt with personally and which need referring to a qualified operator
- ask questions which will help the client to provide the right information in their answer
- take down messages accurately and pass them on, promptly, to the right person
- be able to explain the benefits of the treatments and services available in the salon.

GOOD PRACTICE

You will be able to give quite a lot of information about the treatments you have been trained in. However, do not try and give detailed answers to enquiries about treatments you are unsure about. Get the help of a trained therapist or your supervisor, otherwise you could give wrong information.

Using the telephone

For many clients the telephone is their first contact with the business. A good receptionist never forgets that calls are from people, each of which is a prospective client.

Telephone answering techniques

When you answer the telephone at reception, you must sound professional, courteous and friendly.

You should always:

- answer promptly on the second or third ring: this gives both sides time to prepare themselves without the caller becoming impatient
- smile when you pick up the receiver: your voice is you to a caller. Smiles definitely do travel down the telephone!
- let the caller know that have got through to the salon, give them your name and ask how you can help them. Note the client's name so that you can use it in conversation
- be enthusiastic: enthusiasm is infectious and shows you enjoy being helpful
- listen attentively: it is very off-putting for a caller if they can sense you are being distracted by someone or something else
- repeat back to them any important points discussed and thank them for calling.

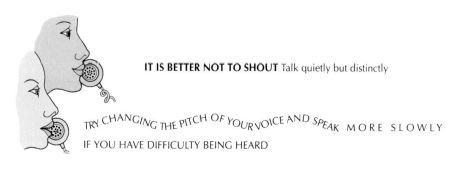

IT IS BETTER NOT TO SHOUT Talk quietly but distinctly

TRY CHANGING THE PITCH OF YOUR VOICE AND SPEAK MORE SLOWLY IF YOU HAVE DIFFICULTY BEING HEARD

Tips for using the telephone

Receiving calls

Here are some reasons why people may call your salon:

- to make, change or cancel an appointment (always repeat the key pieces of information back to your client so that you share the same understanding of what has been agreed)
- to make enquiries about treatments and services offered
- new clients may call to ask for the location of the salon and information on how to get there and where to park
- people may ring up wanting to know if there are any jobs available at the salon, possibly students requesting a work placement (check with your supervisor)
- company representatives may call to check on an order or to make an appointment to discuss products or equipment (you may need to transfer this call to your supervisor or employer)
- someone may make a personal call to a member of staff (check the salon policy about this, some salons will only allow personal calls to staff in an emergency. You might have to take a message).

GOOD PRACTICE

If you have to put a call through to another extension, explain to the caller what you are doing and thank them for waiting. If the extension to which you have transferred the call does not answer after six rings, explain to the caller that you can take a message or, if they prefer, you will ask the person concerned to ring back. Take the caller's name and telephone number.

ACTIVITY

Activity 3.10: Responding to telephone enquiries

Keep a log of five different telephone enquiries you deal with on reception. Give the name of the caller, the date and time of their call and explain what the enquiry was about. Explain how you dealt with the call, highlighting any problems, and state what the outcome was.

Taking messages

When passing on messages, make sure that full and accurate details are written down. Valuable time may be wasted responding to messages if details are missing or unclear. Messages should be written down on a special message or 'memo' pad.

The details should include:

- who the message is for
- who the message is from
- the date and time the message was received
- details of the message
- the telephone number or address of the caller
- the signature of the person taking the message.

TELEPHONE MESSAGE
To   Nishpa
From   Cath Peel
Date 28.3.06   **Time** 17.30
Message
Please ring regarding make-up next Saturday (3 April) Tel 0161 - 741 - 0491
Message taken by Daniel

A completed message slip

REMEMBER

Some messages are confidential. Keep them in a safe place and pass them on to the appropriate person as soon as possible.

Handling enquiries

1 Why should the reception telephone not be used for personal calls?

_____
_____
_____
_____

2 Give three techniques that should be used when answering the telephone at reception.

_____
_____
_____

3 Describe four different types of telephone call that may be received at reception.

_____
_____
_____
_____

4 What action should be taken if the person a caller needs to speak to is not available?

_____
_____
_____
_____

5 How should the receptionist respond to an enquiry left on the salon's telephone answering machine?

_____
_____
_____

Dealing with complaints

Despite everyone's attempts to provide an efficient, personal service, mistakes can sometimes occur. Depending on the circumstances and the mood of the client on the day, some of these can go by more or less unnoticed while others may result in the client becoming upset and complaining quite openly at reception.

Whatever the cause, it is important for problems to be dealt with quietly, tactfully and, if possible, away from the rest of the clients. At Level 1, you will not be expected to deal with problems directly. You will, however, be expected to know who the responsible person is that you should refer problems to and how to look after a client who is complaining at reception.

GOOD PRACTICE

Do not pretend a mistake has not been made when you know very well that it has. Mistakes on the part of the salon must be acknowledged and rectified as soon as possible.

What you must do:

- keep cool and be pleasant and polite with the client
- explain that you will get a senior person to come and speak to them
- ask the client to come with you to a more private area of the salon
- offer the client a seat; a comfortable client is more likely to calm down
- offer the client a drink; this shows the client that you care about them
- do not get involved with the details of the complaint but show concern and understanding for the client being upset, irrespective of who or what is to blame
- do not be tempted to show anger or be rude, even if the client is being unreasonable.

GOOD PRACTICE

The person dealing with the complaint will need to make a record of what has happened. Details of the complaint may need to be referred to, if a client who feels they have suffered damage seeks compensation from the salon.

GOOD PRACTICE

Many businesses openly promote their complaints procedure as part of their customer service policy. This might be displayed or made available in a leaflet at reception.

ACTIVITY

Activity 3.11: Dealing with complaints

Dealing with complaints is always a good basis for role play!

Working with a partner and, if possible, an observer, create a realistic situation which might occur at reception when a client is unhappy with a service or a product received. Have a 'supervisor' on hand in case your client gets out of control! Remember the importance of using the correct body language.

Handling exchanges and refunds

It is usual for the manager to supervise refunds. They will want to find out if the cause of the complaint is due to:

- negligence on the part of the salon: the client may have been given incorrect or incomplete advice. Alternatively, there may have been discrepancies with stock handling or **stock control** procedures
- misunderstandings by the client: sometimes, no matter how much you explain to a client, misunderstandings happen. A product appears not to be working when, in fact, the client is not using it properly
- defective products sold to the salon by a supplier: in this case the terms of the Sale and Supply of Goods Act apply.

REMEMBER

If the client attends the salon for treatment, there may be information on their record card which may be useful when trying to sort out the problem.

A client requesting a refund should be questioned tactfully to determine the cause of the problem

MULTIPLE CHOICE QUIZ

Reception

There may appear to be more than one correct answer. Read each question carefully before making your final decision. Discuss your answers with your colleagues and supervisor and see if you all agree. If you don't, talk through any issues raised.

1 The pages in the appointment book should be made out:
   ☐ at the beginning of each month
   ☐ one week in advance
   ☐ six weeks in advance
   ☐ at the end of each month.

2 If a client arrives at reception while you are speaking on the telephone, you should:
   ☐ finish your telephone call and attend to the client
   ☐ smile at the client and tell her you will only be a minute
   ☐ wave to a colleague to attend to the client
   ☐ smile at the client, gesture to a seat and complete your phone call.

▶▶

3 If a therapist rings reception to say that she will not be coming to work because she is ill, you should:
- ☐ ring up her clients for the day and cancel their appointments
- ☐ move her clients' appointments to another therapist where possible
- ☐ inform the manager
- ☐ wait and see what happens, hoping the problem will get sorted out as the day goes on.

4 The **Data Protection Act** says that:
- ☐ clients are not entitled to see inf ormation about themselves stored on computer.
- ☐ clients are not entitled to see information about other clients stored on computer
- ☐ clients are entitled to see information about themselves stored on computer
- ☐ clients are entitled to see information about other clients stored on computer.

5 You should only deal with problems that are:
- ☐ straightforward
- ☐ routine
- ☐ within your job description
- ☐ within the limits of your authority.

6 Paraphrasing is done to:
- ☐ check that there is no misunderstanding
- ☐ get information from the client
- ☐ provide information for the client
- ☐ check that there is sufficient information.

7 One example of a communication skill is:
- ☐ listening
- ☐ thinking
- ☐ being warm and friendly
- ☐ getting on well with others.

8 'Chip and pin' is a type of:
- ☐ computer software program
- ☐ electrical treatment
- ☐ electronic payment method
- ☐ computerised till.

KEY TERMS

You should now understand the following words and phrases. If you do not, go back through the chapter and find out.

Body language	**Stock control**	**Data Protection Act**
Cash float	**Client confidentiality**	**Communication skills**
Petty cash	**Client database**	**Electronic payments**
Appointment book	**Retail display**	

4 Unit BT1

Prepare and maintain the beauty therapy work area

After working through this chapter you will be able to:
- prepare the beauty therapy work area
- maintain the beauty therapy work area.

Before you work through this chapter: Be wise and revise!
Revision topics to help you achieve this unit:

Prepare and maintain the beauty therapy work area

TOPIC	CHAPTER	PAGE

The information in this chapter will help you to undertstand how to prepare and keep the beauty therapy work area looking professional. The work area should be clean, tidy and contain everything needed by the therapist to carry out beauty treatments. You will learn how to set up the work area for the following treatments:

- waxing
- eye treatments
- make-up
- manicure
- pedicure
- facial treatment.

You will also learn which materials, products and equipment are needed for each treatment.

Creating the right environment for client comfort

Lighting

Correct lighting is important as it can make a client feel relaxed while receiving a treatment. The lighting needs to be bright enough so that the therapist can clearly see the treatment being given. For many treatments it is better to have natural daylight.

The **reception** needs sufficient lighting, although not too bright, so that the appointment book can easily be read. It is a good idea to direct light towards a product display so the client's eyes are drawn towards the products for sale. Treatments such as **manicures** are sometimes carried out in the reception area so adequate lighting will be required for this.

Heating

If the client is too cold or too hot it is unlikely they will enjoy the treatment and may not return to the salon. It is particularly important that a room is warm if the client needs to removing clothing, for example for **waxing** treatment.

Ventilation

Clients will not be able to relax during the treatment if the room is smelly and stuffy. A build-up of strong odours can cause headaches and sickness. If lots of products are being used in a room, for treatments such as manicures, there should be good ventilation so that the fumes can easily escape and that fresh air may enter the room. .

General comfort

In the reception area, the client may be offered a cushion to place behind their back while sitting down. Up-to-date popular magazines and a drink may be offered to the client. A bunch of flowers on the reception desk can help create a relaxing atmosphere. In the work area, clients may require extra pillows, or a blanket to cover them.

ACTIVITY

Activity 4.1: Creating the right environment for client comfort

Briefly describe why each of following factors are important considerations within a treatment or reception area.

Heating

_____

_____

Lighting

_____

_____

Ventilation

_____

_____

Comfort

_____

_____

Preparing the treatment area for waxing

A wax treatment involves the removal of hairs from the body using a sticky substance called wax. The wax is removed from the skin by means of strips, which can be made of either paper or fabric. Areas of the body that are often waxed include the legs, arms, bikini line, underarms, eyebrow, lip and chin. The hairs will take up to six weeks to re-grow.

Client record cards

When a client has any treatment for the first time it is essential that a thorough **consultation** is given and that a record card is filled out. Any information must be clearly written so other therapists can read it.

Wax

There are many different types of wax available.

Warm wax

This type of wax is commonly used in salons and is often made of substances such as glucose syrup, honey and zinc oxide. When cool the wax is solid so special heating containers are used to heat the wax to a temperature of around 43 °C, which will cause the wax to become runny.

Roller wax method

The **roller wax method** involves using a heater to heat up **warm wax**. Wax is contained within cartridges and different-sized heads may be placed onto the cartridge. To wax the legs, a big roller-head will be used and to wax the eyebrows a little roller-head will be used. The wax is rolled onto the skin and a strip may be used to remove the wax and hairs.

Warm wax heater

Hot wax

Hot wax is made up of waxes such as beeswax and also resins. When hot wax is cool it is solid. It is warmed up to a temperature of around 50 °C, somewhat higher than warm wax. Warm wax is mostly supplied in pots but hot wax is often supplied as pellets or blocks. When heated, the hot wax is thicker than warm wax, although still quite runny. It is applied to the skin using a spatula and removed using the fingers. Some hot waxes may be removed from the skin using strips.

> **REMEMBER**
> As hot wax is used at quite a high temperature (50 °C) extra care is required to avoid burning.

A thermostatically controlled hot wax heater

Sugaring

Sugaring is an ancient art of hair removal involving using a sugar paste containing natural products such as sugar, lemon and water. It is supplied in pots and can either be applied to the skin using the fingers and then flicked off, which removes the hairs, or as a traditional warm wax called strip sugar, which is used the same way as warm wax using a wooden spatula and paper or fabric strips.

Roll-on applicator system

GOOD PRACTICE

Many of the health and safety checks you carry out before and after each treatment relate to health and safety legislation.

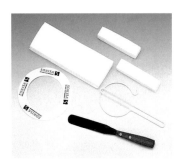

Waxing accessories

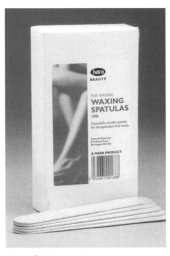

Spatulas

HEALTH MATTERS

The therapist will not reuse a spatula that has been contaminated with blood but will safely dispose of it straight away.

Equipment and materials used for waxing treatment

The following equipment and materials may be used:

- *Couch:* place a plastic protective cover and new couch roll onto the couch
- *Trolley*: disinfect the trolley and place a clean covering such as a couch roll over the top
- *Client record card*: the therapist will need to see the **client record card** in case the client has any contra-indications or allergies or anything else the therapist would need to know before giving a treatment
- *Wax pot:* check that the wax pot is not damaged and that there are no wires coming loose before plugging it in. Ensure it is adequately filled so that the therapist does not run out of wax during a treatment
- *Heater*: turn this on about 20–30 minutes before the start of the treatment depending on which type of waxing system is used
- *Paper or fabric strips*: may be used to carry out waxing treatments. Different therapists may prefer to use different types of strips
- *Wooden spatulas*: can be used to apply wax to the skin. You will need to prepare a selection of different sizes for waxing various areas of the body
- *Pre-wax lotion*: helps to clean and remove any grease from the area to be waxed. If the skin is greasy it may prevent the wax sticking properly to the skin and there may not be sufficient removal of hair
- *Cotton wool pads*: can be used to apply products such as the pre-wax lotion to the area being waxed
- *Tissues*: can be used to protect the client's clothing from products such as wax, or to collect hair that has been removed using tweezers
- *Disposable plastic apron:* for protection and hygiene. Wax is quite sticky and messy so can be hard to remove if it gets onto clothing. Wearing an apron will help to protect the clothing from becoming stained
- *Towels*: are used to cover areas such as the bikini line while waxing so that the client doesn't feel too exposed. However, if wax drips onto a towel it can be difficult to wash out well, so it is a good idea to place tissue on top of the towel
- *Disposable surgical gloves:* it is important to wear gloves to prevent **cross-infection**
- *Bin*: should be placed near to the couch and should be lined with a plastic bin-liner
- *Tweezers*: after a waxing treatment a few hairs may remain and can be removed using clean tweezers
- *Scissors*: can be used to cut long hair, for example the underarm hairs, making it easier for the hairs to be removed when waxing
- *Sanitising solution, for example, disinfectant*: after using items such as tweezers and scissors, they should be thoroughly cleaned and then placed into a jar of sanitising solution

REMEMBER

To **sanitise** means to destroy some **micro-organisms** such as bacteria. To **sterilise** means to destroy all micro-organisms.

- *Powder*: is applied to the skin and is useful if the skin is damp due to sweating, and will help to make the hairs more noticeable
- *Hand mirror*: if the client has a treatment such as an eyebrow wax or lip wax, they can see the final result in a mirror
- *Aftercare leaflet*: may be given to the client after treatment. If the client does not follow the important aftercare advice given on the leaflet they could suffer with a reaction such as an infection of the hair follicles.

HEALTH MATTERS

Talcum powder can irritate the airways in the lungs so many therapists prefer to use a powder such as corn starch.

REMEMBER

Regularly check on the consistency of the wax throughout the day and adjust the thermostat control if necessary.

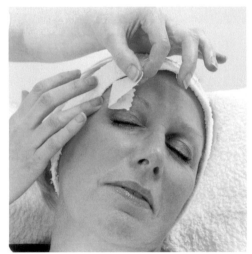

Applying and removing warm wax – eyebrows

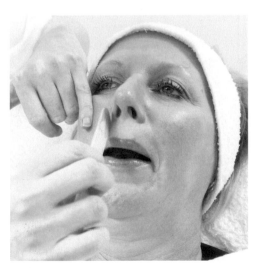
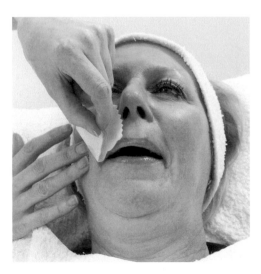

Applying and removing warm wax – upper lip

Setting up the materials and equipment for waxing treatment

Ask yourself the following questions to help you prepare the treatment area:

- Is the room clean and tidy?
- Is everything safe, for example no trailing wires, wax pot safely positioned on trolley?
- Is the room too hot or cold?
- Have the surfaces been disinfected and, if required, covered with couch roll?
- Does the trolley contain everything that is needed to carry out a treatment?
- Have tools such as scissors and tweezers been sterilised properly?
- Is the wax or sugar pot set at the right temperature?
- Is the couch covered with a plastic protective cover and couch roll?
- Are there clean large and small towels available for use?
- Is the bin lined with a bin-liner and positioned near to the couch?

ACTIVITY

Activity 4.2: What do you need?

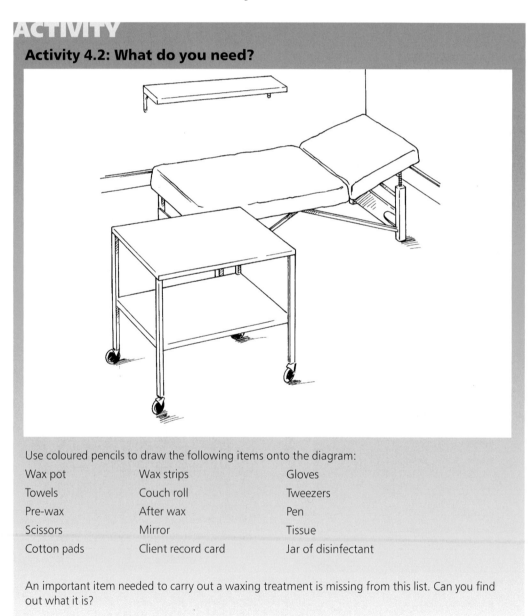

Use coloured pencils to draw the following items onto the diagram:

Wax pot	Wax strips	Gloves
Towels	Couch roll	Tweezers
Pre-wax	After wax	Pen
Scissors	Mirror	Tissue
Cotton pads	Client record card	Jar of disinfectant

An important item needed to carry out a waxing treatment is missing from this list. Can you find out what it is?

A PRACTICAL GUIDE TO BEAUTY THERAPY LEVEL 1

Activity 4.3: Warm wax products

Do some research to find out how many different types of warm wax products are available for use.

After the waxing treatment

After the treatment check the following to ensure you carry out your duties correctly.

You must:

- clean any wax drips that may have fallen onto the wax pot, trolley, couch or floor
- refilled the wax pot using the correct wax
- if required, turned off the wax pot
- dispose of used tissues, cotton pads and so on safely
- place new tissues, cotton wool and so on onto the trolley
- clean and sterilise the tweezers and scissors
- replace dirty towels with clean ones
- store the client card confidentially.

GOOD PRACTICE

Warm wax products take between 20 and 30 minutes to heat up to the required temperature. In the salon, the wax heater is usually switched on first thing in the morning and kept on so it is ready for use at any time.

HEALTH MATTERS

It is a good idea to wear surgical gloves when tidying the work area in case anything is contaminated with blood.

SELF-CHECKS

Preparing the treatment area for waxing

1 State five main items required to carry out a waxing treatment.

_____

_____

_____

_____

_____

2 Name three different types of wax available for use.

_____

_____

_____

3 State two main types of wax strip.

_____

_____

4 How are tweezers cleaned after use?

_____

_____

_____

5 State three safety considerations when setting up a wax pot.

_____

_____

_____

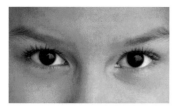

Bright, beautiful eyes

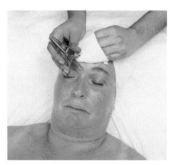

Using automatic tweezers

Preparing the treatment area for eye treatments

Eye treatments help to draw attention to the eyes, which are generally a very attractive feature of the face. Eyebrow shaping and eyelash and eyebrow tinting are popular treatments in the salon. An **eyebrow shape** and tint helps to frame the eyes and treatments involving the lashes helps to accentuate the eyes.
Eye treatments include:

- eyebrow shaping
- eyelash and eyebrow tinting
- false lash application using either strip lashes or individual lashes
- eyelash perming.

Eyebrow shaping

Tweezers are used to remove hairs from the eyebrow to make a new shape or to give a general tidy-up to remove stray hairs. There are two main types of tweezers:

- manual – these tweezers are commonly used to remove stray hairs
- automatic – these tweezers are designed to remove many hairs in a short space of time due to their design.

Eyelash and eyebrow tinting

The eyelashes and brow hairs can be coloured using a dye that darkens the hairs and can also make them appear thicker. An eyelash and brow tint can last up to six weeks.

ACTIVITY

Activity 4.4: Eyelash tints
How many different colours of **eyelash tint** are there? Ask a senior therapist to describe the effects of each when used on eyelashes and eyebrow hairs.

False lashes

False lashes help to make the client's eyelashes look longer and thicker and so draw attention to the eyes. There are two basic types of false eyelashes:

Strip lashes

The whole strip is applied near to the client's eyelashes using a special type of glue. These lashes are only temporary. They can be worn for one day.

Individual lashes

These are available as individual lashes or small groups of two or three. They are attached at the base of the natural lashes with a special type of strong glue. They can be worn for about four weeks

Eyelash perming

Eyelash perming involves using a perming lotion and little rods which help to permanently curl the lashes and also makes the lashes appear longer.

A PRACTICAL GUIDE TO BEAUTY THERAPY LEVEL 1

Equipment and products for eye treatments

General items
The following equipment and products are used for carrying out eye treatments:

- *Couch*: the back of the couch is usually set in a semi-reclined position
- *Trolley*: ensure that everything is clean, that the couch roll is placed on top and the products are neatly presented
- *Towel/tissues*: these can be used to protect the client's clothing from staining
- *Headband*: to prevent any product from coming into contact with the hair
- *Eye make-up remover (non-oily)*: if eye make-up is not removed it can affect the tinting or perming process
- *Cotton wool*: to remove make-up.

Eyebrow shaping
The following items may be used for eyebrow shaping:

- *Tissues*: to collect hairs
- *Tweezers*: to remove the hairs
- *Sanitising solution/cotton wool pads*: to clean the tweezers
- *Eyebrow brush*: to help achieve the desired shape.

Eyelash and brow tinting
The following items may be used for eyelash and brow tinting:

- *Headband:* to prevent products such as tint colouring the client's hair
- *Towels, tissues and gown for protecting clothing*
- *Hand towel* for the therapist: in case they need to wipe their hands
- *Eye make-up remover:* to remove any make-up from the eyes, which may prevent the tint from dyeing the lashes
- *Small non-metallic dish (usually made of glass)*: tint is placed into the dish and mixed with hydrogen peroxide
- *Clean spatula:* to remove products from pots such as petroleum jelly
- *Tint brush*: used to apply the tint onto the hairs
- *Eyeshields:* help to protect staining of the skin around the eyes
- *Eyelash tints in a selection of colours:* include black, blue-black (the darkest), blue, brown and grey (the result of using a grey colour tint is a light brown colour)
- *Hydrogen peroxide 3% (10 Vol):* this product is mixed with the tint
- *Petroleum jelly*: helps to prevent staining of the skin by the tint
- *Scissors*: to cut up cotton pads into eye shield shapes if required
- *Soothing lotion:* to help reduce redness after a treatment such as an eyebrow shape
- *Cotton wool, cotton buds and tissues:* damp cotton wool is used to cleanse the treatment area and to wipe away tint from the eyelashes and eyebrows after it has tinted the hairs
- *Hand mirror*: so the client can see the finished result

- *Record card and pen*: information such as a reaction to a product should be written onto the card. It should also have details of tests performed and any reactions
- *Bin with diposable bin liner.*

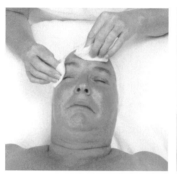

1 *Ensuring lashes are clean and free from make-up*

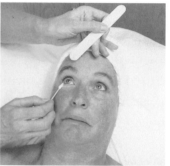

2 *Applying barrier cream*

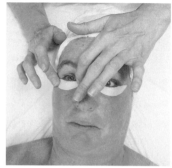

3 *Securing eye shields*

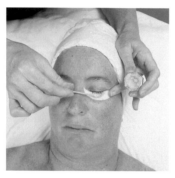

4 *Applying the tint*

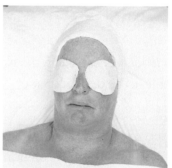

5 *Processing time*

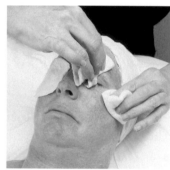

6 *Removing tint*

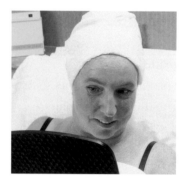

7 *Checking the results*

False lashes/individual lashes

Selection of artificial 'strip' eyelashes

The following items may be used for false eyelashes/individual lashes treatment:

- *Strip lashes*
- *Individual lashes*
- *Adhesive (glue)*
- *Eye make-up remover:* to ensure there is no barrier that would prevent the lashes sticking to the natural lashes
- *Tweezers/orange stick:* to help position the false lashes
- *Sanitiser:* to wipe the ends of the tweezers
- *Scissors:* to trim the false lashes to the desired length
- *Hand mirror:* so the client may see the finished result.

GOOD PRACTICE

Although false eyelash glues are quite safe, some people can be allergic to them. A skin test should be given before treatment. This would be done in the same way as for an eyelash tint.

Eyelash perming

The following items may be used for eyelash perming:

- *Make-up remover:* the treatment may not be successful if make-up is not removed from around the eyes
- *Perming lotion:* to perm the lashes
- *Eyelash curlers:* small, medium and large-sized rods are available. Lashes are wrapped around the rods and perming lotion is applied
- *Perming adhesive:* to secure the lashes to the curlers
- *Fixing lotion:* to ensure the lashes are permanently permed
- *Cotton buds or brushes:* to apply the perm lotion
- *Bin*
- *Record card*
- *Hand mirror.*

Setting up materials and equipment for eye treatments

To prepare the work area for eye treatments, your duties are to:

- make sure the work area is clean and tidy
- keep the couch clean
- place some clean couch roll onto the couch and trolley
- place the products and client's record card neatly onto the trolley and ensure the product bottles are clean
- put any sterilised tools such as tweezers into a jar containing sanitising chemicals
- place some damp cotton wool pads into a bowl and tissues onto the trolley
- place a couple of folded towels neatly onto the couch or trolley.

GOOD PRACTICE

Towels should be boil-washed to destroy harmful germs such as bacteria. This will help to prevent cross-infection.

Applying temporary strip lashes

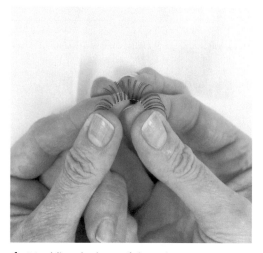

1 *Moulding the base of the strip*

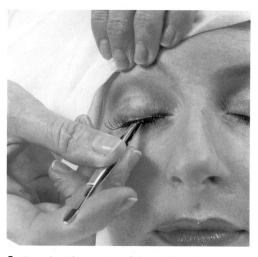

2 *Securing the centre of the strip to the centre of the eyelid*

3 *Securing the inner and outer edges of the strip*

4 *Blending the false eyelashes with the natural ones*

5 *The final effect*

A PRACTICAL GUIDE TO BEAUTY THERAPY LEVEL 1

ACTIVITY

Activity 4.5: Wordsearch

Can you find the following words?

s	p	x	i	n	t	u	v	l	f	y	l	l	e	j	m	u	e	l	o	r	t	e	p	s
v	e	s	i	w	i	a	h	b	d	r	a	c	d	r	o	c	e	r	e	q	i	y	j	d
j	r	c	o	t	t	o	n	b	u	d	s	t	e	d	s	p	a	t	u	l	a	k	q	n
g	m	i	o	t	n	i	t	i	u	p	w	p	l	e	e	n	r	a	m	a	n	a	r	a
n	r	s	l	i	o	o	w	t	d	r	z	e	e	m	g	u	t	i	s	s	u	e	s	b
u	o	s	n	o	i	t	o	l	g	n	i	m	r	e	p	i	r	j	u	a	t	p	v	d
t	p	o	r	g	t	w	s	a	f	h	u	r	s	j	d	r	e	v	i	s	e	h	d	a
g	h	r	e	c	o	f	v	i	s	k	o	t	p	e	o	e	c	k	t	p	e	r	v	e
n	s	s	c	r	l	i	b	e	e	d	i	x	o	r	e	p	n	e	g	o	r	d	y	h
i	a	c	e	i	g	p	y	a	j	c	o	i	d	d	u	i	i	g	t	c	w	e	n	t
p	l	e	n	f	n	e	d	p	k	x	k	e	n	h	z	t	n	f	o	a	b	e	k	l
i	e	s	t	r	i	p	l	a	s	h	e	s	t	i	s	u	b	i	j	u	i	l	l	d
b	y	s	d	b	x	i	n	s	e	h	s	a	l	l	a	u	d	i	v	i	d	n	i	s
p	e	d	u	u	i	d	i	e	p	l	a	b	k	s	d	y	r	b	n	o	x	a	f	p
i	r	u	t	q	f	i	t	w	e	e	z	e	r	s	n	j	s	b	j	d	i	s	w	s

eyelash perm	strip lashes	individual lashes	tint
towels	cotton buds	bin	record card
mirror	fixing lotion	brush	tissues
perming lotion	adhesive	tweezers	orange stick
scissors	petroleum jelly	hydrogen peroxide	eyeshield
spatula	headband		

SELF-CHECKS

Eye treatments

1   State three different types of eye treatments.

   _____

   _____

   _____

2   What is the difference between manual tweezers and automatic tweezers?

   _____

   _____

3   How could you sterilise tweezers?

   _____

   _____

4   What hygiene precautions should be taken before, during and following an eyebrow shaping treatment?

   _____

   _____

   _____

5   State the two types of false lashes.

   _____

   _____

After treatment

Your duties are to:

● put on gloves in case anything is contaminated with blood

● empty the bin and place a new liner into it

● store away products and equipment safely and in the correct place

● store the client record card confidentially.

Preparing the treatment area for manicure and pedicure treatment

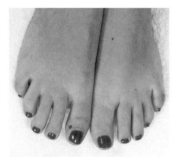

Toenail and nail polish

Manicures and **pedicures** are treatments carried out to the hands or feet:

● A manicure involves treating the hands to improve the health and appearance of the skin and nails.

● A pedicure involves treating the feet to improve the health and appearance of the nails and skin.

Products, materials and equipment required for manicure and pedicure treatment

The following may be used for manicure and pedicure treatments:

● *Manicure trolley:* ensure the trolley is clean and lined with couch roll

● *Manicure bowl:* contains warm water, perhaps with some oil or antiseptic solution

● *Foot spa or bowl:* contains warm water; products such as detergents or essential oils are often added

● *Emery boards* (also known as nail files): used to file and shape the nails.

● *Nail polish remover:* removes unwanted polish from the nails

● *Buffers:* buffers can be made of leather or be disposable

● *Buffing paste:* used together with a buffer and consists of a gritty substance

● *Nail scissors:* used to cut the nails.

A foot spa

Professional, cushioned emery boards

- *Toenail clippers:* used to cut the nails of the toe
- *Cuticle knife:* a metal tool that needs to be handled with care as it is quite sharp
- *Orange sticks:* cotton wool is placed at either end of the orange stick. The stick is used to apply products such as cuticle and buffing cream to the skin and nails
- *Hoof stick:* used to push back the cuticle if required
- *Cuticle cream/oil:* cuticle cream or oil is used to soften the cuticles so that the cuticle may be gently pushed back if required
- *Cuticle remover:* helps to soften the skin of the cuticle and also to loosen it from the nail plate. This will make it easier to remove excess cuticle

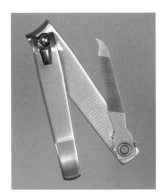
Toenail clippers

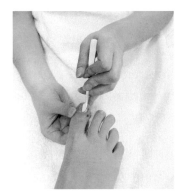
A cuticle knife

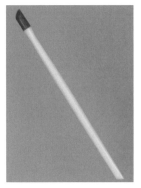
A hoof stick

HEALTH MATTERS

If the cuticle remover is not thoroughly removed it may damage the skin.

- *Cuticle nippers:* a metal tool that should be handled with care. It is used to remove excess cuticle
- *Foot files/pumice stones:* these items are used to remove hard, excess skin from the feet
- *Cotton wool pads/tissues:* can be used to apply and remove products and may be placed into clean bowls
- *Hand cream/oil or lotion:* used to massage and/or moisturise the skin
- *Foot cream, oil or lotion:* used to massage and/or moisturise the skin of the feet
- *Exfoliate cream:* helps to remove dead skin cells from the skin so will help to improve the skin's appearance and the feel of the skin.

A callus file

Le Remedi hand treatment programme

- *Base coat*: helps to prevent staining of the nails when using a coloured nail varnish. It also provides a base on which to apply nail polish
- *Nail polish*: there are many coloured nail polishes that can be applied to the nails
- *Top-coat*: helps to protect the nail polish and so it is less likely to peel or chip as quickly

Nail polishes

Manicure range

- *Nail strengthener*: helps to strengthen the nails to prevent breakage
- *Polish thinner*: used to thin the polish if it has become thickened
- *Paraffin wax heater:* used to heat paraffin wax
- *Paraffin wax:* there are many different types of paraffin wax products. A brush is often used to apply it onto the skin. Foils and towels will also be required
- *Thermal mittens*: used to apply warmth to the hands
- *Thermal boots*: used to apply warmth to the feet

Paraffin wax heater and accessories

Thermal manicure mittens

Thermal boots

- *Sanitising solutions:* after using items such as tweezers and scissors they should be thoroughly cleaned and then placed into a jar of sanitising solution
- *Towels:* medium-sized towels are used for drying the client's hands and feet
- *Bin:* should be placed near to the couch and should be lined with a bin-liner.

ACTIVITY

Activity 4.6

Do some research to find out why a therapist would use the following: paraffin wax, thermal mittens and heated booties.

HEALTH MATTERS

The therapist will need to see the client record card in case the client has any contra-indications or allergies or anything else the therapist should know before giving a treatment.

REMEMBER

An aftercare leaflet may be given to the client after treatment which will provide information about how to look after the skin and nails.

Setting up materials and equipment for manicure and pedicure treatment

When setting up the treatment area, your duties are to:

- ensure the area is clean and tidy
- ensure everything is safe, for example no spillage of products on the floor
- ensure the room is not too hot or cold
- disinfect all surfaces and if necessary cover them in couch roll
- ensure the trolley contains everything that is needed to carry out a treatment
- sterilise tools such as scissors and clippers
- place a clean bin near to where the treatment is being carried out
- If a particular light is positioned so that it shines onto the treatment area, ensure that it is working
- position the towels correctly and fold them neatly and ensure there are enough towels
- place a towel on the floor in **preparation** for pedicure treatment.

REMEMBER

To sterilise tools, an **autoclave** or a **glass bead steriliser** may be used but remember to wash the instruments thoroughly otherwise they will not sterilise effectively.

ACTIVITY

Activity 4.7: Label the items

Label the following items used for manicure and pedicure treatment:

cuticle knife	manicure bowl	thermal boots
orange stick	pedicure bowl	buffer
emery board	spatula	thermal mittens
nail polish	foot file	

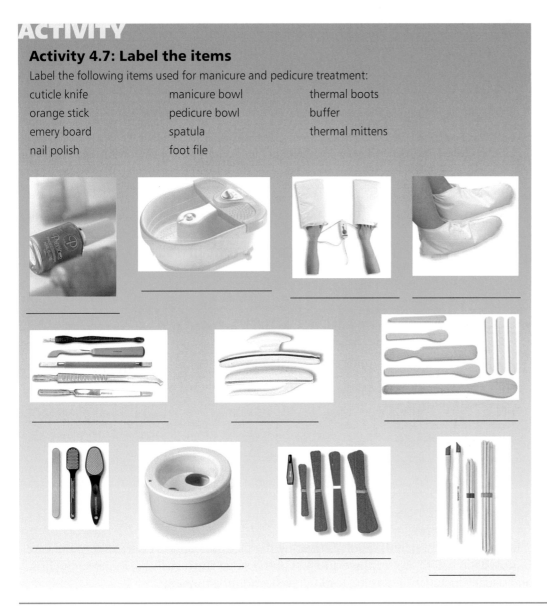

After the treatment

After the manicure or pedicure treatment your duties are to:

- dispose of used tissues, cotton pads and so on safely
- place new tissues, cotton wool and so on onto the trolley
- clean the equipment such as the manicure and pedicure bowls
- clean the plastic equipment and buffer (if leather) in warm soapy water, dry and then sanitise it
- place metal tools such as the cuticle knife and cuticle nippers into the steriliser, for example autoclave or glass bead steriliser
- clean the tops of bottles and products
- clean the tweezers and scissors
- empty the bin
- replace used towels with clean ones
- return the client card to the place where it is confidentially stored.

SELF-CHECKS

Manicures and pedicures

1   Why is a sanitising solution such as disinfectant required for a manicure?
_____
_____

2   Name five products you would need to put on the trolley for manicure treatment.
_____
_____
_____
_____
_____

3   How would you describe a pedicure treatment to a client?
_____
_____
_____

4   How would you sterilise the cuticle knife?
_____
_____

5   Why should you wear surgical gloves when clearing away waste?
_____
_____

A facial treatment improves the health and appearance of the skin

Preparing the treatment area for facial treatments

A **facial** treatment mainly involves treating the face and neck. The treatment helps to improve the health, appearance and feel of the skin. The facial lasts for about an hour and usually includes cleansing, toning, mask and moisturising.

Products, materials and equipment for facial treatments

The following products, materials and equipment are commonly used when carrying out a facial treatment:

- *Cleanser:* to cleanse the face. There are different types of cleansers to suit various skin types

Cleansing products

- *Eye make-up remover:* removes all traces of eye make-up
- *Toner:* there are different types of toners to suit various skin types
- *Moisturiser:* there are different types to suit various skin types
- *Mask:* different types of mask are available with different actions
- *Exfoliater:* to remove dead skin cells
- *Massage oil/cream:* used when carrying out a massage
- *Spatulas:* used to remove products from pot
- *Cotton wool pads/cotton buds:* used to remove products from the skin. Dampened cotton pads can be used to cover the eyes during a mask treatment
- *Sponges:* used to remove products such as a mask from the skin
- *Tissues:* used to blot the skin after applying toner
- *Bowls:* a large bowl is filled with warm water; small bowls are used to store cotton wool pads and so on
- *Headband:* protects the client's hair
- *Towels:* one towel may be placed across the client's chest. The therapist will also need a towel to dry their hands
- *Mask brush:* used to apply the mask to the face
- *Comedone extractor:* a metal tool used to remove blackheads
- *Record card and pen:* useful information can be written onto the card, for example which products are preferred by the client, or if there was reaction to a product
- *Hand mirror:* so the client can see the final result
- *Magnifying lamp:* so the therapist can assess the client's skin type
- *Steamer:* to apply steam to the face, which helps to cleanse and improve the bloodflow to the skin.

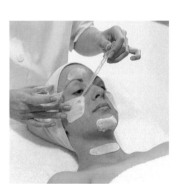

Peel-off mask applied to the face on pre-cut shapes

GOOD PRACTICE

A thermos flask may be filled with very warm water and stored under the couch if required, which means you will not need to get water directly from the tap and risk spilling water onto the floor.

Setting up materials and equipment for facial treatments

As a beauty assistant you will need to prepare the work area for the facial treatment.

Your duties are to:

- make sure everything is clean and tidy
- ensure that the room is not too hot or cold, stuffy or smelly
- make sure there are enough pillows and bedding for the client's comfort
- ensure that there is a clean gown for the client to put on
- make sure that there is a couch roll placed onto the couch
- make sure the trolley contains everything that is needed to carry out a treatment
- sterilise items such as scissors and tweezers
- fill the water container on the steamer with distilled water and switch it on
- ensure there is a clean bin near to where the treatment is being carried out
- if a particular light will be used to assess the skin type, ensure that it is working
- position the towels correctly and fold them neatly and ensure there are enough towels
- put a full selection of facial products onto the trolley so that the therapist may treat all skin types.

ACTIVITY

Activity 4.8: Can you match the item with its correct description?

Using coloured pencils, shade the item and its correct description using the same colour.

Item	Description
Moisturiser	Used to protect the client's hair
Large bowl	Metal tool used to remove blackheads
Eye make-up remover	Helps to moisturise skin
Small bowls	Removes all traces of eye make-up
Cleanser	Often made of wood and used to remove products from pots
Comedone extractor	Used to apply mask onto the skin
Massage oil/cream	Used to blot the skin after applying toner
Headband	Used to provide massage to the face
Tissues	Used to remove products from the skin
Magnifying lamp	Used to store items such as cotton pads and jewellery
Mask brush	Helps to remove dirt from the skin
Cotton pads	Useful for assessing the client's skin type
Spatula	Filled with warm water and the water is used to remove products from the face

After the treatment

Your duties are to:

- dispose of used tissues, cotton pads and so on safely
- place new tissues, cotton wool and so on onto the trolley
- clean tools such as a **comedone** extractor and ensure they are sterilised
- clean the tops of bottles and products
- replace dirty towels with clean ones
- return the client card to the place where it is confidentially stored.

SELF-CHECKS

Facial treatments

1 Why should you ensure that bottles and containers are clean?

_____

2 State five products that would be required to carry out a facial treatment.

_____

_____

_____

_____

_____

3 Why would a therapist use a comedone extractor?

_____

_____

4 What is the purpose of a steamer?

_____

5 Why is a spatula used to remove products and not a finger?

_____

_____

Preparing the treatment area for make-up treatments

A **make-up** treatment involves using a range of cosmetics such as eyeshadows and lipsticks to help enhance the appearance of the face. Make-up can be used to bring out good features of the face and can help to disguise other features, for example a big nose, that are not so flattering.

A client may request a make-up lesson to learn the correct way to apply cosmetics and to find out which colours suit her face. Other clients may have a special occasion such as a wedding so want to look their best.

Products, materials and equipment for make-up treatment

The following products, materials and equipment may be used for make-up treatment:

- *Headband*: to protect the hair

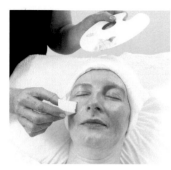

Applying foundation

Blusher colours

- *Hair clips*: to clip the hair back away from the face
- *Gown*: to protect the client's clothing
- *Tissues*: many uses
- *Sponges*: to apply make-up onto the face such as foundation
- *Make-up brushes*: to apply make-up such as eyeshadow and blusher to the face
- *Disposable applicators*: to apply make-up such as eyeshadow. Can be thrown away after use
- *Eyebrow brush*: used to brush eyebrow hairs to give a nice shape
- *Spatula*: to remove products from pots
- *Orange sticks/cotton buds*: orange sticks may be tipped with cotton wool and used to remove excess make-up around the eyes
- *Make-up palette*: cosmetics such as eyeshadow may be placed onto the palette.
- *Cotton wool pads*: to remove make-up or other products from the skin
- *Record card and make-up chart* used to record information such as the products and make-up colours chosen
- *Hand mirror*: so that the client may see the completed make-up treatment
- *Pencil sharpener*: to sharpen eye-liner and so on
- *Cleanser/toner/moisturiser*: to prepare the skin before make-up application
- *Concealers*: to help conceal blemishes, for example dark circles around the eyes
- *Foundation*: to help give an even colour to the whole face
- *Blusher*: to help to emphasise the cheek bones
- *Shaders*: to help draw attention away from an area
- *Highlighter*: to highlight a particular area so that attention is drawn towards it
- *Eye shadows*: to help bring out the eye colour

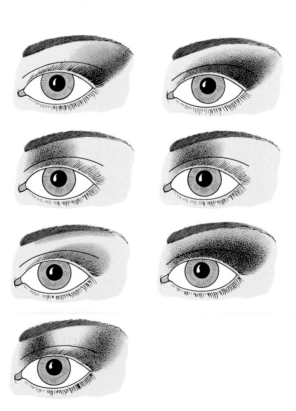

Some eyeshadow effects

- *Eyeliners*: an eyeliner is mainly applied around the eyes and helps to accentuate them
- *Eyebrow pencil*: helps to make the eyebrows more noticeable, especially if the hairs are fair
- *Mascara*: makes the lashes look longer and thicker

Applying eyeliner

Applying mascara to upper eyelashes

- *Lipstick/lip gloss*: helps to draw attention to the lips
- *Lip pencil*: outlines the shape of the lips and can make them appear slightly bigger
- *Eyelash curlers*: helps to make the lashes appear longer.

Lip make-up shades

Eyelash curlers

ACTIVITY

Activity 4.9: Cosmetics and tools used during make-up treatment

Match the terms below with the correct description in the list:

Highlighter	Lip pencil	Blusher	Eyebrow pencil	Foundation
Shader	Mascara	Concealer	Eyeshadow	Make-up brush

1 Helps to bring out the colour of the eyes... _____
2 Outlines the lips to help draw attention to them... _____
3 Makes the eyelashes look longer and thicker... _____
4 Applied to the eyebrows to make them more noticeable... _____
5 Helps to highlight a particular feature of the face... _____
6 Helps to bring out the cheek bones... _____
7 Helps to give an even colour to the whole face... _____
8 Helps to draw attention away from a particular area of the face... _____
9 Helps to conceal blemishes, for example dark circles under the eyes... _____
10 Eyeshadow and blusher is applied using this... _____

Setting up materials and equipment for the make-up treatment

The make-up area must be well organised before the client arrives.

Your duties are to:

- ensure everything is clean and tidy
- ensure there are enough pillows and bedding for the client's comfort
- ensure there is a clean gown for the client to put on
- make sure the trolley contains everything that is needed to carry out a treatment
- place a clean bin near to where the treatment is being carried out
- if a particular light will be used to assess the skin type, ensure that it is working
- ensure there is sufficient lighting to carry out a make-up treatment
- position the towels correctly and fold them neatly and make sure there are enough towels
- put a full selection of facial products on the trolley so that the therapist may treat all skin types.

Applying make-up

1 *Vena before make-up is applied*

2 *Concealer applied*

3 *Foundation and face powder applied*

4 *Blusher applied*

5 *Eyeshadows applied*

6 *Mascara, eyeliner and eyebrow powder applied*

7 *Mouth outlined, lipstick and lip gloss applied*

8 *Evening make-up*

After the treatment

After the make-up treatment, your duties are to:

- dispose of used tissues, cotton pads and so on safely
- clean the tops of bottles and products
- replace the tops of the lipsticks and other cosmetics
- empty the bin
- replace dirty towels with clean ones
- return the client card to the place where it is confidentially stored.

GOOD PRACTICE

Make-up products come in a range of attractive colours. When setting up the trolley, try to arrange the products so that they are pleasing to the eye.

SELF-CHECKS

Make-up

1 Why would the client wear a gown and a headband during a make-up treatment?

2 Give three reasons why a client would come for a make-up treatment.

3 Why are diposable brushes and applicators used to apply make-up?

4 State five products that would be found on the trolley for a make-up treatment.

5 Why do think it is important to have good lighting when giving this treatment?

MULTIPLE CHOICE QUIZ

Decide which is the correct answer and tick the box.

1 The correct storage of client records relate to which Act?
- ☐ Electricity at Work Act
- ☐ Data Protection Act
- ☐ Fire Precautions Act
- ☐ Employer's Liability Act.

2 It is very important that the therapist follows health and safety legislation. What are your responsiblities relating to this legislation?
- ☐ to ensure the work area is tidy
- ☐ only to report obvious problems to your supervisor when available
- ☐ to take action to prevent health and safety hazards and report breaches to your supervisor
- ☐ to ensure the correct disposal of waste.

3 When should you report a health and safety hazard?
- ☐ immediately
- ☐ during your break
- ☐ when the hazard becomes dangerous
- ☐ at the end of the day.

4 Which of the following environmental conditions would be unacceptable in the salon?
☐ good lighting
☐ warmth
☐ good supply of fresh air
☐ very cold wind.

5 Which of the following may cause cross-infection to occur?
☐ using sterilised tools
☐ using clean towels
☐ not washing your hands
☐ throwing away disposable items after use.

6 Which of the following is *not* used for sanitising?
☐ moisturiser
☐ ultraviolet cabinet
☐ disinfectant
☐ antiseptic.

7 Sterilisation destroys bacteria and viruses. What is meant by sanitisation?
☐ destroys all bacteria
☐ destroys some of the bacteria and viruses

☐ increases the number of bacteria and viruses
☐ sterilises tools and equipment.

8 Which of following would not be used during a waxing treatment?
☐ spatula
☐ mask brush
☐ afterwax lotion
☐ tweezers.

9 Which of the following would be used during a facial treament?
☐ toner
☐ pre-wax lotion
☐ cuticle cream
☐ eyeshadow.

10 Which of the following would you check before each treatment?
☐ that waste has been disposed of correctly
☐ everything is clean and tidy
☐ everything is safe
☐ all of the above.

KEY TERMS

You should now understand the following words and phrases. If you do not, go back through the chapter and find out what they mean:

Waxing	**Roller wax method**	**False lashes**
Eye treatment	**Sugaring**	**Patch test**
Make-up	**Cross-infection**	**Contamination**
Manicure	**Sanitise**	**Autoclave**
Pedicure	**Sterilise**	**Glass bead steriliser**
Facial	**Micro-organism**	**Comedone**
Reception	**Ultraviolet cabinet**	**Hygiene**
Consultation	**Eyebrow shape**	**Maintain**
Warm wax	**Eyelash tint**	**Preparation**
Hot wax	**Eyelash perming**	**Client record card**

5 Unit BT2

Assist with facial treatments

After working through this chapter you will be able to:

- prepare for facial treatment
- set up the work area
- use **consultation** techniques
- perform a **skin analysis**
- prepare the client
- assist with a facial treatment
- complete the treatment.

Before you work through this chapter: Be wise and revise!
Revision topics to help you achieve this unit:

Assist with facial treatments

TOPIC	CHAPTER	PAGE

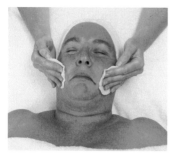

A facial

REMEMBER

Men, as well as women, are having regular facials!

HEALTH MATTERS

A full facial lasts for at least an hour. Check your posture when sitting or standing (try to keep the back straight) to avoid developing back ache and tension in your neck and shoulders.

What is a facial?

A facial treatment involves treating the face and neck, and will help to improve the health and appearance of the skin. A facial treatment lasts for around an hour depending on which type of facial the client is receiving. During a facial treatment, a therapist will usually carry out all or some of the following:

- cleanse
- tone
- exfoliation
- massage
- mask application
- moisturise.

To carry out a facial treatment it is important the therapist has knowledge of the structure and functions of the skin.

Anatomy and physiology: the skin

The skin is a protective, waterproof covering and is made up of millions of **skin cells**. It consists of layers called the **epidermis** and **dermis**. The layer beneath the dermis is called the **subcutaneous layer**.

Epidermis

The upper part of the skin consists of five layers called the epidermis.

ACTIVITY

Activity 5.1: The five layers of the epidermis

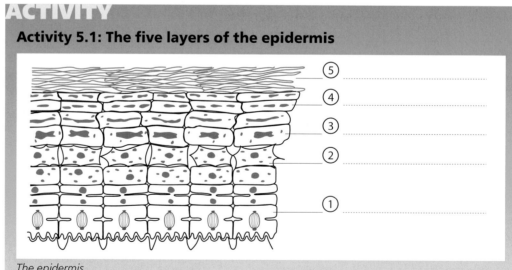

The epidermis

Label the diagram matching the numbers to the numbered terms in the following text.
Use this key to colour the diagram:

Yellow – layers 1 and 2   Red – layers 4 and 5

Red and yellow (i.e. some cells red, some yellow) – layer 3

1. Basal layer (stratum germinativum)

The basal layer is the deepest layer in the epidermis and is in contact with the dermis directly beneath it. These cells are living and divide to make new skin cells. As new cells are produced they push older cells above them towards the surface of the skin, until they finally reach the horny layer. It takes 3–6 weeks for the skin cells to be pushed up from the basal layer to the horny layer.

2. Prickle cell layer (stratum spinosum)

In the prickle cell layer the cells are living. The cells join by arm-like fine threads, which give the cells a prickly appearance.

3. Granular layer (stratum granulosum)

The granular layer contains cells that have a granular appearance. As the cells die they fill with tiny granules.

4. Clear layer (stratum lucidum)

The clear layer is found below the horny layer. This layer is only found on the fingertips, the palms of the hands and the soles of the feet.

5. Horny layer (stratum corneum)

The top layer of the epidermis is called the horny layer, and consists of flat, overlapping, dead cells.

The horny layer helps to prevent bacteria entering through the skin and protects the body from minor injury. Cells of the horny layer are continually being rubbed off the body by friction and are replaced by cells from the layers beneath. The shedding of dead skin cells is known as **desquamation**.

REMEMBER

The rate of new cells being produced in the basal layer slows down as we get older and so there is less shedding of dead skin cells. Mature skins appear quite dull as dead skin cells build up on the skin's surface.

Skin pigmentation

Melanin is responsible for the pigment (colour) of the skin and is stimulated by ultraviolet rays from the sun. This is why the skin develops a tan after sunbathing. Its function is to protect the deeper layers of the skin from damage. Everyone has about the same number of melanocytes but produces varying quantities of melanin. This will determine the depth of skin colour. More melanin is produced in black skins than white skins, and this extra protection can help black skins to age more slowly than white skins.

REMEMBER

Fair skins are more at risk in the sun than dark skins but all skin needs protecting from the damaging effects of ultraviolet rays from the sun.

HEALTH MATTERS

The lips do not contain melanin, the protective pigment in the skin, and burn more easily in the sun. The mouth is a prime site for skin cancer.

Activity 5.2: Inside the skin

Hair

Epidermis

Dermis

Subcutaneous layer

The skin and its structures

Label the diagram matching the numbers to the numbered terms in the following text. Use this key to colour the diagram:

Pink – arrector pili muscle and the muscle below the subcutaneous layer

Blue – sweat gland

Yellow – adipose tissue and sebaceous gland.

Red – blood vessels.

Dermis

Below the epidermis lies the dermis, which connects with the basal layer. It consists of two layers:

- The upper section is called the **papillary layer** and contains small tubes called **capillaries**, which carry blood and a fluid-like substance called lymph.

- The **reticular layer** contains **collagen** and **elastin**. Collagen gives the skin strength and elastin gives the skin its elasticity. Wavy bands of tough collagen fibres restrict the extent to which the skin can be stretched, and elastic fibres return the skin back to shape after it has been stretched.

The dermis also contains **sebaceous glands**, **sweat glands** and arrector pili muscles, nerves, hair follicles and blood vessels.

1. Sebaceous glands

These are small, sac-like structures, which produce a substance called **sebum**. Sebum is a fatty substance and is the skin's natural **moisturiser**. These glands are found all over the body, but are more numerous on the scalp and areas of the face such as the nose, forehead and chin. **Hormones** control the activity of these glands and as we get older less sebum is produced, which means the skin becomes drier.

Sebum and sweat mix together on the skin to form an **acid mantle**. The acid mantle maintains the pH (acid/alkaline level) of the skin at 5.5–5.6. This helps to protect the skin from harmful **bacteria** and **fungi**.

2. Eccrine glands

These are sweat glands. They are found all over the body and they produce sweat. The sweat duct opens directly onto the surface of the skin through an opening called a **pore**. Sweat consists of 99.4 per cent water, 0.4 per cent toxins and 0.2 per cent salts.

3. Arrector pili

These are small muscles attached to the hair follicles. When we are cold the contraction of these muscles causes the hairs to stand on end. This results in the appearance of goose bumps.

4. Sensory nerve endings

These are found all over the body but are particularly numerous on our fingertips and lips. These nerves will make us aware of feelings of pain, touch, heat and cold by sending messages through sensory nerves to the brain.

Messages are sent from the brain through **motor nerves**. Motor nerves stimulate the sweat glands, arrector pili muscles and sebaceous glands to carry out their functions.

5. Blood vessels

Blood within the **blood vessels** provides the skin with **oxygen** and **nutrients**. The living cells of the skin produce waste products such as carbon dioxide. These waste products pass from the cells and enter into the bloodstream to be taken away and removed by the body.

Subcutaneous layer

The subcutaneous layer is situated below the dermis. It mostly consists of **adipose tissue** (fat).

6. Adipose tissue

The adipose tissue helps to protect the body against injury and acts as an insulating layer against heat loss, helping to keep the body warm.

7. Muscle

Muscle is found below the subcutaneous layer and is attached to bone.

Functions of the skin

Sensation

The skin contains sensory nerve endings that send messages to the brain. These nerves respond to touch, pressure, pain, cold and heat and allow us to recognise objects from their feel and shape.

Heat regulation

It is important for the body to have a constant internal temperature of around 37 °C. The skin helps to maintain this temperature by:

Vasoconstriction

This occurs when the body becomes cold. The blood vessels become narrower so that the blood flow is reduced through the capillaries. Heat lost from the surface of the skin is therefore reduced.

HEALTH MATTERS

Smoking causes vasoconstriction of the blood vessels. As a result less blood is able to reach the skin tissue, which affects the health of the skin.

Vasodilation

This occurs when the body becomes too hot. The capillaries get bigger and the blood flow increases; this allows heat to be lost from the body.

Shivering

Shivering when we are cold helps to warm the body, as the contraction of the muscles produces heat within the body.

Absorption

The skin is largely waterproof and absorbs very little, although certain substances are able to pass through the basal layer. Essential oils such as lavender can pass through the hair follicles and into the bloodstream. Ultraviolet rays from the sun are also able to penetrate through the basal layer.

HEALTH MATTERS

Certain medications such as hormone replacement therapy can be given through patches placed on the skin.

Protection

The skin protects the body by keeping harmful bacteria out and provides a covering for all the organs inside. It also protects underlying structures from the harmful effects of ultraviolet light. The other functions of the skin also help to protect the body.

Excretion

You have probably noticed that when you get hot, you sweat. The eccrine glands send out sweat onto the skin surface and so heat is lost as the water evaporates from the skin.

Secretion

Sebum helps to keep the skin moisturised and also to make it waterproof.

Vitamin D

The ultraviolet rays from the sun enter through the skin's layers and activate a chemical, which changes into vitamin D. Vitamin D is needed for strong bones and teeth.

REMEMBER

Skin that produces excess sebum can still become dehydrated if it is not looked after properly.

REMEMBER

Think of SHAPES VD to help you remember the functions of the skin.

Skin diseases and disorders

Skin diseases and disorders can be classified as bacterial infections, viral infections, fungal infections, **infestations**, **allergies** and **non-infectious** conditions. Some infections, such as ringworm and athlete's foot, can be caught by **direct contact** with an infected person. Infections can also be caught by **indirect contact** with contaminated items such as towels, coins, door handles, crockery, and so on, which can store germs such as bacteria.

Boils

A boil is an infection of the hair follicle, which begins as a tender, red lump and develops into a painful pustule containing pus. Once a head is formed the pus is discharged, leaving a space, and so scarring of the skin often remains after the boil has healed. Poor general health, overwork, tiredness and an unhealthy diet are factors that increase the chance of developing a boil. Sufferers may be treated with antibiotics. Boils should be avoided during **massage** treatment. Boils may be dangerous if they occur near to the eyes or the brain. Several connected boils are known as a **carbuncle**.

A boil (furuncle)

Stye

A stye is a small boil on the edge of the eyelid and is caused by an infection of an eyelash follicle. The area will be inflamed and swollen. The area should be avoided during treatment.

Conjunctivitis

This is inflammation of the conjunctiva, the membrane covering the eye. The inner eyelid and eyeball appear red and sore. It is caused by a bacterial infection following irritation to the eye, such as grit or dust that enter the eye, and is further aggravated by rubbing. Pus is often present and may ooze from the area. Conjunctivitis is **infectious** and cross-infection can occur through using contaminated towels or tissues.

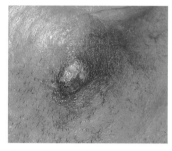

Conjunctivitis

Impetigo

This infection begins when bacteria invade a cut, cold sore or other broken skin. It can be seen as weeping blisters that form golden or yellow-coloured crusts. The area around the crusts is inflamed and red. Impetigo is highly infectious and spreads quickly on the surface of the skin. Usually the outbreaks are among children. If this condition is suspected, the sufferer must be referred to the doctor and treated with antibiotics.

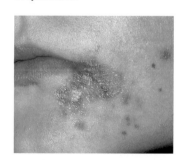

Impetigo

Cold sore

Cold sores are a common skin infection caused by the herpes simplex **virus**. The virus is usually passed on in early childhood, probably after being kissed by someone with a cold sore. The virus passes through the skin, travels up a nerve and lies dormant at a nerve junction. When the virus is stimulated, it travels back down the nerve and forms a cold sore. It begins as an area of **erythema** (redness) on the skin, which blisters and forms a crust, usually around the mouth. Cold sores often appear after a period of stress. They can also be caused by exposure to bright sunlight, menstruation or accompany colds and flu. Cold sores are highly infectious so the area must be avoided during facial treatment.

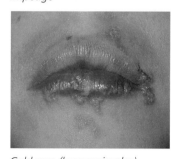

Cold sore (herpes simplex)

The blisters of a cold sore contain the virus. A cold sore is most infectious when the blisters have formed and shortly afterwards, when they break and weep.

Allergies

An allergy is an abnormal response by the body's immune system to a foreign substance (**allergen**). Some people can react to ordinary substances, that are normally harmless to most other people. Irritation to the skin causes some of its cells to release a substance called **histamine**, causing the skin to become warm, red and swollen.

It is advisable to give an allergy test to someone with sensitive skin; otherwise there may be a reaction to the product being used. You should also ensure that the client is not allergic to wheat or nuts if you intend to use wheatgerm or oils extracted from nuts. An irritated skin due to an allergy is not infectious, but it is advisable not to work over the affected area.

A doctor may prescribe antihistamine tablets and a **cortisone cream** for relieving the symptoms of an allergic skin reaction. When the specific cause of the allergy is not known, the patient is usually referred to a **dermatologist**, a doctor specialising in skin problems.

Eczema

Milia

Eczema used to be considered to be different from dermatitis but it is now generally accepted that both terms may be used to describe the same condition. Eczema is inflammation of the skin and is commonly found inside the elbows and behind the knees. There may be itchy, dry, scaly red patches present on the skin and small blisters may burst, causing the skin to weep. **Hereditary** factors or external irritants such as detergents, cosmetics and soaps can cause eczema. Internal irritants such as dairy products can also be a trigger. This condition is not infectious, although it is advisable to avoid working over the affected areas during treatment, especially if there is weeping or bleeding.

Whiteheads (milia)

When sebum becomes trapped inside a hair follicle it may form a hard lump called a whitehead. A whitehead (milium) can be seen as a small white spot and may accompany dry skin. This condition is not infectious.

Blackheads (comedones)

Comedones

When sebum becomes trapped in a follicle and the head is black in colour, it is known as a blackhead or comedo. The head of the comedo becomes black in colour because it combines with the oxygen in the air (oxidises). The black of the blackhead is due to skin pigment (melanin), not dirt. Comedones generally occur on greasy skin types and are not infectious.

Acne vulgaris

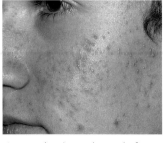

Acne vulgaris on the male face

Acne is a common complaint and usually affects teenagers. It is caused by an overproduction of sebum, usually due to stimulation of the sebaceous glands by hormones called testosterone and progesterone. During teenage years the levels of these hormones rise. The sebum, along with dead skin cells, becomes trapped in the openings of the sebaceous glands and, if they become infected, red and swollen spots will appear. Comedones (blackheads) also form and, if they become infected, the typical red and swollen spot appears. The spots are mainly found on the face, neck and back. Acne is not infectious but it is advisable for the client to consult their doctor before massage treatment.

Rosacea

This condition is often referred to as **acne rosacea**. It mainly affects people over the age of 30 and is more common in women than men. Rosacea affects the nose, cheeks and forehead, giving a flushed, reddened appearance. The blood vessels, which are dilated in these areas, produce a butterfly shape. Pus-filled spots may appear and the affected area may also become lumpy, because of swollen sebaceous glands. Causes include stress, eating spicy or hot food and drinking alcohol. It is not an infectious condition but care needs to be taken when massaging over the affected areas. It is wise to avoid the area if a client has a severe case of rosacea.

Psoriasis

In people with psoriasis, the skin cells reproduce too quickly in certain areas of the skin. This results in thickened patches of skin, which are red, dry, itchy and covered in silvery scales. Psoriasis may be mild and only affect the elbows and knees or may cover the whole body, including the scalp. The cause is unknown although the condition tends to be hereditary and stress can be a factor. Psoriasis is not infectious so treatment can be given providing there is no bleeding or weeping and the client will not feel any discomfort.

Skin tags

Skin tags can affect most parts of the body, often the neck. They are made of loose fibrous tissue, which protrudes out from the skin, and are mainly brown in colour. They are harmless and are not infectious. Removal of skin tags can be carried out by a doctor or certain beauty clinics. It is advisable not to work over the skin tags as it may be uncomfortable for the client.

HEALTH MATTERS

You should not apply any stimulating facial treatments to a client suffering with rosacea or psoriasis.

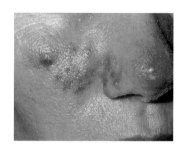

Rosacea

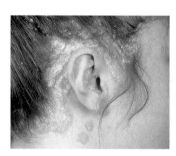

Psoriasis on the scalp

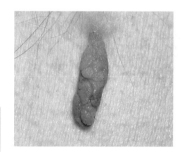

A skin tag

ACTIVITY

Activity 5.3: Skin conditions

Research the following skin conditions and tick the correct box for each.

Skin condition	Infectious	Non-infectious
Boil		
Stye		
Conjunctivitis		
Impetigo		
Cold sore		
Allergy		
Eczema		
Whitehead (milium)		
Blackhead (comedo)		
Acne vulgaris		
Acne rosacea		
Psoriasis		
Skin tag		

Skin

1   Name the five layers of skin that make up the epidermis.

_____
_____
_____
_____
_____

2   State five structures that are found within the dermis.

_____
_____
_____
_____
_____

3   What is sebum and what is its purpose?

_____
_____
_____
_____

4   What is the cause of goose bumps?

_____
_____
_____

5   Eccrine glands produce which substance?

_____

6   What is responsible for producing the colour of the skin?

_____

7   State three functions of the skin.

_____
_____
_____

8   Why would you not work directly over cold sores or impetigo?

_____
_____
_____
_____
_____

9   State three infectious skin conditions.

_____
_____
_____

10 State three non-infectious skin conditions.

_____
_____
_____

Activity 5.4: Infections and non-infectious skin conditions

Make a list of all the infectious skin conditions and a list of all the non-infectious skin conditions.

Infectious skin conditions

_____

_____

_____

_____

_____

_____

_____

_____

Non-infectious skin conditions

_____

_____

_____

_____

_____

_____

_____

_____

Contra-indications to facial treatment

A beauty therapist may not be able to carry out a facial treatment if a client has a **contra-indication**. Contra-indications to facial treatment include:

- infectious skin condition
- infectious eye condition
- bruising
- sunburn
- injury to the area being treated
- any bleeding or weeping
- recent scar tissue (up to six months)
- cuts and **abrasions**.

Consultation form

A consultation form should be completed before the treatment is carried out. It helps the therapist to find out information relating to the client's health, their expectations of the treatment and if they have any contra-indications. The therapist can also look at the client's skin to see its condition and make notes on the consultation form. An example of a consulatation form/record card is provided on pages 45-46.

An example of a consulatation form/record card is provided on pages 45-46.

GOOD PRACTICE

Always examine the face in good light. Using an illuminated magnifier allows you to give the skin a detailed, close-up inspection.

Skin types

You will need to conduct a skin analysis before carrying out a facial treatment. A magnifying lamp may be used to look closely at the skin on the face. **Skin types** vary from person to person and can be described as being normal, dry, oily, combination, sensitive, dehydrated or mature.

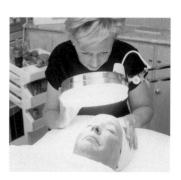

Magnifying lamp

Normal

This skin type will look healthy, clear and fresh. It is often seen in children, as external factors and ageing have not yet affected the condition of the skin, although the increased activity of hormones at puberty may cause the skin to become greasy. A normal skin type will look neither oily nor dry and will have a fine, even **texture**. The pores are small and the skin's elasticity is good so it feels soft and firm to the touch. It is usually free of spots and **blemishes**.

Dry

This skin type may look thin and fine, and broken capillaries can often be seen around the cheek and nose areas. The skin will feel and look dry because little sebum is being produced and the skin is also lacking in moisture (water). This skin type will often tighten after washing and there may be some dry, flaky patches. There will be no spots or comedones (blackheads) and no visible **open pores**. This skin type is prone to premature wrinkling, especially around the eyes, mouth and neck.

Oily

This skin type will look shiny, dull and slightly yellowish (sallow) in colour because of the excess sebum production. Oily skin is coarse, thick and will feel greasy. Enlarged pores can be seen and may be due to the excess production and build-up of sebum. Open pores can let in bacteria, which cause spots and infections. Blocked pores often lead to comedones (blackheads). Oily skin tends to age more slowly, as the grease absorbs some of the ultraviolet rays of the sun and so can protect against its damaging effects. The sebum also helps to keep the skin moisturised and prevents drying.

Combination

With this skin type there will be areas of dry, normal and greasy skin. Usually the forehead, nose and chin are greasy (this is known as the **T-zone**). The areas around the eyes and cheeks are usually dry and may be sensitive.

Sensitive

This skin type is often dry, transparent and reddens easily when touched. **Broken capillaries** may be present, especially on the cheeks, which give the face a red colour. Hereditary factors may be a cause of sensitive skin. Certain substances may easily irritate a sensitive skin so care should be taken when choosing products for this type. If a white skin is sensitive to a product it will show as a reddened area, but on black skin it will show up as a darkened area.

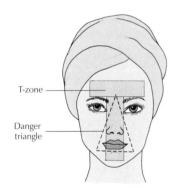

T-zone

Danger triangle

The T-zone

> **REMEMBER**
>
> Sensitivity will show up as a darkened area on black skin rather than the pink or reddened colour that will show on lighter skins.

Dehydrated

This skin type lacks moisture (water) and so is dry. The causes include illness, medication, too much sun, dieting and working in a dry environment with low humidity, such as an air-conditioned office. Sebum helps to prevent evaporation of water from the skin, so when insufficient sebum is produced, moisture is lost from the skin. The skin feels and looks dry and tight. There may be flaking and fine lines present on the skin. Broken capillaries are also common with this skin type.

Skin that produces too much sebum can still become dehydrated if it is not looked after properly.

Mature

This skin type is dry as the sebaceous and sweat glands become less active. The skin may be thin and wrinkles will be present. There are usually broken capillaries, often around the nose and cheek areas. The bone structure can become more prominent as the adipose (fat) and supportive tissue become thinner. **Muscle tone** is often poor so the contours of the face become slack, causing sagging skin. Because of the poor blood circulation, waste products are removed less quickly so the skin may become puffy and pale in colour. **Liver spots** may also appear on the face and hands. The cause of this skin type is ageing and altered hormone activity.

Activity 5.5: Skin types

Briefly describe the following skin types.

Skin type	Brief description
Normal	
Dry	
Oily	
Combination	
Sensitive	
Dehydrated	
Mature	

Equipment and products needed to carry out a facial treatment

- *Treatment couch*: should be disinfected and covered with either towels or a blanket. Clean couch roll should be placed on top
- *Trolley*: should be disinfected and lined with couch roll
- *Magnifying lamp*: is used to help examine the skin. Clues such as spots and blackheads will help you to decide the client's skin type
- *Stool*: should ideally be height adjustable and have a back rest
- *Large bowl*: should be filled with warm water
- *Small bowls*: will be used for items such as cotton pads and to put jewellery into
- *Headband*: will ensure the hair is tied away from the face and will help prevent products from getting onto the hair
- *Facial tissues*: There are many uses for tissues such as blotting the skin after applying **toner**
- *Towels*: used to cover the client and also to dry the hands
- *Cotton wool*: some products will be applied and removed using cotton wool pads

- *Spatulas*: used to remove cream from a pot. The fingers are not used as it is unhygenic
- *Mirror*: can be used for consulting with the client before and after the treatment
- *Gowns*: a client may wear a gown to help protect her clothing and also it is easily removed when carrying out a treatment
- *Facial cleanser*: usually consists of water and oil and helps to get rid of grease and dirt from the skin's surface
- *Facial toner*: is applied after the skin has been cleansed. It helps to remove any **cleanser** that remains on the skin and to tighten the pores
- *Mask*: can be applied to the skin for between about 10 and 15 minutes. Different types of **masks** can be used and have various benefits
- *Mask brush*: used to apply the mask onto the face
- *Sponges*: used to remove products from the skin such as masks.

HEALTH MATTERS

If the client is pregnant, it is recommended that the headrest should be slightly raised during treatment so that the client is not lying flat.

REMEMBER

A metal tool with a loop at one end, called a comedone extractor, is used to remove blackheads.

GOOD PRACTICE

Sponges and mask brushes are difficult to clean and sterilise. They should be washed in very hot soapy water, dried and sanitised.

A PRACTICAL GUIDE TO BEAUTY THERAPY LEVEL 1

Preparing the client for facial treatment

Consultation

1 Carry out the consultation preferably in a private, quiet place.
2 Find out if the client has any contra-indications.
3 Questions can be asked about the client's skincare routine for example:

- How often do you cleanse, tone and moisturise your skin?
- How much water do you drink a day? (This will help hydrate (add water) the skin)
- Do you use soap? (Soap can be drying to the skin)

4 Ask the client what she would like to gain from the treatment, for example would she like help with a particular problem such as greasy skin. This information would be written onto your **treatment plan.**
5 You can explain to the client what is involved in the treatment and how long it takes and how much the treatment will cost.

Preparing your client

Your duties are to:

- ask the client to remove any jewellery, such as a necklace and earrings, and place it into a bowl on the trolley. (If the client wore a necklace during the treatment it could get broken or covered in a product)
- check there are pillows and bedding for the client's comfort
- the client may be given a gown to wear and asked to get onto the couch. If the couch is quite high they may need help to do this
- wash your hands in front of the client so they can see you are hygienic
- a large towel/blanket can be used to cover the client and a small towel may be placed over the shoulder and chest area
- put a headband onto the client's head. A wooden spatula may be used to tuck stray hairs under the head-band
- discuss your facial treatment plan with your senior therapist.

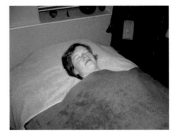

Conducting the facial treatment

Basic facial treatment procedure

Most facials follow a basic facial treatment routine, such as the procedure below:

- giving a consultation
- looking at the skin, known as skin analysis, to find out the client's skin type
- removal of eye make-up
- removal of lipstick
- cleansing of the skin
- skin toning (first)
- exfoliation
- massage to face and neck
- application of a mask
- skin toning (second)
- skin moisturising

Skin cleansing

The skin is cleansed to remove make-up, remove dirt and grease and increase the effectiveness of other products used during the facial treatment.

There are generally two types of skin cleansing:

Superficial cleansing

This type of cleansing often involves cleansing the skin only once and may be used if the client is not wearing make-up, or is having a mini facial.

Deep cleanse

This involves the use of special massage movements to help to give a thorough deep cleanse. The skin is often cleansed twice.

Always treat the eyes and lips first before moving onto the larger areas of the face and neck. This is more hygienic and helps to prevent spreading dark-coloured make-up products over the face.

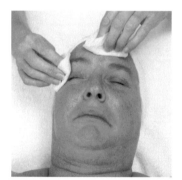

Cleansing the eye area

Cleansing the skin

Even if the client claims not to be wearing make-up, always give a superficial cleanse. This will help you to make an accurate assessment of the skin. It will also help the other skin treatments to be more effective by removing make-up and other surface debris.

Superficial cleanse

Always treat the eyes and lips first before moving to the larger areas of the face and neck. This is more hygienic and prevents spreading heavily pigmented make-up products over the face.

1   Instruct the client to keep their eyes closed.
    (a) Apply a small amount of cleansing milk or eye make-up remover to the eyelids. Spread the cleanser over the upper eyelids with small, gentle, rotary massage movements. Use the pads of the 'ring' fingers and avoid applying pressure over the eye.
    (b) Alternatively, apply the cleanser directly to the eyelids on damp cotton wool pads, supporting the skin at the temples and ensuring cleanser does not penetrate the eye.

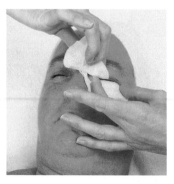

Dissolving and removing mascara

2   Stroke a little cleanser underneath the eyes, working towards the nose. Ensure that cleanser does not penetrate the eyes.

3   Use damp cotton wool pads to wipe away cleanser from around the eyes. Treat one eye at a time. Stroke outwards over the upper eyelid and then keep the skin supported while cleaning underneath with a second pad.

4   For removing mascara, place damp cotton wool pads beneath the lashes and dissolve mascara with a suitable eye make-up remover. A tipped orange stick or cotton bud is useful for getting to the base of the lashes.

5   Remove make-up from the lips with small, rotary massage movements, and wipe away cleanser and dissolved make-up with a damp cotton wool pad.

6   Apply the appropriate cleansing product to the neck and main facial areas, omitting the eyes and lips.

7   Use gentle upward stroking and rotary massage movements to spread the cleanser and work it well into the skin creases (for example above the chin and at the sides of the nose), where grease and make-up tend to build up.

8   Remove the cleanser with firm upward and outward movements, using damp cotton wool pads.

9   Wipe over the skin with a mild toner (low **alcohol** content) on damp cotton wool pads. This should remove the greasy film remaining after the cleanse without disturbing the skin's surface.

10 Blot any excess moisture on the skin. Split a tissue into single ply and create a hole in the centre for placing over the nose. Lay the tissue over the face and gently press it against the skin. Gradually roll the tissue down the face and onto the neck.

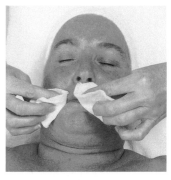

Cleansing the lips

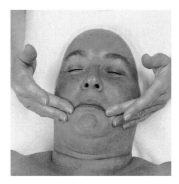

Cleansing the face and neck

Deep cleanse

Once the type and condition of the skin has been assessed, choose a suitable deep-cleansing product and apply it to the face and neck.

The deep cleanse involves the use of special massage movements which:

● are relaxing

● stimulate the flow of blood and lymph through the skin

● assist the penetration of cleanser into the hair follicles, dissolving make-up or dirt that has penetrated them

● help soften and loosen surface blockages

● aid desquamation (shedding of surface cells).

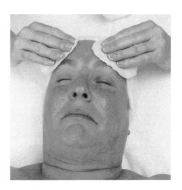

Removing cleanser with damp cotton wool pads

REMEMBER

The ring fingers exert the least pressure. They are the best ones to use when working over the very thin and delicate skin around the eyes.

GOOD PRACTICE

Use an oily eye make-up remover to remove stubborn waterproof mascara.

REMEMBER

The cleansing products work by either dissolving grease or by using a detergent action, which suspends dirt and make-up so that they can be wiped off the skin.

Applying toner

Blotting the face with a tissue

Procedure for deep cleanse

The following sequence ensures that all areas of the face and neck are cleansed thoroughly, and that the movements flow smoothly into one another so that a relaxing rhythm is maintained.

Whichever procedure you use, make sure that:

- your hands are clean, smooth and relaxed. Stiff hands put extra pressure on the face, which is less comfortable for the client
- the movements are adapted to the size and shape of the area being treated, for example over the cheeks and forehead
- pressure is reduced when working over bony areas and sensitive skin.

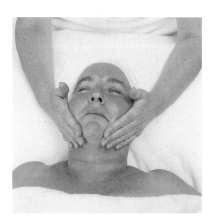

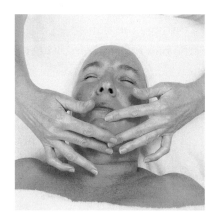

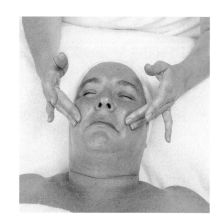

1 *With hands resting on jawline, stroke them towards the angles of the jaw, then down the sides of the neck and firmly upwards from the base, avoiding pressure over the trachea (wind pipe); repeat six times*

2 *Slide hands up over the chin and work into the crease with the index fingers, one after another, sliding them back under the chin to repeat the movements; repeat six times for each hand*

3 *Perform small circular movements with the pads of the fingers, covering the cheeks from the corners of the mouth to the sides of the nose and carrying on up to the temples. Slide hands back gently to the corners of the mouth to repeat the movements (six times)*

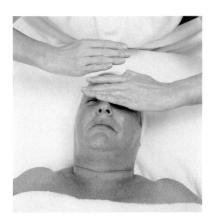

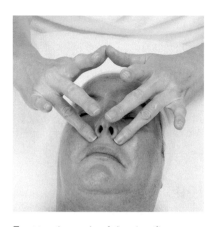

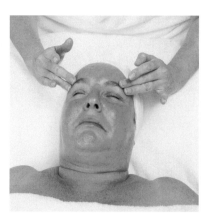

4 *Slide hands from the temples to the centre of the forehead and, keeping the fingers straight but relaxed, stroke them down the nose, one after another, six times for each hand*

5 *Use the pads of the ring fingers to work thoroughly, upwards and downwards, into the creases at the sides of the nose; repeat six times in each direction*

6 *Slide the hands back up the sides of the nose. Stroke out over the eyebrows and then inwards, underneath the eyes, producing a big circular movement; repeat six times*

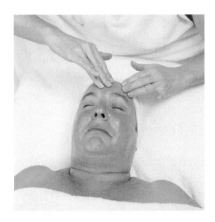

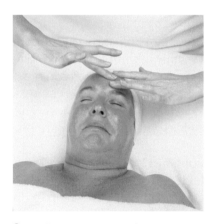

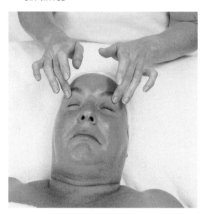

7 *Perform circular movements over the forehead with the pads of the fingers. Work across from temple to temple, one hand following the other, so that the forehead is covered (six times), finishing in the centre*

8 *Still using the pads of the fingers, work from temple to temple across the forehead, with small interlocking zig-zag movements. Cover the forehead six times, finishing in the centre*

9 *Stroke the ring fingers out over the eyebrows and then inwards underneath. As a circle is completed, gently perform three very light lifting movements beneath the brow, starting with the index finger. The ring finger should then be correctly positioned to repeat the whole movement*

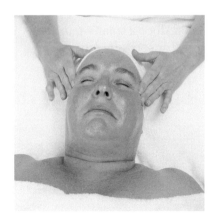

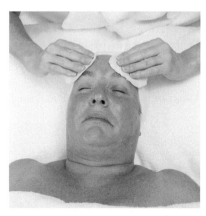

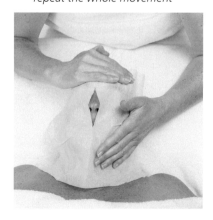

10 *Finally, slide the fingers up the sides of the nose, over the forehead and apply a little pressure at the temples to let your client know the routine has finished*

11 *Complete removal of cleansing product with skin toner*

12 *Blot the skin with a tissue*

GOOD PRACTICE

It is important to use the ring finger (the one next to your little finger), when applying and massaging skin care products to the skin around the eyes as these fingers apply the least pressure.

Skin toning

After cleansing the skin it should be toned. There are different products that may be used to tone the skin. Toning lotion has various uses such as helping to:

- remove oil from the skin, especially the toners that contain alcohol
- create a skin-tightening effect known as an **astringent** effect, which reduces the release of sweat and sebum onto the skin and helps to tighten the pores
- cool and refresh the skin.

Milder toners contain little or no **alcohol** and so have a gentler effect on the skin. They consist mainly of purified water and floral extracts such as rose. They are often used on dry, mature and sensitive skin types.

Skin tonics are slightly stronger toners. They may contain alcohol and an astringent substance, such as witchhazel. They are often used on normal skin types.

Astringents contain a lot of alcohol and so are the strongest toners. They may contain **antibacterial** ingredients which help to treat spots and blemishes. Their anti-bacterial effects and the fact they help to dissolve oil make them ideal to use on oily skin types.

Applying toner to the skin

Your duties are to:

- apply toner to the face either using cotton wool pads or, if in a spray bottle/container, spray onto the face ensuring you cover the eyes
- use two damp cotton wool pads to gently wipe in an upward direction over the neck and face or spray onto the face
- after applying toner blot the skin with a facial tissue. Produce a small rip in the centre of the tissue for the client's nose. The tissue will absorb any moisture remaining on the skin.

The skin will also be toned before the moisturiser is applied.

Mask treatment

The face mask is applied after the skin has been cleansed and toned. Some facials include **exfoliation** (a product used to remove the dead skin cells) and massage before the mask treatment is given.

There are two types of mask:

Setting masks
These are applied to the face and neck in a thin layer and allowed to dry out, for example clay masks. The effects of the mask depend on their ingredients and the length of time they are left on the skin.

Non-setting masks
These consist of ready-prepared substances such as cream, oil or natural ingredients taken from flowers, plants, herbs and vegetables. Each mask is designed to treat different skin conditions.

Applying a non-setting face mask

Your duties are to:

- select the **non-setting mask** that will benefit your client's skin type
- ensure you have enough mask in your bowl so that it will cover your client's face and neck
- use a mask brush to paint the mask onto the skin. Start at the neck and move in an upwards direction. The whole face should be covered except the eyes, nostrils, lips and hair line. If the hairband is in place you should not get mask onto the hair
- when you have finished applying the mask, you can put two round pieces of dampened cotton wool onto the eyes
- leave your client to rest for about ten minutes
- after ten minutes remove the eye pad. Pick up two damp sponges and press them down onto the mask. Leave for a few seconds so that the dampness helps to remove the mask. Work over the whole face

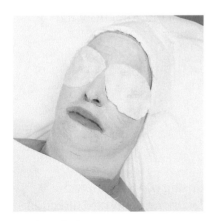

Mask applied, eye pads in place

Removing the mask with damp sponges

- begin at the neck using upwards strokes to remove the face mask
- when all of the mask has been removed you can tone the skin. This will also help to remove any trace of the mask.

GOOD PRACTICE

As a general rule, apply the mask quite thinly. There is no need to apply it thickly as the result will be the same.

Benefits of mask treatment

The benefits of a mask treatment depend on which mask is applied. General benefits include:

- helping to hydrate (add moisture) the skin
- giving a firming and lifting effect
- improving the blood circulation
- deeply cleansing the skin
- tightening the pores
- exfoliating the skin so removing dead skin cells.

Moisturising the skin

The skin should be protected during the day against the ravages of the sun, wind, cold and air pollution. Moisturisers help protect the skin, nourish it and replace lost moisture. Moisturisers are mostly made up of oil and water. The water helps to put moisture back into the skin and the oil helps to stop loss of moisture from the surface of the skin.

A **humectant** such as glycerine is added to a moisturiser. This attracts water from the air and helps prevent the moisturiser from drying out.

Man with clean, glowing skin

Applying moisturiser

To apply moisturiser:

- put some moisturiser into your hand
- using similar strokes to those used during the cleansing process, apply the moisturiser to the skin. Begin at the neck area and work in an upward direction until you reach the forehead
- blot excess moisturiser from the skin using a facial tissue.

Woman with clean, glowing skin

Benefits of using a moisturiser

A moisturiser helps to plump out the skin with moisture, which helps to reduce the appearance of fine lines. It also helps to improve the feel and look of the skin as it softens it. Many moisturisers contain UVA and UVB sunscreens which help protect the skin from the damaging effects of the sun's ultraviolet rays.

SELF-CHECKS

Facials

1 Give three reasons why you would apply toner to the face.

_____

_____

_____

2 Which areas of the face are not usually treated with a face mask?

_____

_____

3 For how long should a face mask be left on the face?

4 What action would you take if a client complains of a 'burning' skin sensation while the face mask is applied?

_____

_____

5 What does moisturiser mostly consist of and why would you apply it to the skin of the face and neck?

_____

_____

ACTIVITY

Activity 5.6: Record cards

Look at some of the record cards at your salon which have been completed for facial clients.

1 Read the information given about the client's skin and see what **recommendations** have been made for their skin care.

2 Look at the products that have been used during the client's treatment and also note which products have been purchased by the client.

Completing the facial treatment

When the treatment has finished, check that your client is happy with the results (you may use a mirror). The head of the couch should be slowly lifted to an upright position. If a client gets up too quickly, there will be a sudden rush of blood away from the head, which may cause dizziness.

The last few minutes of the treatment should be spent discussing what has been achieved during the facial. Make sure the client's record card has been correctly filled in. Home care advice may also be given and you can also check if your client wishes to purchase any retail products.

ACTIVITY

Activity 5.7: Facial treatment sequence

Can you remember the sequence of the basic facial treatment? Place the correct letter in each box. (A letter may be used twice)

a Apply moisturiser

b Apply toner

c Massage

d Skin analysis

e Apply mask

f Consultation

g Remove eye make-up

h Deep cleanse

1	2	3	4	5	6	7	8	9

Home care advice

When advising on home care, your duties are to:

- advise your client on how to apply a product
- tell your client not to overload the eye area with greasy cream at night. The cream may melt and get into the eye area and make the eyes appear puffy next morning
- recommend that the skin is cleansed, toned and moisturised twice each day; morning and night
- a day moisturiser may be used during the daytime and another moisturiser may be applied during the night-time. Night-time moisturisers are generally thicker in consistency
- inform your client to use a product with a SPF (sun protection factor) of at least 15. This will help to protect the skin from harmful UVA and UVB rays given off by the sun
- recommend that your client has regular facials to maintain a healthy skin.

REMEMBER

Enter all details of treatments and purchases on the client's record card and help them to book their next appointment.

Facial treatments

Decide which is the correct answer and tick the box.

1 Which of the following would *not* be included during a facial treatment?
   ☐ cleanse
   ☐ buff
   ☐ tone
   ☐ moisturise

2 If a skin is spotty with blackheads present, which skin type do think it is most likely to be?
   ☐ dry
   ☐ sensitive
   ☐ mature
   ☐ oily.

3 The purpose of toner is to:
   ☐ remove traces of cleanser and help tighten the pores
   ☐ moisturise the skin
   ☐ deeply cleanse the skin
   ☐ remove dead skin cells.

4 A mask applied to the face and neck in a thin layer and allowed to dry out is known as a:
   ☐ non-setting mask
   ☐ facial mask
   ☐ setting mask
   ☐ jet set mask.

5 The purpose of exfoliating the skin is to:
   ☐ remove blackheads
   ☐ remove dead skin cells
   ☐ help reduce **erythema**
   ☐ help moisturise the skin.

6 Comedones are:
   ☐ whiteheads
   ☐ spots
   ☐ dry patches
   ☐ blackheads.

7 Which of the following is not a benefit of receiving a mask treatment?
   ☐ removes comedones
   ☐ deeply cleanses
   ☐ improves the circulation
   ☐ helps to exfoliate the skin.

8 An adverse reaction is:
   ☐ an unwanted reaction to the treatment
   ☐ a hostile client
   ☐ a product that has 'gone off'
   ☐ too much product applied to the skin.

9 Which of the following would *not* prevent the therapist carrying out a full facial treatment?
   ☐ impetigo
   ☐ cold sore
   ☐ freckles
   ☐ boils.

10 Some moisturisers contain an SPF. For what do the initials SPF stand?
   ☐ Standard Professional Facial
   ☐ Sun Protection Factor
   ☐ Special Product Facial
   ☐ Skin Peeling Factor.

KEY TERMS

You should now understand the following words and phrases. If you do not, go back through the chapter and find out what they mean.

Consultation	Acid mantle	Blemishes
Skin analysis	Bacteria	Texture
Cleanser	Viruses	Hormones
Toner	Fungi	T-zone
Moisturiser	Infestations	Open pores
Massage	Allergies	Broken capillaries
Mask	Direct contact	Skin tone
Exfoliation	Indirect contact	Muscle tone
Oxygen	Infectious	Liver spots
Nutrients	Non-infectious	Treatment plan
Posture	Allergen	Aromatherapy
Skin cell	Histamine	Alcohol
Epidermis	Cortisone cream	Astringent
Dermis	Dermatologist	Antibacterial
Subcutaneous layer	Hereditary	Setting mask
Desquamation	Milia	Non-setting mask
Melanin	Contra-indication	Humectant
Sweat glands	Abrasion	Sun protection factor
Adverse reaction	Skin type	Recommendation
Erythema	Collagen	
Sebaceous gland	Elastin	

A PRACTICAL GUIDE TO BEAUTY THERAPY LEVEL 1

6 Unit BT3

Assist with nail treatment on the hands

After working through this chapter you will be able to:

- carry out a basic nail treatment on the hands that includes filing, buffing, moisturising and applying nail polish
- prepare the work area for nail treatment
- carry out consultation techniques and advise on home care products.

Before you work through this chapter: Be wise and revise!
Revision topics to help you achieve this unit:

Assist with nail treatment on the hands

TOPIC	CHAPTER	PAGE

A manicure treatment will help to improve the health and appearance of the hands and nails. Your client may have a particular problem such as overgrown cuticles and would like you to help with this condition, or they may have an event such as a wedding and would like their hands and nails to look attractive. A treatment will usually take between 30 and 45 minutes.

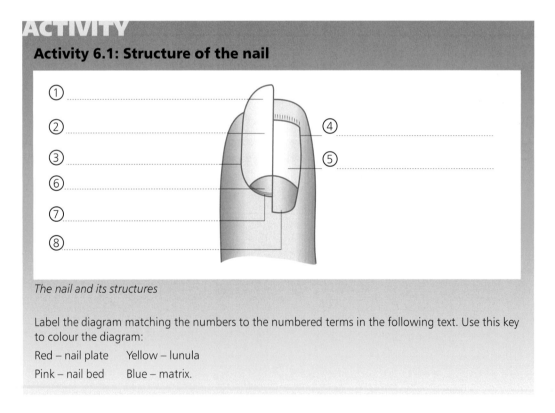

REMEMBER

The technical name for the nail is **Onyx**.

Benefits of receiving a nail treatment

Benefits include:

- **filing** the nails with an emery board, providing it is carried out correctly, will prevent splitting and breakage of the nails
- nails become stronger and more attractive which will help to improve the client's confidence
- nails are **buffed** which helps to improve the circulation to the nail resulting in nails that grow faster and stronger
- **nail polish** will help to make the hands look more attractive
- the client is given **home care advice**, which helps them to look after their hands and nails.

Anatomy and physiology: nails

It is important to have a good knowledge of the structure and function of the nail if providing nail treatment.

Nails

Nails help to protect the ends of fingers and are also useful for picking up small objects. The nails contain a protein called **keratin**, which is also found in the hair. The nails also contain water and fat.

ACTIVITY

Activity 6.1: Structure of the nail

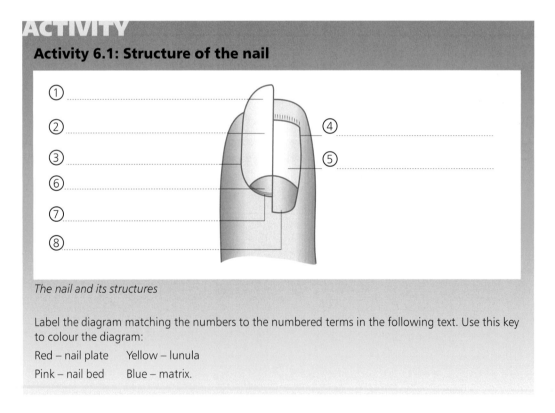

The nail and its structures

Label the diagram matching the numbers to the numbered terms in the following text. Use this key to colour the diagram:

Red – nail plate   Yellow – lunula

Pink – nail bed   Blue – matrix.

1. Free edge

The **free edge** is an extension of the nail plate and is the part that we cut and file. If you have long enough nails, look at the palm of your hand and notice the nails protruding over the fingertips. You will be looking at the free edge.

2. Nail plate

This is the tough part of the nail that we can see. It appears pink in colour because of the blood vessels in the nail bed below it. It contains no blood vessels or nerves so can be cut without pain. It helps to protect the nail bed beneath it.

3. Nail walls

These are overlapping folds of skin found at the side of the nails that protect the edges of the nail plate.

4. Nail grooves

Grooves at the side of the nails between the nail plate and nail wall act as guidelines for growing nails so that they grow in a straight line.

5. Nail bed

The nail bed is found underneath the nail plate and is rich with nerves and blood vessels. The nail bed and nail plate contain grooves and ridges, which enable them to stick together perfectly.

6. Lunula

The lunula is crescent-shaped and mostly white in colour. It is found at the base of the nail plate.

7. Cuticle

The **cuticle** is the overlapping skin at the base of the nail. It prevents bacteria and any other harmful substances entering the **matrix** and causing infection.

When in good condition the cuticles will be soft and can be gently pushed back. If the cuticles are dry, they may split and can also overgrow and stick to the nail plate.

8. Matrix

The nail plate is made up of cells. The cells divide in the matrix to make the nail plate. The matrix has lots of nerves and blood vessels. Injury to this area can mean temporary or permanent damage to the growing nail. It takes about five to six months for the nail to grow from the matrix to the free edge.

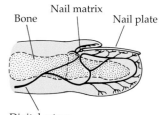

The digital artery divides and subdivides to supply blood to the skin and nail bed

Blood supply to the nail and nail bed

Nail shapes

It is important that the nail shape suits the client's hands. Nail shapes include oval, pointed, square, round and wide.

Oval nail
Generally considered to be the most attractive nail shape. Oval nails give the effect of length without producing a fragile point.

Pointed nail
Clients who are impatient for their nails to grow sometimes shape them into a point so that they look longer. This is the worst thing they could do: a pointed nail will soon snap off

Square nail
Short, square nails are often preferred by clients because of their jobs, for example people who handle food, and beauty therapists

Wide nail
Wide nails can be made to appear slimmer by leaving a narrow strip free from enamel at either side of the nail. This creates an illusion of extra length, which draws attention away from the width.

Oval

This shape is generally considered to be the most attractive shape. It is an ideal shape for short, thick fingers as it helps to make the fingers look longer.

Pointed

A pointed nail can break easily as this shape weakens the nail, so ideally the nails should not be filed into this shape.

Square

The free edge is filed into a straight line. This shape is recommended for people who have jobs requiring short nails such as beauty therapists.

Round

This is a practical nail shape as it is hardwearing, strong and neat. It is a popular shape for male clients.

Wide nails

Wide nails can be made to appear slimmer by leaving a narrow strip free from nail polish at either side of the nail. This will help to make the nail look longer.

Structure and nail shapes

1 Name the protein found in the nail and state what its function is.

_____

_____

2 Which part of the nail do we cut and file?

_____

3 What is the name of the overlapping flaps of skin found at the sides of the nail?

_____

4 What is the function of nail grooves?

_____

_____

5 What is crescent-shaped and mostly white in colour?

_____

6 How long does it take for a nail to grow from the base to the tip?

_____

7 Injury to this part could mean temporary or permanent damage to the nail. What is it?

_____

8 What is the function of the cuticle?

_____

_____

9 It is not recommended to file a nail into which shape?

_____

10 Which nail shape is considered to be the most attractive?

_____

Nail diseases and disorders

Nail diseases are conditions of the nail and surrounding skin which result from bacterial, fungal and viral infections. Nail diseases **contra-indicate manicure**. A client with a diseased nail should be referred to their doctor for medical treatment.

Nail disorders do not usually create a problem for the beauty therapist. The basic manicure and pedicure procedures can be adapted for most conditions, supported with appropriate home care advice.

Nail diseases

The general signs of disease are inflammation, swelling and pus around, and sometimes underneath, the nail plate. Some conditions show a green, yellow or black discoloration of the nail, depending on the nature of the infection. The main route for infection is through broken skin or damaged cuticle.

REMEMBER

You can save your client a lot of discomfort by identifying the early signs of disease and advising them to get prompt medical attention.

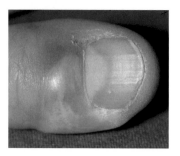
Paronychia

Paronychia (pa-ro-nic-ee-ah)

This is the most common of all nail diseases; it usually starts off as a torn cuticle or following the loss of cuticle from all or part of the nail. Bacteria enter the 'live' tissue behind the nail fold and a swollen, throbbing condition results with the formation of pus around the nail border. People who have their hands in and out of water a lot can develop an advanced form of the condition which involves infection by a fungus as well as bacteria. A doctor will usually prescribe an anti-fungal ointment and antibiotics to clear the infection.

HEALTH MATTERS

The best way of preventing paronychia is to keep the hands dry and the cuticles soft and pliable.

REMEMBER

The warm, moist environment of a shoe creates ideal growing conditions for a fungus. Feet and shoes should be kept as cool and dry as possible.

Ringworm

Ringworm of the nail (onychomycosis or tinea unguium) is a fungal infection that can appear either as whitish patches, which can be scraped off the nail surface, or as yellow streaks, which appear in the main body of the nail. The disease invades the free edge and spreads down to the nail root. The nail plate becomes spongy and furrowed, and is sometimes completely detached. Often, after medical treatment, the nail remains malformed.

Nail disorders

A nail disorder does not usually contra-indicate manicure, but special care may be required during treatment to prevent the condition from worsening. If you are concerned about the severity of a disorder and are unsure whether to proceed or not, ask the advice of your supervisor. They may recommend the client to get written permission from their doctor or suggest you omit the affected nail from some or all parts of the manicure procedure.

Transverse furrows

When caused by ill health, transverse furrows (Beau's lines) appear across every nail as the affected cells emerge from under the nail fold. Of course, the furrows cannot be seen until two or three weeks after the illness. As the general state of health improves, so does the health of the matrix and new, normal cells replace the damaged ones. Bad manicure practices can cause furrows when too much pressure is applied at the base of the nail.

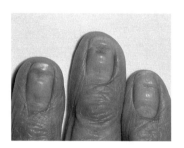
Beau's lines – transverse furrows

HEALTH MATTERS

Always take care when pushing back and removing excess cuticle from the base of the nail. Too much pressure in this area can disturb the matrix cells situated behind the base of the nail. If the matrix cells are damaged, the resulting nail growth is malformed.

A PRACTICAL GUIDE TO BEAUTY THERAPY LEVEL 1

Bruised nail

A blue–black nail indicates bruising of the nail bed as a result of injury, for example trapping a finger in a car door or dropping a heavy weight on the foot. The injury causes bleeding under the nail plate. As the injury heals, the bruise changes colour and eventually disappears. The finger or toe should be excluded from treatment if the injury is painful. A dark-coloured nail polish may be used to disguise the bruise.

Dry, flaking nails

Fat and moisture keep the nails flexible, and the layers of cells compacted into a smooth plate. Both fat and moisture can be removed easily if the hands are not properly cared for. Dry, flaking nails (onychorrhexis) and chapped skin are usually caused by inadequate protection. Exposure to harsh weather conditions, contact with solvents, and poor diet can all cause dry, flaking nails. Salon treatments and home care focus on smoothing and strengthening the free edge, lubricating the nail plate and softening the cuticles and skin. In some cases, the client's diet may need to be revised.

Split nails

Split nails are usually brittle nails. The most common causes are excessive use of solvents and detergents, careless filing, poor diet and ill health. If the condition is accompanied by dry hair and skin, there may be a glandular disorder. Regular manicures and a good home care routine are important for preventing split nails.

REMEMBER

Detergents are designed to dissolve grease, and they are just as effective on skin and nails as they are on dirty dishes and laundry!

Pitted nails

A few isolated pits or dimples in the nail are common and do not usually indicate a serious disorder. Deep pitting of the nails may be caused by psoriasis, in which case there is usually an accompanying skin condition.

Longitudinal ridges

Ridges that appear down the length of the nails often accompany the ageing process. They result from irregular keratin production and can also appear as a result of minor external injury. The ridges may split, allowing dirt to enter. As the nail grows, healthy cells replace the damaged ones and the problem disappears.

HEALTH MATTERS

Normally, the nails contain 18 per cent water. If this amount is increased greatly, for example after soaking, the nails become very soft and less effective for protection. If the amount is reduced considerably, the nails become brittle and prone to snapping or splitting.

GOOD PRACTICE

Nail polish should not be applied to nails with severe ridging because it is difficult to achieve a good finish. Buffing with paste helps to smooth ridges and creates an attractive shine. Special basecoats (ridge fillers) help to even out the surface of slightly ridged nails before applying enamel.

Clients should be advised against 'digging' under the free edge. The area where the hyponychium attaches to the nail plate creates a seal which protects the nail bed. If this seal is broken, minor separation of the nail plate from the nail bed occurs, opening up a route for infection.

Loose nails

Loose nails (onycholysis) may be due to an internal disorder or may accompany certain skin diseases such as psoriasis, eczema and fungal infections. The nail gradually separates from the nail bed until the whole nail becomes loose or sheds completely. Severe nail separation contra-indicates manicure and pedicure treatments. Further disturbance to the nail could result in premature shedding of the nail and exposure to infection.

Discoloured nails

Some deeply pigmented nail varnishes produce yellow stains on the nails if worn without a basecoat. The stains are unsightly but harmless. Brown staining of the nails may be evident in people who smoke heavily.

White spots

White spots (leuconychia) usually occur as a result of minor injury to the nail when air becomes trapped between the layers of cells. The spots are harmless and disappear as the nail grows out. White spots present on every nail can indicate a calcium deficiency but you are not likely to come across this in the salon.

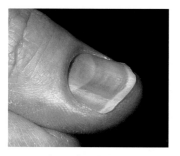

Spoon-shaped nails (koilonychia)

Spoon-shaped nails

Some people are born with the condition, but, for others, it can be a symptom of anaemia and, when this is treated, the nail condition disappears. Spoon-shaped nails (koilonychia) are due to an accumulation of cells under the free edge. They sometimes occur in people who have an over-active thyroid gland.

Very thick nails

When present on the fingers, very thick nails (onychauxis) may accompany the ageing process, but they can also be caused by an internal disorder. Very thick, disoloured toenails may be the result of constant irritation by ill-fitting shoes.

Eggshell nails

Eggshell nails are thin, pale and much more flexible than normal nails. They curve upwards easily at the free edge. The usual causes are chronic illness or a nervous disorder.

GOOD PRACTICE

Treat eggshell nails as fragile nails. Although they are more flexible than normal, they are also much thinner and therefore not as strong.

REMEMBER

The cuticles will not split if they are kept soft and pliable and prevented from becoming overgrown.

Excess cuticle

Some cuticle is necessary to protect the nail matrix, but an excessive amount of cuticle (pterygium) looks unattractive. Most people have a little excess cuticle, which can be removed during a manicure treatment. However, in extreme cases, the whole nail is virtually covered in cuticle skin and medical treatment is required to remove it.

Blue nails

The nails may appear blue when there is poor blood circulation to the fingers. The fingers have a bluish tinge and the hands feel cold. The nails do not actually turn blue, but they lack the healthy pink colour which would normally show through the nail plate.

Dark pigmentation

The nails of black clients often have areas of dark pigmentation which appear in linear streaks or bands. These are harmless and due to clusters of melanocyte (pigment-forming) cells present in the matrix.

Hangnail

A hangnail is a small piece of horny epidermis which has split away from the cuticle and nail walls. Sometimes hangnails 'catch' and tear the skin, providing a route for bacteria. Hangnails are common in nail biters and also occur as a result of dry cuticles.

Ingrowing toenails

The nails of the big toes are the ones most commonly affected. Instead of moving along the nail bed in the nail grooves, the sides of the nail cut into the nail walls causing skin damage. The condition can be very painful. Inflammation, swelling and pus often occur and the condition has to be treated medically. The two most common causes of ingrowing toe nails are (a) wearing ill-fitting shoes, which put pressure on the toenails from above, and (b) cutting the toenails down their sides instead of straight across; sharp 'spicules' of nail become embedded in the nail walls.

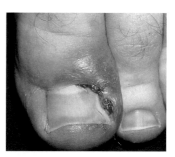
Blue nails

Ingrowing toenail

GOOD PRACTICE

Always cut toenails straight across and never down their sides which would force them to grow into the skin.

Bitten nails

In most cases, only a small portion of the nails is visible, the edges of which are rough and uneven. The finger tips appear bulbous; there is no free edge. Frequently the cuticles become involved and constant biting causes them to grow thicker and harder. Severe nail biting can lead to hangnails, warts and bacterial infection around the nails. The disturbance of the matrix cells over a long period of nail biting can affect the formation of the replacement nail.

Bitten nails

Bitten nails: how manicures can help

Professional manicures encourage the client by improving the appearance of the nails and making them less easy to chew! This is achieved by:

- filing the nails into a regular shape
- bevelling the split layers together so that the edges become smoother
- softening, lifting and removing excess cuticle from the nail plate (a warm oil treatment is particularly useful before doing this)
- buffing the nails, which helps them to grow and gives them a healthy glow.

HEALTH MATTERS

Treatments that stimulate the blood supply help to improve poor blood circulation. Hand massage and buffing warm the tissues, bringing blood to the surface and improving skin colour.

Diseases and disorders of the nails

1 Give two reasons why a client with a nail disease should be referred to their doctor.

_____
_____
_____
_____

2 Name two fungal infections of the nails and describe their appearance.

_____
_____
_____
_____

3 Give two examples of how bad manicure techniques can damage the nails.

_____
_____
_____
_____

4 Why are strong solvents bad for the nails?

_____
_____
_____

5 State two ways in which ageing affects the nails.

_____
_____
_____
_____

6 Why is buffing good for the nails?

_____
_____
_____
_____

Diseases and disorders of the hands and feet

It is not just the nails that are examined before a manicure or pedicure. The condition of the skin of the hands and feet also influences the treatment procedures and advice for home care.

Diseases and disorders of the skin

Many skin diseases involve the hands but some are more likely to appear there than on other parts of the body. This is mainly due to them being exposed and in contact with potentially harmful substances or other sources of infection through touch. Most damage to the skin of the feet occurs as a result of pressure, friction and congestion in footwear (which includes shoes, tights, socks and stockings). Problems arise if the toes are not able to move freely and the feet are not adequately ventilated.

Eczema and dermatitis

Eczema and dermatitis have the same symptoms but their causes are different. Both conditions start off with redness or duskiness of the skin. Small lumps appear, which blister and form scales. The skin is very dry and there is usually intense itching.

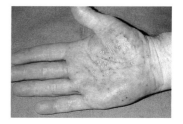

Eczema

Eczema is usually caused by factors inside the body or by an inherited or acquired instability of the skin. People suffering from eczema often suffer from asthma or hay fever as well.

Dermatitis results from factors outside the body, for example contact allergies. An allergic dermatitis reaction usually shows up within 24 hours of contact with the offending substance.

HEALTH MATTERS

Both these conditions should be treated by a doctor. The skin of the hands should be excluded from the manicure. Basic nail shaping, cuticle work and buffing is permissible. Nail polish is not contraindicated, but it will draw attention to the hands, which is not always advisable.

REMEMBER

An allergy to nail polish affects the skin of the face. Advise against nail polish if the client suffers from eczema of the face.

Psoriasis

Psoriasis appears as irregularly shaped plaques of red skin, covered in waxy, silvery scales. The skin feels very rough and, if the scales are removed, tiny spots of bleeding occur. Psoriasis is thought to be an inherited condition which flares up during times of stress or illness. It is caused by an abnormally rapid rate of cell turnover in the epidermis. Unfortunately, psoriasis can be very itchy and if the scales are disturbed through scratching, bleeding may occur, leaving the skin open to infection. The limbs, elbows and knees are common sites of psoriasis.

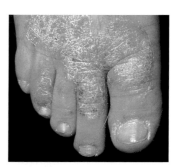

Psoriasis

HEALTH MATTERS

If the condition is present in a very mild form, the client may have a manicure or pedicure as long as stimulating treatments are avoided and the skin plaques are not disturbed. If the psoriasis is severe, the skin will be particularly sensitive and contra-indicated to salon treatments. Psoriasis is not contagious and treatment is medical.

Warts

Warts occur commonly on the fingers and, less frequently, on the palms of the hands. They are usually skin-coloured or greyish-brown, raised and with a rough surface, which tends to itch. The centre of the wart is often depressed with a dark centre. Warts are due to a virus and contra-indicate manicure treatment. Warts occurring on the soles of the feet are called verrucas.

Warts are due to a virus and contra-indicate manicure because they are contagious. Substances can be bought from a chemist which help to destroy the wart chemically. There are medical treatments for warts, but most tend to disappear spontaneously.

Whitlow

A whitlow is a bacterial infection of the soft pad at the tip of the finger or thumb. There is a build-up of pus which cannot escape due to the thickness of the skin. As a result, intense pain occurs which reaches a peak after two or three days.

A whitlow contra-indicates manicure because of the infection present. Treatment is medical and usually involves lancing the swelling and prescribing a course of antibiotics.

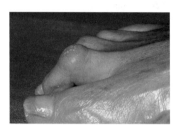

A corn

Corns

Corns consist of a central core surrounded by thick layers of skin. They appear frequently over the **joints** in the toes and the soles of the feet. The skin thickens up in response to friction, then pushes down into the dermis. Corns are not usually infectious. Sometimes, soft corns develop between the toes and these can become infected.

Never let a client talk you into cutting away a corn. The treatment of corns should be left to a qualified chiropodist.

Corns are painful due to the pressure put on underlying nerve endings. Special plasters and pads are available which ease the pressure. Ointment can be bought from the chemist which causes the hard skin to peel.

Calluses

These are larger areas of hard skin caused by friction, but they are less painful than corns because they do not push down into the dermis. Calluses often occur on the pads of the toes and the heels, and sometimes on the palms of the hands after doing heavy work. Calluses usually clear up quite quickly once the source of pressure has been removed.

Contagious skin diseases can be picked up from infected skin cells left on floors, in shower trays, from towels – in fact from anything that may have previously been in contact with the disease.

Callus files and pumice stones are available for rubbing away patches of hard skin, but, of course, they work by friction and friction causes the skin to thicken! Cleansing scrubs and exfoliating creams are available which gently soften, loosen and remove hard skin.

Athlete's foot

Athlete's foot (tinea pedis) is a form of ringworm which affects the skin of the foot. The fungus invades between the toes and spreads to the soles and sides of the feet. The first signs are itching, flaking, cracking and weeping of the skin between the fourth and little toe. Small blisters and rashes occur. When the soles and heels are involved, the skin develops bright red inflammation covered with white scales. Athlete's foot is extremely contagious and is contra-indicated to salon treatment.

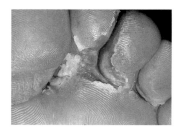

Athlete's foot

HEALTH MATTERS

Anti-fungal preparations are available from the chemist and they are usually effective within two weeks. The feet should be kept scrupulously clean, cool and dry, and protected in high-risk areas such as swimming pools, changing rooms and gymnasiums.

Verrucas

Verrucas (plantar warts) are firm and round with a rough surface. They may occur singly or in groups. If the top is scraped off, small dark spots (blood vessels supplying the verruca) can be seen. Verrucas are caused by a virus and are contagious; they are picked up easily by bare feet. Because they occur commonly on the soles of the feet, the weight of the body pushes the verrucas inwards and they become deeply embedded in the skin, which can be very painful.

HEALTH MATTERS

Verrucas contra-indicate pedicure. A client with a verruca should be referred to a chiropodist. Chemists supply preparations for the home treatment of verrucas.

Disorders of the joints

Rheumatism is a general term for pain, with or without stiffness, which affects the muscles and joints. It describes a symptom of a disorder rather than being a disorder itself. Rheumatism covers many conditions including arthritis.

Arthritis

Arthritis is a general term for inflammation of a joint. The condition can follow injury or bacterial infection, but, more commonly, it results from the wear and tear of ageing. The joint swells, stiffens and becomes painful. The overlying skin takes on a red, shiny appearance. When the joints of the hand are affected, in severe conditions, the whole hand appears deformed.

GOOD PRACTICE

A bunion does not contra-indicate pedicure, but care should be taken when massaging the foot if the bunion is painful.

GOOD PRACTICE

Great care is required when massaging the hands of a client with arthritis. Joints that are inflamed must not be over-stimulated.

Bunion

A bunion is a harmless swelling of the joint of the big toe which is particularly common in middle-aged women. It usually affects both feet. As the joint swells, the skin over it becomes hard, red and tender. The big toe usually becomes displaced, turning inwards towards the other toes.

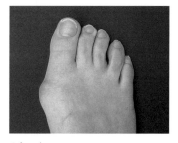

A bunion

Skin and nail conditions

1   State three causes of nail disease.

_____
_____
_____

2   Describe the appearance of paronychia.

_____
_____
_____
_____

3   Name one fungal infection of the skin.

_____

4   What is the most common cause of white spots on the nails?

_____

5   How would you recognise psoriasis on the nail?

_____
_____

6   State two ways in which illness may affect the appearance of the nails.

_____
_____

7   State three reasons why ridges may appear on the nail.

_____
_____
_____

8   What advice would you give to someone who had splitting and flaky nails?

_____
_____
_____

9   Name one viral infection of the skin.

_____

10 State five clues that may indicate there is a problem with the nails or the skin around it.

_____
_____
_____
_____
_____

ACTIVITY

Activity 6.2: Revision chart

Put together a revision chart to help you learn the diseases and disorders of the nails and hands. You can draw pictures, describe the disease/disorder's appearance and cause, state if it is infectious and decide if it is a contra-indication or if it is a condition you can help to treat.

Consultation form

The **consultation** form below can be used for a nail treatment.

Consultation form for a nail treatment

MANICURE/PEDICURE CONSULTATION FORM
NAME: TEL NO:
ADDRESS: EMAIL ADDRESS: DOB: OCCUPATION:
CONTRA-INDICATIONS: EQUIPMENT AND PRODUCTS USED: TREATMENT PLAN: HOMECARE ADVICE: PRODUCTS PURCHASED: NOTES: Client signature...Date................................

GOOD PRACTICE

When examining a client's hands, make sure you include the palms and the backs of the hands.

HEALTH MATTERS

If a contra-indication is found and prevents treament taking place, explain to your client that if you continued with treatment it could make the condition worse.

Equipment and materials: general

There are various products and equipment required to carry out a manicure and pedicure. The following are usually required.

Manicure trolley

Ensure that the trolley is clean and lined with a towel and couch roll.

Manicure bowl

The bowl should contain warm water, perhaps with some oil or antiseptic solution. Soaking the client's fingers in the water helps to soften and cleanse the skin.

> **REMEMBER**
>
> Tools that have been cleaned, sterilised and stored hygienically can be used safely, even at a moment's notice, to treat an unexpected client.

Manicure workstation

Emery boards (also known as nail files)

A wooden emery board is mostly used to file and shape the nails. The darker, coarser side of the emergy board is used to remove length from the nail. The finer, less rough side is used to file nails into shape. It should be used at a 45 degree angle and in one direction only. Never use the emery board in a back and forth motion (sawing) on the nails. It can also be used to bevel the nail after shaping.

> **REMEMBER**
>
> **Bevelling** is a term used to describe the removal of roughness from the free edge using an emery board. The fine side of the emery board is used in an upward stroke across the free edge to help make it smooth.

> **HEALTH MATTERS**
>
> The emery board may be given to the client for home use as it is difficult to sterilise. If a metal file is used it may be cleaned and stored inside an ultraviolet cabinet.

Emery boards

Buffers

A nail buffer helps to stimulate the blood circulation to the nail and this will help to improve the health of the nails. Buffers also help to give the nails a slightly shiny appearance. They can be disposable or have a leather surface.

If the buffer is disposable it may be given to the client. Otherwise, wipe it over with antiseptic and store in an ultraviolet cabinet.

Nail scissors

Scissors are used to cut the nails. Nail scissors often have curved blades which help to cut the nails without weakening them.

To avoid **cross-infection**, the scissors may be cleaned with disinfectant and sterilised in the **autoclave**.

Cuticle knife

A cuticle knife is a small metal tool and needs to be handled with care. It is used to remove dead skin from around the cuticle and nail wall. It must be used flat and must not be poked into the cuticle. It should be kept wet by dipping into water containing some antiseptic to prevent scratching of the nail plate.

GOOD PRACTICE

A cuticle knife may be sterilised in an autoclave. It can be placed into solution such as barbicide to help disinfect it.

REMEMBER

Always wrap or lay your sterilised tools on a tissue when preparing the treament area.

Cuticle nippers

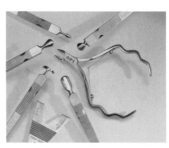

Manicure tools

If there is too much cuticle, or hangnails present, the **cuticle nippers** can be used to remove it. The cuticle nippers should be handled with care and must not pull or tear the skin.

GOOD PRACTICE

Cuticle nippers may be sterilised in the autoclave. They can be placed into a solution such as barbicide to disinfect them.

HEALTH MATTERS

Always take care when pushing back and removing excess cuticle from the base of the nail. Too much pressure in this area can damage the matrix, resulting in damage to the nail.

Orange sticks

An orange stick is a wooden stick with a pointed end and a hoof end. The hoof end is used to apply products such as cuticle and buffing cream to the skin and nails and also for pushing back pre-softened cuticles. The pointed end is tipped with cotton wool and used to clean around the nail and under the free edge.

GOOD PRACTICE

The orange stick may be thrown away after use because it is difficult to sterilise.

Cuticle remover

This product helps to dissolve dead cuticle and skin around the nail. It must only be applied to the direct area, otherwise irritation may occur.

Other items needed for manicure include:

- *Cotton wool pads*: can be used to tip the orange sticks and to apply and remove products and should be placed into clean bowls

- *Spatulas:* used to take a product out of a pot, for example moisturising cream. The spatula can be thrown away after use
- *Tissues:* there are many uses for tissues. They can be used to protect the clothing. You could also give them to the client if they need to blow their nose
- *Towels:* medium-sized towels are used for drying the client's hands and feet
- *Antiseptic wipes:* to clean the hands
- *Bin:* the bin should be placed near to the couch and should be lined with a plastic bin-liner
- *Surgical spirit/Sanitising solution:* after using items such as tweezers and scissors, they should be thoroughly cleaned with surgical spirit and then placed into a jar of **sanitising solution** such as barbicide.

Equipment and materials: manicure products

Nail polish remover

Nail polish remover is applied to the nails using cotton wool. It usually contains **acetone**, which dissolves the polish although acetone-free remover is available for nail extensions.

Collection of manicure products

Buffing paste

A buffing paste is used together with a buffer. It consists of a gritty substance and helps to improve the blood circulation, remove ridges on the nail and make the nails look shiny.

Cuticle cream/gel/oil

Cuticle cream, gel or oil is used to soften the cuticles so that the cuticle may be gently pushed back if required.

Hand cream, oil or lotion

These products may be used to massage and/or moisturise the skin which will help to soften, condition and improve the circulation to the hands.

Basecoat

A **basecoat** helps to prevent staining of the nails when using a coloured nail polish. It also provides a base on which to apply nail polish and helps the nail polish to last longer.

Nail polish

There are many coloured nail polishes that can be applied to the nails.

Collection of nail polishes

You need to know the following:

- dark nail polishes will make the nails look smaller
- bright nail polishes draw attention to the nails, so is not suitable for use on someone with arthritis or any other skin or nail problem
- a French manicure involves applying a white nail polish to the free edge and then covering the nail in a light pink polish. It can help make the nails appear longer
- a pearlised nail polish contains ingredients that make it shiny and glossy. No **top-coat** is required if this polish is used.

Top-coat

A top-coat helps to protect the nail polish so it is less likely to peel or chip as quickly. Therefore the polish will last longer. The top-coat also gives a glossy finish.

Nail strengtheners

A **nail strengthener** is a clear varnish and is applied to the nail to make it stronger. It helps to prevent breakage and splitting of the nail.

Equipment and materials

1   What is the purpose of each side of an emery board?

2   What is the main difference between a cuticle cream and a cuticle remover?

3   What would you use to remove excess cuticle?

4   Give two reasons for applying a basecoat.

5   Which product would you use if a client had ridges in their nails?

6   Why is a top-coat not required with pearl nail polish?

7   What could you do if a nail polish became thick?

8   How should manicure tools be stored?

ACTIVITY

Activity 6.3: Visit a wholesaler

Visit a beauty wholesaler and look at the full range of manicure products and equipment. Try to find manicure mittens and paraffin wax and find out the purpose of using them during a manicure treatment. Compare the different products and take away product information leaflets and price lists to keep for future reference.

Activity 6.4: Complete the diagram

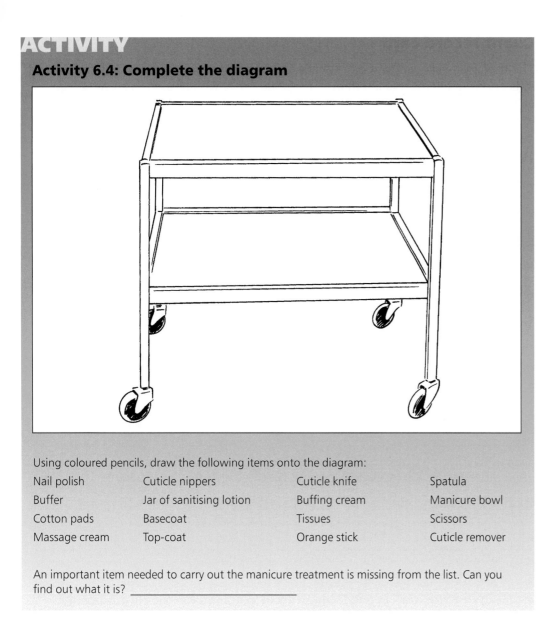

Using coloured pencils, draw the following items onto the diagram:

Nail polish	Cuticle nippers	Cuticle knife	Spatula
Buffer	Jar of sanitising lotion	Buffing cream	Manicure bowl
Cotton pads	Basecoat	Tissues	Scissors
Massage cream	Top-coat	Orange stick	Cuticle remover

An important item needed to carry out the manicure treatment is missing from the list. Can you find out what it is? _____

Preparing the treatment area

Make sure everything is either new, has been **sterilised** and is tidy. If a manicure cushion is not available, folded towels may be used instead for the client to place their hands. A treatment couch roll or a disposable manicure mat may be placed over the top.

GOOD PRACTICE

An aftercare leaflet may be given to the client to provide information about how to look after the skin and nails at home.

It is important to ensure the client is in a comfortable and relaxed position. Make sure they do not have to lean forward over the workstation because this will cause aching in the back and shoulders. There should also be adequate back support on the chair.

The therapist should assess the condition of the hands and nails before treatment takes place in case any contra-indications are present.

Client record card

The therapist will need to see the client record card in case the client has any contra-indications or allergies or anything else the therapist would need to know before giving a treatment.

Manicure procedure

'Are you sitting comfortably?' This is probably the first question you will ask your client at the beginning of the manicure and it is just as important that you can answer 'yes' as well. The effects of bad posture get worse over the course of a working day, causing premature fatigue and aches and pains.

HEALTH MATTERS

Slouching strains the back, neck and shoulders and restricts proper breathing, reducing the oxygen supply to the body.

GOOD PRACTICE

Ensure that the client's hands and arms are free from clothing and jewellery. Offer the client a lightweight gown to protect their clothing. Additional protection may be provided by placing a towel over the client's knees if treatment is not being provided at a manicure station.

The following checklist will ensure comfort both for you and your client:

- sit close enough to your client to avoid stretching and straining arms during the manicure
- sit upright with back straight and shoulders relaxed
- your seating should be firm and at the correct height
- sit with your legs together and not crossed
- make sure you work in good light to avoid 'peering' over the client's hands.

HEALTH MATTERS

Surgical spirit, unlike many other liquid antiseptics, is tolerated by most skins. It is very effective when used in a manicure. The only drawback is that it smells very clinical. This could 'put off' some clients but reassure others!

REMEMBER

Do not rub the nail with the cotton wool pad and remover, or the nail polish colour may spread over the surrounding skin. This will need treating with more nail polish remover, which is bad for the skin and takes up time during the manicure.

1 Wash and dry your own hands, preferably where the client can see you. Evidence of good hygiene practice is always reassuring for a client and shows that you are working to professional standards.
2 Examine the hands and nails. If nail polish is being worn it will have to be removed before you can make an accurate assessment.

3   While you are checking that there are no contra-indications to manicure, note any conditions that may need special attention. If there are signs of neglect they will need discussing with the client and advice should be given regarding home care.

4   Explain the purposes of the manicure relative to the condition of the client's hands and nails. If the client wishes to wear enamel, establish which one they require and check that the texture is suitable for application.

5   Wipe over both sides of the hands with a mild liquid antiseptic on a cotton wool pad. This cleans the hands without softening the nails before filing.

6   Establish whether the client is left-handed or right-handed; proceed on the opposite hand. This ensures that the hand that suffers the most wear and tear has a longer soaking period, which benefits the nails, skin and cuticles.

7   Apply nail polish remover with a cotton wool pad held between your index finger and middle finger. Press the pad firmly onto the nail for a couple of seconds, then slide it off the nail, squeezing gently against the nail plate to remove all traces of dissolved enamel.

8   Pull back the nail walls gently from the sides of the nail plate to expose any enamel which might otherwise be hidden. Use a tipped orange stick and nail polish remover around the nail border so that the nails are left absolutely clean.

9   Nails that are excessively long may need cutting before filing. Apply a little pressure from above with your thumb when using the scissors. This helps to give support and minimises disturbance at the base of the nail.

10 Cut across the free edge of the nail, leaving the nail slightly longer than the desired length.

11 Working on the first hand, file the nails from sides to centre towards the nail tip. Hold the emery board as near to the end as possible. This produces long, flowing strokes and gives the nails a smooth edge.

12 Buffing can be done after filing without paste polish to stimulate the blood supply to the nail bed, or with paste polish to help smooth the nail for a later application of nail polish. Use the buffer briskly but lightly, applying approximately 15–20 strokes per nail in one direction only, towards the free edge.

13 Use the blunt end of an orange stick to transfer a little cuticle cream to the client's nails. Massage the cream well into the cuticles, using both of your thumbs.

14 Soak the fingers in the prepared soapy water and repeat the filing and cuticle massage on the second hand. Dry the first hand thoroughly and put the second hand in to soak.

15 Apply cuticle remover with the pointed end of an orange stick tipped with cotton wool. With the flat side of the stick resting on the nail plate, gently push back the cuticles, working around the nail border with small, circular movements.

16 Gently lift and clean under the cuticles with the tipped end of the orange stick and cuticle remover. Use the same stick to clean under the free edge.

17 Use the cuticle knife gently to loosen eponychium from the nail plate. The blade should be used wet and kept as flat to the nail surface as possible to avoid scratching it. Work round the nail border with small circular movements, keeping the cutting edge facing towards the main body of the nail.

18 Take the other hand out of soak and dry it thoroughly. Rinse the nails of the first hand and scrub them to remove all traces of debris and cuticle remover. Dry the nails, pushing the cuticles back gently with the towel. Repeat steps 15–17 on the second hand.

GOOD PRACTICE

Work on building up your speed, using the emery board in the correct way. Find as many volunteers as you can to let you practise. Keep a check on the nail shapes and ask for your clients' comments regarding the final results.

HEALTH MATTERS

Never use a two-way sawing action with the emery board. This creates heat, which dries out some of the moisture within the nail and causes the layers to separate.

REMEMBER

There is no point in buffing at this stage of the manicure if buffing with paste is required later on as an alternative to nail polish. Make sure you know what the client wants before starting the treatment.

REMEMBER

Cuticle remover has a bleaching effect which helps to whiten the free edge.

GOOD PRACTICE

Never angle the knife so that the cutting edge is vertical. The blade may not look sharp; but it can penetrate the nail if not used carefully.

19 Use the cuticle nippers to remove any excessive or damaged cuticle. Place the pointed end of the nippers slightly under the lifted cuticle. Squeeze the blades together to ensure a clean cut is made before releasing the blades and moving further along the cuticle.

20 Use the smooth side of the emery board to remove any roughness that may have developed around the free edges of the nails. Stroke the pad of your thumb around the free edge to check that it is smooth.

21 Apply either hand cream or lotion to the hand and forearm and proceed with the massage. Reapply lotion or cream as necessary during the massage to prevent friction. See page 199 for the massage sequence.

22 The massage leaves a film of grease on the nails which must be removed before the next stage of the manicure. Wipe over the nails with nail polish remover on a cotton wool pad.

23 If buffing is required as an alternative to nail polish, apply a tiny amount of paste to the centre of each nail with an orange stick and smooth it towards the free edge with the pad of the ring finger or thumb. Buff the nails until you have created a healthy-looking shine. Take care not to spread paste over the surrounding skin.

24 If nail polish is going to be applied, make sure that the client replaces jewellery beforehand to prevent smudging.

25 Apply a basecoat, then two coats of a coloured enamel and then a top-coat. Pearlised enamels do not require a top-coat.

Applying nail enamel

26 Following the application of each coat, lightly touch the tip of the thumb nail to test whether the enamel has dried. It is important to allow each coat to dry before applying another, otherwise the enamel smudges easily and the effect of the treatment is spoiled.

27 While the nails are drying, advise the client about products that may be purchased from the salon for home use.

28 Record details of the client's treatment and escort them to reception.

29 Record details of the client's retail purchases.

Step-by-step manicure procedure

1 *Apply nail polish remover*

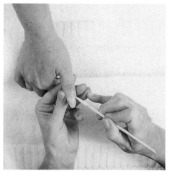

2 *Remove polish from nail border*

3 *File nails from sides to centre*

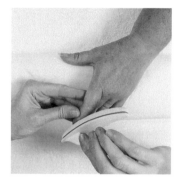

4 *Buff the fingernails*

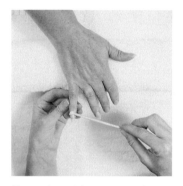

5 *Apply cuticle cream and massage into cuticles (a)*

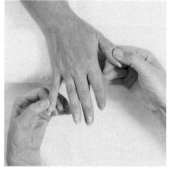

6 *Apply cuticle cream and massage into cuticles (b)*

7 *Soak first hand, repeat filing and cuticle massage*

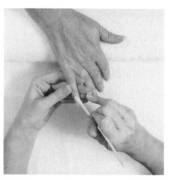

8 *Apply cuticle remover*

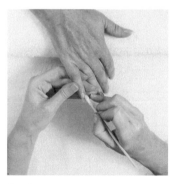

9 *Clean under cuticles*

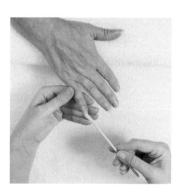

10 *Clean under free edge*

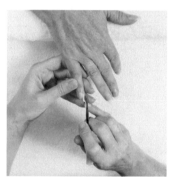

11 *Use the cuticle knife*

12 *Scrub the fingernails*

13 *Push back the cuticles*

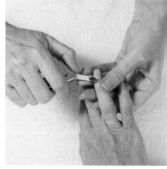

14 *Use the cuticle nippers (a)*

15 *Use the cuticle nippers (b)*

16 *Check the free edge is smooth*

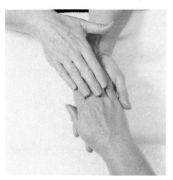   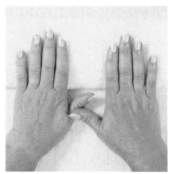

17 *Massage the hands*

18 *Remove grease from the nails*

19 *Apply nail polish*

20 *Finished effect*

SELF-CHECKS

Manicure procedure

1 State three ways of avoiding backache when giving a manicure treatment.

2 Give three reasons for examining the client's hands before a manicure.

3 Why should the nail polish colour be chosen at the beginning of the manicure?

4 Why is the orange stick used tipped with cotton wool?

5 How does buffing the nails without paste polish benefit the nails?

6 Why is cuticle cream used before cuticle remover in the massage sequence?

7 State two precautions that should be taken to avoid scratching the nail plate with the cuticle knife.

8 How should the nails be prepared for nail polish after the hand massage?

9 Why is it important to apply nail polish with the minimum number of strokes?

10 What details should be entered on the client's record card after a manicure treatment?

Manicure treatments for men

The male market is becoming increasingly important to the beauty therapy industry. Male grooming has become big business and manicure treatments play their part in that. A male client may attend for manicure treatment either because their occupation means that their hands are continuously on show and they want them to look good, for example they work as a croupier, or because they have become interested as a result of other treatments they are receiving at the salon.

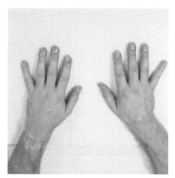
Male manicure

Whatever the motivation of the client, the following guidelines for adapting the manicure procedure apply:

- concentrate on those aspects of the manicure that are designed to produce natural-looking, healthy nails
- file the nails to a short, square shape rather than oval
- push back and remove excess cuticle from the nail plate
- buff with paste to (a) remove ridges in the nail plate and (b) produce the final, healthy shine
- use unperfumed products throughout
- use an oil or lotion, rather than cream, to massage the hands. This will provide 'slip' and help prevent discomfort when massaging over hairy areas
- use deeper movements during the hand and arm massage.

Hand massage

Massage is not just rubbing hand cream into the skin. If that was the case, the client might just as well be handed the bottle and be told to get on with it! Skilfully applied massage movements help to relax the client, make the joints more supple and leave the skin feeling smooth and refreshed. Besides helping the skin to absorb the hand cream or lotion, the massage increases the flow of blood to the area, providing essential nutrients for the muscles, bones, skin and nails. The removal of waste products from the area is also speeded up. Exercises are included in the sequence which help to ease stiffness and improve the mobility of the joints.

Le Remedi hand treatment programme

The basic procedure is made up of **effleurage** and **petrissage** massage movements:

- *Effleurage*: long, flowing, stroking movements performed with the fingers and palms of the hand. Very little pressure is used. Every massage sequence begins and ends with effleurage. Effleurage soothes the nerve endings and helps to remove loose surface skin cells.
- *Petrissage*: deeper, rhythmic, localised circular kneading or friction-type movements, which have stimulating effects. Petrissage increases the rate at which blood flows through the skin and underlying muscles, and removes loose surface skin cells and waste matter.

HEALTH MATTERS

During a hand massage, the joints of the fingers and wrists are put through their full range of movement, sometimes against a resistance. This stimulates the circulation of blood through the joints and helps to increase their suppleness and flexibility.

Hand massage

1 Name three beneficial effects of hand massage.

_____
_____
_____

2 State the names of two types of massage movements.

_____
_____

3 Give two effects upon the skin of petrissage movements.

_____
_____

4 Why is a cream or lotion used when massaging the hands?

_____
_____
_____
_____

5 Give two contra-indications to hand massage.

_____
_____

ACTIVITY

Activity 6.5: Manicure treatments

You need to get experience of treating as many different clients as possible. This way, you are more likely to come across a range of conditions and problems, and that will help you to apply your knowledge. Always make out a treatment plan and fill in a record card when giving a manicure treatment. Make a note of any conditions and problems you encounter below. These will go towards your portfolio of assessment evidence. Check with your supervisor how many manicure treatments you need to complete.

_____
_____
_____
_____
_____
_____
_____
_____
_____
_____
_____
_____
_____
_____
_____
_____

Massage sequence

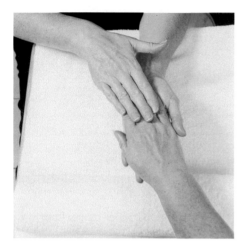

1 *Stroking from fingers to elbow (a) six times with each hand*

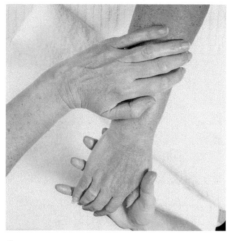

2 *Stroking from fingers to elbow (b) six times with each hand*

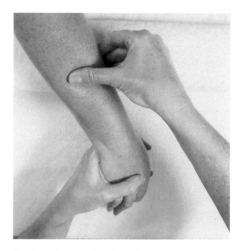

3 *Thumb kneading (petrissage) to forearm*

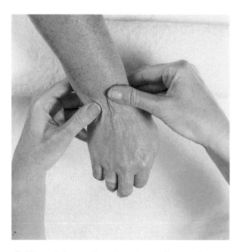

4 *Thumb kneading (petrissage) to wrist*

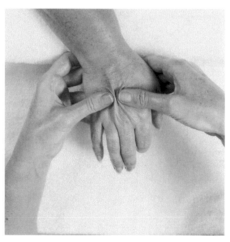

5 *Thumb kneading (petrissage) to back of hand*

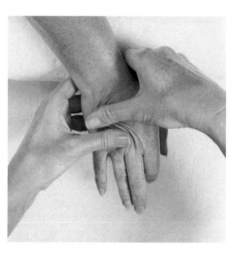

6 *Cross-thumb frictions (petrissage) to back of hand*

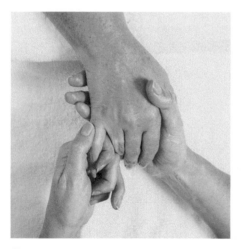

7 *Thumb kneading (petrissage) to joints of fingers*

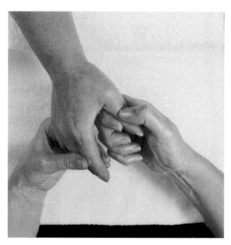

8 *Thumb kneading (petrissage) to joints of thumb*

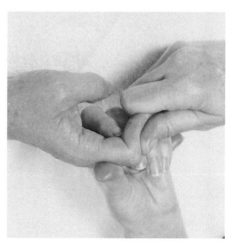

9 *Pushing against a resistance (exercise) six times to each finger and thumb*

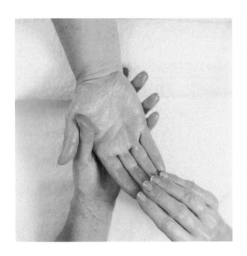

10 *Turning the hand over*

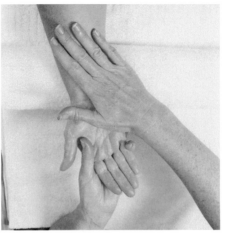

11 *Stroking (effleurage) from fingers to elbow (hand upwards) six times*

12 *Thumb kneading (petrissage) from elbow to palm*

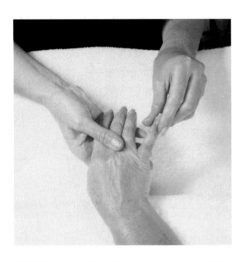

13 *Finger rotation (exercise) six times with each finger and thumb*

14 *Wrist rotation (exercise) six times in each direction*

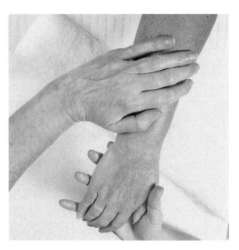

15 *Stroking (effleurage) from fingers to elbow (hand downwards) six times*

ACTIVITY

Activity 6.6: Sequence of a manicure

Decide the order of sequence of events during a manicure treatment and place the correct letter in each box.

a Nail polish application

b Buffing

c Massage

d Filing

e Basecoat

f Top-coat

1	2	3	4	5	6

Completing the nail treatment

At the end of the treatment you need to make sure that the client record card is up-to-date and stored confidentially. Home care advice can then be given.

Home care advice

Home care advice is an important part of giving a professional service. You can also recommend retail products to your clients. Home care advice includes:

- wearing rubber gloves while washing up
- drying the hands throughly after washing (or the skin may become dry)
- moisturising the hands using hand cream
- frequently using an emery board to keep the nails smooth and free of splits
- wearing gloves while gardening
- not using the nails as tools, for example, for opening a drinks can
- inform the client that it is important to have regular manicure treatments
- recommend a manicure treatment every two weeks.

MULTIPLE CHOICE QUIZ

Decide which is the correct answer and tick the box.

1 When using an emery board to shape the nails you must ensure which of the following:
   - ☐ you carry out a back and forth (sawing) action
   - ☐ you work from the side to the centre in one direction only
   - ☐ you file the nails into a point
   - ☐ the client helps to file the nails.

2 The free edge of the nail is:
   - ☐ the nail plate
   - ☐ the nail bed
   - ☐ the part of the nail that extends over the finger tip.
   - ☐ the skin around the nail.

3 The typical nail shape is?
   - ☐ oval
   - ☐ triangle
   - ☐ diamond
   - ☐ rectangle.

4 Which of the following is not used during a nail treatment?
   - ☐ cuticle cream
   - ☐ towel
   - ☐ buffing paste
   - ☐ headband

5 Which of the following is the medical term for white spots on the nail plate?
   - ☐ fungus
   - ☐ psoriasis
   - ☐ paronychia
   - ☐ leuconychia

6 Nail polishes should not be stored:
   - ☐ in a cupboard
   - ☐ on a shelf
   - ☐ in a drawer
   - ☐ on a window ledge in direct sunlight.

7 The buffing method involves:
- ☐ buffing in one direction from the cuticle to the free edge
- ☐ banging the buffer directly onto the nail plate
- ☐ vigorous strokes from side to side across the nail plate
- ☐ working in fast circular motions across the nail plate.

8 A wart is caused by:
- ☐ a bacterial infection
- ☐ a viral infection
- ☐ a fungal infection
- ☐ a parasite.

9 To check that the free edge is smooth the therapist should:
- ☐ use an emery board to bevel the end of the nail
- ☐ pick off rough bits of the nail
- ☐ buff vigorously
- ☐ use some cuticle cream.

10 The nails should be free of grease when:
- ☐ appling cuticle cream remover
- ☐ applying nail polish
- ☐ rubbing cuticle cream into the cuticles
- ☐ when placing the fingers into the manicure bowl.

KEY TERMS

You should now understand the following words or phrases. If you do not, go back through the chapter and find out what the mean.

Filing	**Contra-indicate**	**Bevelling**
Buff	**Inflammation**	**Contaminate**
Nail polish	**Antibiotics**	**Sanitising solution**
Home-care advice	**Nail disease**	**Acetone**
Adverse reaction	**Consultation**	**Nail ridges**
Keratin	**Cuticle nippers**	**Ridge filler**
Cuticle	**Cuticle remover**	**Basecoat**
Matrix	**Cuticle cream**	**Top-coat**
Free-edge	**Nail strengthener**	**Cross-infection**
Nail grooves	**Sterilise**	
Nail infection	**Autoclave**	

Glossary

abrasion grazing of the skin and perhaps some bleeding, which occurs as a result of rubbing or wearing away of the skin, for example when falling over and grazing the skin of the knee

accident book kept in a salon for the reporting of accidents and personal injuries to staff and members of the public

acetone a solvent often found in nail polish remover and nail polish thinners that dissolves and removes nail polish

acid mantle a slightly acid coating on the skin, made up of sebum, sweat and keratin. The acid mantle helps to prevent the growth of harmful bacteria and fungi on the skin

adverse reaction an undesirable reaction of a client to a treatment that may occur during or after the treatment

alcohol a spirit used for its de-greasing properties, for example in brush cleaners and 'strong' toning lotions

allergen a substance that causes an allergic reaction

allergic reaction an abnormal reaction of the skin to something it has been brought into contact with – irritation, itching, inflammation, swelling, rash, blisters

antibacterial destroys or stops the growth of bacteria

antibiotics medicines used to help destroy harmful bacteria

aromatherapy a treatment that involves using oils extracted from plants, herbs and trees to help improve health and well-being

astringent substance that helps to tighten the skin temporarily. Witch hazel is an astringent

autoclave a piece of sterilising equipment in which water is boiled, under pressure, at a high temperature. Used for sterilising stainless steel and glass items

bacteria tiny organisms that can be harmful (pathogenic) and cause infection

basecoat a product, applied before nail polish to smooth the nail and prevent staining of the nail plate by pigments contained in the nail polish

beauty industry the industry of providing treatments and selling beauty products and services to customers

beauty therapist a fully trained therapist, qualified to provide beauty treatments and services and advise on a range of beauty subjects

bevelling method of using an emery board to remove roughness and excess bits of nail from around the free edge

blemishes for example, marks, spots and discoloured areas of skin

body language non-verbal communication that gives physical 'cues' to one's mood, feelings or behaviour

broken capillaries	damaged blood capillaries, often seen as little red lines on the skin of the cheeks and around the nose
buffing	the method of using a 'buffer' to create a natural looking shine on the nails. Buffing stimulates the blood circulation and helps to provide a smooth surface to the nail
career	successful progression along a career path
career path	the progression route of qualifications and experience leading to particular career aims
cash float	the cash put in the till at the start of the day for giving change
cleanser	a cosmetic product used to remove make-up, dirt and dead skin cells from the skin
client database	a record keeping system for maintaining information about clients, their treatments and purchases
client confidentiality	the entitlement of a client to not have their personal details revealed to third parties
client record card	a card containing the client's relevant personal details and important information relating to their beauty treatments and purchases
code of ethics	professionally recognised standards of behaviour
collagen	protein fibres found in the dermis that help give strength and support to other structures in the skin
comedone	a blackhead, caused by a build-up of sebum which turns 'black' through a process of oxidation at the mouth of the hair follicle
communication skills	the skills by which people communicate with each other, for example by talking, listening, writing and using body language
consultation	the process of questioning and physical examination that takes place between a therapist and a client in order to agree a treatment plan
consumer protection	the legal rights of customers when making a purchase
contamination	pollution or infection, for example, placing fingers into a pot, rather than using a spatula, risks the contents of the pot becoming contaminated with any bacteria present on the fingers
Continuing Professional Development (CPD)	further training and work experience available to qualified professionals for enhancing their career progression
contra-indication	a sign that a treatment must not go ahead, for example symptoms of a skin disorder that could be made worse by the treatment
cortisone cream	a steroid cream that helps to relieve swelling, burning and itching of the skin
COSHH	Control of Substances Hazardous to Health (Regulations 2002)
cross-infection	the transfer of infection directly through personal contact or indirectly through contact with a contaminated article
customer service	all aspects of looking after customers and their individual needs
cuticle	fold of thickened skin found around the base of the nail

cuticle cream	a product used to soften the cuticle and make it more pliable so that it can be pushed back more easily
cuticle nippers	cutting tool used in a manicure to remove excess cuticle skin and hard, dry split skin (hangnails) from the sides of the nails
cuticle remover	a product used to break down excess cuticle so that it can be scraped away gently from the nail plate with a cuticle knife. Also has a bleaching effect
Data Protection Act	legislation protecting individuals from having personal information about them passed on to third parties
dermatologist	a medically qualified skin specialist
dermis	layer of skin found beneath the epidermis, in which many of the structures such as sebaceous glands and nerves are found
desquamation	the shedding of dead skin cells
elastin	protein fibres found in the skin that help to make it elastic and flexible
electronic payments	payments by credit/debit card that are made electronically, by swiping a card or by 'chip and pin'
employer's liability	compulsory insurance required to cover an employer for claims that might arise when an employee suffers injury at work
employment rights	the legal rights of an employee
Environmental Health Officers	inspectors from the Local Authority who check up on standards of health and safety
epidermis	the uppermost layer of skin which is, itself, made up of five layers
erythema	redness of the skin
exfoliation	a product that helps to remove dead skin cells from the skin
eyebrow shape	method of using tweezers or wax to improve the shape and appearance of the eyebrows
eyelash perming	a permanent method of curling eyelashes with the use of small rods and a chemical 'perm' lotion
eyelash tint	treatment in which eyelashes are permanently coloured to enhance the appearance of the eyes
eye treatment	includes eyebrow shaping, eyelash tinting, eyebrow tinting and eyelash perming
facial	treatment involving cleansing, massage and, sometimes, a face mask that helps to improve the health and appearance of the skin of the face and neck
false lashes	artificial individual or strip lashes, applied to make the natural eyelashes appear longer and thicker
filing	method of shortening nails and smoothing rough edges using an emery board
free edge	the part of the nail at the tip of the finger
fungi	plant-like organisms responsible for certain diseases such as ringworm and athlete's foot

glass bead steriliser	small, electrically heated container that contains glass beads that heat up and help to sterilise small objects such as tweezers
hazard	something which is a hazard has the potential to cause harm
hazard data sheet	an information sheet explaining the potential of a product or process to cause harm and the precautions that should be taken to prevent the risk of it causing harm
Health and Safety at Work Act	identifies the responsibilities of employers and employees to provide a safe working environment, not just for themselves but for anyone present on the business premises
Health and Safety Executive	the 'lead' authority on health and safety which enforces health and safety legislation
hereditary	transmitted from parents to children
histamine	a substance produced by special cells in the dermis in reaction to skin damage or an allergy. The extent of the histamine reaction depends on the nature of the injury, but includes itching, erythema, pain, swelling, inflammation and pustules
home-care advice	advice given to a client to carry out at home to ensure he/she gains maximum benefit from their salon treatment
hormones	chemical 'messengers' made by the body. Hormones released by one part of the body travel in the blood to other parts of the body to tell cells how to function or when to grow, divide or die
hot wax	a mixture of beeswax and resin used during a 'waxing' treatment to remove hair from the skin
humectant	a substance that attracts moisture (water)
hygiene	practices that ensure cleanliness and good health and that help to protect against cross-infection
infectious	a disease capable of being 'spread', for example from one person to another
infestations	invasions by parasites that cause harmful conditions such as scabies and head lice
inflammation	redness and swelling
keratin	a protein found in the skin, hair and nails
liver spots	darkened, flat spots that often appear on sun-exposed areas of skin
maintain	to keep up
make-up treatment	the application of make-up to the face to enhance facial features and improve the appearance of the face
manicure	a treatment that helps to improve the health and appearance of the skin and nails of the hands
mask	a product or formulation often applied with a brush during a facial, to help improve the appearance and condition of the skin
massage	a sequence of special manipulations (massage movements) applied to the body for improving the appearance and condition of the skin and underlying structures

matrix	the 'living' part of the nail, situated at the base of the nail, which produces the cells that make up the nail plate. Damage to this area may cause permanent damage to the nail
melanin	the dark pigment that produces a sun tan. Melanin protects the deeper layers of the skin by absorbing the sun's ultraviolet rays
micro-organism	a tiny single-celled living organism too small to be seen by the naked eye
milia	small, solid, white pearly nodules which form when skin grows over the mouths of hair follicles, obstructing the passage of sebum onto the surface of the skin
moisturiser	a product that is a mixture of oil and water with a 'humectant' added that attracts water and helps 'fix' it in the upper layers of the skin. Moisturisers lubricate and soften the skin. Some moisturisers have UV filters that help to protect the skin from the damaging effects of the sun.
muscle tone	the state of 'tension' when a muscle is relaxed. 'Good' muscle tone keeps the contours firm and well defined
nail disease	an infection of the nail, usually by a fungus
nail grooves	grooves found at the sides of the nail that help it to grow in the right direction
nail infection	an infection affecting the nail and skin around it, often caused by bacteria and fungi
nail polish	also known as nail varnish or nail enamel, it is used to enhance the appearance of the nails
nail ridges	ridges found on the nail plate which may be caused by injury or illness
nail strengthener	a product applied during a manicure to help strengthen the nail plate
non-infectious	cannot be transferred, for example from one person to another
non-setting mask	a mask used for treating the skin that does not dry and remains soft, for example, cream, warm oil and fruit masks
nutrients	nourishment (food) carried by blood to the cells
open pores	enlarged pores caused by an over-production of sebum, which stretches the mouths of the hair follicles situated on the surface of the skin
oxygen	a colourless, odourless, tasteless gas, essential for sustaining life
patch test	a 'skin compatibility' test that is carried out to determine if the client is suitable for or 'contra-indicated' to treatment
pedicure	a treatment that helps to improve the health and appearance of the skin and nails of the feet
petty cash	a small amount of cash kept on hand by a business for incidental expenses
posture	the way we position ourselves when, for instance, standing or sitting
prepare	to arrange and set up
product data sheet	information listing all the general characteristics and components of a product

product liability	liability of a manufacturer or seller of a defective product for any injuries or damages suffered as a result of the defective product
product sales	the value of products sold to customers
professional beauty treatments	treatments provided by a qualified beauty therapist
professional image	the way you present yourself at work
professional indemnity	insurance taken out, by an individual, to protect themselves against claims by clients, from injuries incurred as a result of their treatments
professional standards	the standards of competence and behaviour expected of someone operating at a 'professional' level
public liability	a form of insurance taken out by employers to cover them for claims made by members of the public as a result of injury, or damage to personal property, caused by the employer or an employee at work
reception	the 'control centre' for salon operations where appointments, enquiries, sales and payments are managed
recommendation	suggestion or advice given
regular clients	clients who attend the salon regularly for treatment and are 'loyal' to the salon
regulations	specific laws making up the legal framework in which the industry operates
retail display	the method of promoting and providing retail products for purchase
RIDDOR	The Reporting of Injuries, Diseases and Dangerous Occurrences Regulations (1995)
ridge filler	a manicure product, applied before nail varnish, to help even out ridges in the nail so that they appear smoother and provide a better 'finish' for the nail varnish
risk	the potential harm that may arise from a process or treatment
risk assessment	an assessment of the likelihood of a hazard occurring
roller wax method	a method of hair depilatory in which cartridges containing warm wax, and which have rollers at one end, are rolled onto the skin to remove hairs
sanitise	to make sanitary by cleaning or sterilising
sanitising solution	a cleaning product used to prevent the growth of micro-organisms such as bacteria
sebaceous gland	a gland found in the dermis that produces a fatty substance called sebum
setting mask	a mask which dries on the face in order to achieve its therapeutic effects. Examples of setting masks are clay masks, peel-off masks and thermal masks
skin analysis	a process of looking at the skin to determine the skin type and its condition
skin cell	the smallest structure that makes up part of the skin
skin tone	the strength and elasticity of the skin

skin type	the classification of skin for treatment purposes. Skin types include normal/balanced, oily, dry, combination, sensitive and mature
sterilise	to destroy all disease-causing organisms, such as bacteria
subcutaneous layer	'fatty' layer of skin found beneath the dermis
sugaring	a method of removing hair with a sugar-based preparation
sun protection factor (SPF)	the degree to which a sunscreen product provides protection from the harmful effects of the sun
sweat glands	structures situated in the dermis that produce sweat. Sweating helps to control body temperature
team work	the combined efforts of everyone in the team to work together
texture (skin)	the feel of the surface of the skin
toner	a product used to remove any traces of excess grease from the skin and to prepare the skin for the next stage of treatment. Some toners have a tightening effect on the skin
top-coat	a product applied to the nails to seal and protect the nail polish application, to add shine to the nails and to make the nail polish last longer
treatment plan	a plan of action agreed between the beauty therapist and the client to ensure that the best possible treatment is given
t-zone	an area of the face including the forehead, nose and chin
ultraviolet cabinet	a piece of equipment that uses ultraviolet light to sanitise small items of equipment
viruses	small disease-causing micro-organisms that are too small to be seen, even with microscopes
warm wax	a mixture of a low melting-point wax such as paraffin wax, synthetic resins and other materials used to carry out a depilatory waxing treatment
waxing	a treatment involving the use of wax for temporarily removing the appearance of hairs from the face and body
workplace policies	the expressed commitments of an employer to standards of conduct and behaviour expected in their workplace

Index

accidents 70
acetone 188
acid mantle 149
acne rosacea 153
acne vulgaris 152–3
adipose tissue 149
adverse reactions 45
AIDS (Acquired Immune Deficiency Syndrome) 64
allergies 152
antiperspirants 59
appearance, personal 13–14, 56–60
appointments, making 109–12
arrector pili 149
arthritis 183
associations, professional 12, 13
astringents 164
athlete's foot (tinea pedis) 65, 183
autoclaves 66

bacteria 63, 64–5
basal layer of the skin 147
basecoat (for nails) 189
Beau's lines (transverse furrows) 176
beauty consultants 21
beauty industry 1–2
  career opportunities 16–23
  legal framework 7–11
  product sales 2–3
  professional framework 12–13, 15–16
  professional treatments 3–5
  qualifications 23–5
  'regular' clients 6
  types of business 5
beauty salons see salons
beauty technicians 19
blackheads 152, 153
blood vessels 149
body language 105
boils 65, 151
buffers, nail 186, 193, 194
buffing paste 188, 194
bunions 183

calluses 182
capillaries 148
  broken 156, 157
carbuncles 151
card payments 95
career opportunities 16
  career paths 17, 25
  continuing professional development (CPD) 25
  qualifications 23–5
  specific jobs 18–23
cash tills 94–5
chemicals 81–2
  sterilisers and disinfectants 67
'chip and PIN' 95
cleansing, skin 160
  deep 160, 161–4
  superficial 160, 160–2
clear layer of skin 147
clients
  buying products 2–3
  complaints 115–17
  confidentiality 10
  consumer protection 9–10
  dealing with on arrival 106–7
  dealing with problems 108
  health and safety 44–5
  protecting against theft 86–7
  records 10, 45–6, 107
  'regular' 6
closed questions 104
code of ethics 12–13
cold sores 64, 151
colds 64
collagen 148
comedones 152, 153
communication skills 100–1
  asking questions 104–5
  body language 105
  listening 103
  reading 101–2
  speaking 102–3
  writing 102
complaints, dealing with 115–17
computers 94
  tills 94–5
conjunctivitis 151

A PRACTICAL GUIDE TO BEAUTY THERAPY LEVEL 1

consultants, beauty   21
consultations
    consultation forms   45–6, 155, 185
    for facial treatments   159
consumer protection   9–10
continuing professional development
    (CPD)   25
contra-actions   45
contra-indications   45
    to facial treatment   155
contracts of employment   11
Control of Substances Hazardous to
    Health Regulations 2002 (COSHH)
    34
corns   182
cosmetic camouflage   19
cosmetics see make-up treatments
CPD (continuing professional
    development)   25
cross-infection   63
cruise therapists   19
customers see clients
cuticle cream/gel/oil   188
cuticle knives   187, 193
cuticle nippers   187, 194
cuticle removers   187, 193
cuticles   173
    excess   178

Data Protection Act 1998   10
databases   94
deodorants   59
dermatitis   181
dermis   148–9
desquamation   147
Disability Discrimination Act 1995   11
disinfection   66, 67

eccrine glands   149
eczema   152, 181
effleurage   197
elastin   148
electric shock   77
electrical safety   76–8
Electricity at Work Regulations 1989
    36
electrologists   20
electronic point of sale (EPOS)   95
emergency services, calling   75–6
emery boards   186
Employer's Liability (Compulsory
    Insurance) Act 1969   36

employment rights   10–11
Employment Rights Act 1996   11
enquires, handling   114
Environmental Health Officers   9
Environmental Protection Act 1990
    35
epidermis   146–7
epilation, electrical   20
EPOS (electronic point of sale)   95
equipment
    for eye treatments   127–8, 129
    for facial treatments   137–8, 158
    health and safety   30–1, 78
    for make-up treatments   139–42
    for nail treatments   132–5, 186–9
    for wax treatments   122–3, 124
European Union (EU)   8
exchanges and refunds   116–17
exfoliation   165
eye treatments   126
    applying temporary strip lashes
        130
    duties after treatment   132
    equipment and products for
        127–8, 129
    preparing for   129
    tinting eyelashes   128
eyebrows
    shaping   126, 127
    tinting   126, 127
    waxing   123
eyelashes
    false   126, 128, 129, 130
    perming   126, 129
    tinting   126, 127, 128
eyeliner, applying   141
eyeshadows   140

facial treatments   136, 146
    basic routine   159
    completing the treatment   167
    consultation with client   159
    contra-indications   155
    duties after treatment   139
    equipment, products and materials
        137, 158
    face masks   165–6
    home care advice   168
    preparation for   138
    preparing the client   159
    skin analysis   155–7
    skin cleansing   160–4

skin moisturising   166–7
skin toning   164–5
fax (facsimile transmission service)
   95
feet
   diseases and disorders of   180–3
   therapist's   13, 57
field sales representatives   21–2
Fire Precautions Act 1971   33
Fire Precautions (Workplace)
   Regulations 1999   33
fire safety   33–4, 73, 75
   calling emergency services   75–6
   electrical equipment   77
   firefighting equipment   73–4
first aid   33, 78–9
   first aid kits   79
   problems and actions   80
float, cash   95
foundation, applying   140
free edge of nails   172
freelance beauty therapists   18

germs   61–2, 64
glass bead sterilisers   66
glass, broken   49
granular layer of skin   147

hair, therapist's   13, 58
hand cream/oil/lotion   189
hands
   diseases and disorders of   180–3
   massage   197, 199–200
   therapist's   13, 57
   washing   69
hangnails   179
HASAWA (Health and Safety at Work
   Act) 1974   29
hazardous substances   34–5, 81–2
hazards   40–1
head lice   65
health farms   5
health and safety
   accidents   70–1
   at reception   47–8, 54
   client care   44–6
   electrical safety   76–8
   employee's responsibilities   39
   fire safety   73–6
   first aid   78–80
   legislation   8–9, 28–36
   personal presentation   56–60

product safety   81–2
responsibility for   39–40, 54
risks   40–2
security   83–7
   in stock room   46–7, 53
   in treatment areas   53
   treatment hygiene   61–7
   when assisting with treatments
      43–4
   working environment   48–51
   workplace policies   38
Health and Safety at Work Act 1974
   (HASAWA)   29
Health and Safety (Display Screen
   Equipment) Regulations 1992   31
Health and Safety Executive (HSE)   9
Health and Safety (First Aid)
   Regulations 1981   33
Health and Safety (Training for
   Employment) Regulations 1990   37
heating   50–1, 120
hepatitis B   64
histamine   152
HIV   64
home care advice   4
   after facial treatments   168
   after nail treatments   201
hormones   148, 152–3
horny layer of skin   147
hot wax   121
HSE (Health and Safety Executive)   9
humectants   166
hygiene   61
   bacteria   64–5
   hand washing   69
   infection   62–3
   parasites   65
   personal   13–14, 56–9
   sanitisation   65–7
   viruses   64

impetigo   65, 151
improvement notices   9
infection   62–3
   cross-infection   63
   secondary infection   63
   skin infections   151
ingrowing toenails   179
injuries   34
insurance   36

jewellery, therapist's   14, 56
joints, disorders of   183

keratin   172
koilonychia   178

lashes
   false   126, 128, 129, 130
   perming   126, 129
   tinting   126, 127, 128
lecturers   22–3
legal framework   7–8
   consumer protection   9–10
   employment   10–11
   health and safety   8–9, 28–36
leuconychia   178
lifestyle, therapist's   60
lifting and handling   31, 70–1
lighting   51, 120
listening skills   103
liver spots   157
Local Government (Miscellaneous
   Provisions) Act 1982   32
lunula   173

make-up artists   19–20
make-up, therapist's   13
make-up treatments   139
   applying make-up   140, 141, 142
   duties after treatment   143
   eyeshadow effects   140
   preparation for   142
   products, material and equipment
   139–41
Management of Health and Safety at
   Work Regulations 1999   29
manicures   132
   benefits of   172
   completing   201
   consultation forms   185
   duties after   136
   home care advice   201
   manicure procedure   192–6
   for men   197
   preparation for   135, 191–2
   products, material and equipment
   132–5, 186–9
Manual Handling Regulations 1992   31
mascara, applying   141
masks, face   165–6
massage   20
   hand massage   197, 199–200

massage therapists   20–1
materials
   for eye treatments   127–8, 129
   for facial treatments   137–8, 158
   for make-up treatments   139–42
   for nail treatments   132–5, 186–9
   for wax treatments   122–3, 124
matrix   173, 194
media make-up artists   19–20
melanin   147
men   6
   manicures   197
milia   152
moisturisers and moisturising   166–7
motor nerves   149
muscles   149

nail bars   5
nail files   186
nail polish   189, 194
nail polish remover   188, 193
nail strengtheners   189
nail technicians   20
nail treatments   132
   benefits of   172
   completing   201
   consultation forms   185
   duties after   136
   equipment, products and materials
      132–5, 186–9
   home care advice   201
   manicure procedure   192–6
   manicures for men   197
   preparation for   135, 191–2
nails
   anatomy and physiology   172–3
   bitten   179
   diseases and disorders   175–9
   shapes   174
   therapist's   58
   see also hands
NVQs (National Vocational
Qualifications)   23–4

onychauxis   178
onycholysis   178
onychomycosis   176
onychorrhexis   177
open questions   104
oral hygiene, therapist's   14, 58
orange sticks   187
overalls   13–14, 56

papillary layer of the skin   148
parasites   65
paronychia   176
patch tests   126
pedicures   132
  benefits of   172
  completing   201
  consultation forms   185
  duties after   136
  equipment, products and materials
    for   132–4, 186–8
  preparation for   135, 191–2
perming, eyelash   126, 129
personal hygiene, therapist's   13, 59
Personal Protective Equipment (PPE)
  at Work Regulations 1992   30
petrissage   197
petty cash   95
piercings   56
pigmentation
  nails   179
  skin   147
pilfering   85
plantar warts   183
pores   149, 156
posture, therapist's   59
PPE (Personal Protective Equipment)
at Work Regulations 1992   30
presentation, personal   13–14, 56–60
prickle cell layer of skin   147
Prison Service, career opportunities in
  23
probationary period of work   11
products
  for eye treatments   127–8, 129
  for facial treatments   137–8, 158
  for make-up treatments   139–42
  for nail treatments   132–5, 186–9
  safety   46–7, 53, 73, 81–2
  sales   2–3, 21–2, 96–7
  security   86
  stock handling and storage   97–8
  for wax treatments   122–3, 124
professional indemnity insurance   36
professionalism
  code of ethics   12–13
  continuing professional development
    25
  image   13–14, 56–60
  professional associations   12
  qualifications   23–5
  working relationships   15–16

prohibition notices   9
Provisions and Use of Work
  Equipment Regulations 1998   30
psoriasis   153, 181
public liability insurance   36
pus   63

qualifications   23–5
questions, asking   104–5

reading, effective   101–2
reception   92, 93
  creating right environment   120–1
  dealing with clients on arrival   106–7
  dealing with client's problems   108
  dealing with complaints   115–17
  electronic equipment   93–5
  handling telephone enquiries
    112–14
  health and safety   47–8, 54
  items at desk   93
  making appointments   109–12
  retail displays   96–7
receptionists   100
  communication skills   100–5
records, client   10, 45–6, 107
refunds   116–17
relationships, professional   15–16
Reporting of Injuries, Diseases and
  Dangerous Occurrences Regulations
  1995 (RIDDOR)   34
retail displays   96–7
reticular layer of the skin   148
ringworm of the nail   65, 176
risks and risk assessment   40–2, 54
roller wax method   121
rosacea   153

safety *see* health and safety
Sale and Supply of Goods Act 1994
  117
sales   2–3
  career opportunities in   21–2
  retail displays   96–7
salons   5
  career opportunities in   18, 22
  client care   106–17
  creating the right environment
    120–1
  health and safety   38–9, 48–51,
    53–4
  reception   92–8

security   83–7
sanitisation   65
   disinfection   66–7
   sterilisation   66, 67
scabies   65
scissors, nail   186, 193
Scottish Vocational Qualifications
   (SVQs)   23–4
sebaceous glands   148
sebum   148, 150, 152, 153
secondary infection   63
security   83–4
   during business hours   85
   outside business hours   84–5
   personal safety   87
   theft   85–7
sensory nerve endings   149
shivering   150
shoes, therapist's   13, 57
skin   146
   anatomy and physiology   146–9
   cleansing   160–4
   diseases and disorders   151–3, 180–3
   functions of   149–50
   moisturising   166–7
   toning   164–5
   types   155–7
skin cells   146, 147
skin tags   153
smoking   73
spa assistants   22
spas   5
speaking skills   102–3
staff
   employment rights   10–11
   and health and safety   39–40
   and security   87
   teamwork   16
   see also therapists
sterilisation   66, 67
stock
   handling and storage   97–8
   health and safety   46–7, 53
   retail displays   96–7
   security   86
stratum corneum   147
stratum germinativum   147
stratum granulosm   147
stratum lucidum   147
stratum spinosum   147
styes   151
subcutaneous layer of the skin   149

sugaring   121
SVQs (Scottish Vocational
   Qualifications)   23–4
sweat   56, 149, 150

T-zone   156
teachers   22–3
team work   16
technicians, beauty   19
teeth, therapist's   14, 58
telephone calls
   answering techniques   113
   reasons for   114
   taking messages   114
   transferring   114
telephones   93
theft   85–6
therapists
   career opportunities   16–23
   continuing professional development
     25
   employment rights   10–11
   personal presentation   13–14,
     56–60
   professionalism   12–13
   qualifications   23–5
   teamwork   16
tills   94–5
tinea pedis (athlete's foot)   65, 183
tinea unguium (ringworm of the nail)
   65, 176
tinting, eyelashes and eyebrows   126,
   127, 128
toenails, ingrowing   179
toners and toning, skin   164–5
top-coat (for nails)   189
trainers/lecturers   22–3
transverse furrows on nails   176
treatments
   creating the right environment
     120–1
   eye   126–32
   facial   136–9, 146, 155–68
   hand massage   197, 199–200
   health and safety   43–6, 53
   hygiene   61–7
   make-up   139–43
   nail   132–6, 172, 185–97, 201
   professional   3–5
   timings   110
   wax   121–5

ultraviolet cabinets   66
ultraviolet rays of the sun   147, 148

vasoconstriction   150
vasodilation   150
VDUs (visual display units)   31
ventilation   50–1, 120
verrucas   183
viruses   64, 151
visual display units (VDUs)   31
vitamin D   150

warm wax   121, 123
warts   64, 181, 183
waste, dealing with   49
watches   14
water supply   50

wax treatments   121
   duties after treatment   125
   equipment and materials   122–3
   eyebrows   123
   treatment area preparation   124
   types of wax   121
   upper lip   123
whiteheads   152
whitlows   65, 182
Working Time Regulations 1998   37
Workplace (Health, Safety and
   Welfare) Regulations 1992   30
workplaces
   health and safety   38, 48–51, 53–4
   see also salons
written communication   102